PELICAN BOOKS

A396

SOCIAL WELFARE AND THE CITIZEN

EDITED BY PETER ARCHER

SOCIAL WELFARE AND THE CITIZEN

Edited by Peter Archer

PENGUIN BOOKS

Penguin Books Ltd, Harmondsworth, Middlesex
U.S.A.: Penguin Books Inc., 3300 Clipper Mill Road, Baltimore 11, Md
AUSTRALIA: Penguin Books Pty Ltd, 762 Whitehorse Road,
Mitcham, Victoria

—

First published 1957

Made and printed in Great Britain
by The Whitefriars Press Ltd
London and Tonbridge

Contents

The information given in the text is correct as at the time of going to press, February 1957, but in certain respects (e.g., rates of insurance contributions, income tax, etc.) may need modification in the light of later changes in the law.

Introduction

PETER ARCHER

SLOGANS about Liberty, Equality, and Fraternity have become somewhat hackneyed in two hundred years. But the aspirations which they express have lost none of their importance. A government which fails at least to recognize their desirability (other considerations permitting) offers no plausible reason why the majority of its citizens should lend it their support. Liberty implies that the citizens should be consulted in the selection of rulers and policies, and that the rulers should have no greater power to interfere in their affairs than is necessary to implement the policies. Equality entails that the legitimate interests of all the citizens should be given proper weight in deciding on a course of action. (Of course, the use of the words 'legitimate' and 'proper' leaves many questions unanswered.) And Fraternity means that the community sympathetically interests itself in the well-being of each of its members.

Liberty has long been achieved in Britain, although events occasionally remind us of the need for eternal vigilance. Equality still provides a subject for political disagreement, but the contents of this book bear witness to many bygone battles from which its supporters emerged triumphant, and which are no longer in issue. These contributions are really about Fraternity. And this is less a subject for disagreement than an attitude of mind, to which some are addicted less ardently than others.

Law and social services represent the interest of the community in the problems of the individual. Frequently, social services arise from the concern of a number of citizens who voluntarily join together to assist those facing a particular problem. But to an increasing degree they take the form of intervention by the Government, using the resources of the whole people. And where there is a general feeling that a certain type of problem should be of general concern, those who, whether from a callous selfishness or a sturdy self-sufficiency, have no wish to be fraternal may have to be coerced in order that the scheme shall function. Those who are happily free from the problem are expected to contribute to the relief of the less fortunate.

This communal interest in the relief of misfortune has fluctuated in intensity and varied in form from time to time, from the bread and circuses which the citizens of Ancient Rome demanded from the private purses of their politicians, to the friendly societies formed by the thrifty town-dwellers of Britain in the eighteenth century. But the idea that the Government itself should become a Robin Hood, redistributing financial resources between the more and the less fortunate, is scarcely earlier (except for the relief by local authorities of extreme poverty) than the last hundred years.

The modern Welfare State in this country accepts as its aims the famous 'Three Principles' set out in Part I of the Beveridge Report: first, that the wishes of any one section of the community are not given undue weight as against those of other sections (what one is tempted to call 'the acknowledgement to Equality'); secondly, to curtail and ultimately to abolish the 'Five Giants' with which the Report is chiefly concerned – poverty, disease, ignorance, squalor, and idleness; thirdly, so far as possible to preserve individual initiative.

Standards vary, of course, with the period at which they are set up, and what is regarded to-day as a satisfactory social service may not be so regarded in another generation. Nor can it be disputed that very much remains to be done, even within the limits originally set. But it would be unfair to underrate the advance which has been made within the present century. Constitutional liberty may itself have been an early achievement, but a great deal is being effected towards training in democratic techniques. Workers' participation in industry, school 'parliaments', and membership of boards of school managers and advisory committees, all conduce to a virile democracy. This in turn, by encouraging citizens of varying backgrounds to become articulate, assists in the achievement of the first 'Beveridge Principle'.

The second was widely implemented in the years immediately following the Second World War. If to the Five Giants are added tyranny and loneliness, the subject-matter of this book is defined. The attack on the Five Giants is directed towards two ends. First, to establish a minimum standard of living below which no household shall fall – that is, to provide a 'subsistence' income for everyone. Secondly, essential services are to be provided by the community, and they are to be in the nature not of basic minimum services, for those who can afford nothing better, but of services which are the best that the community can afford. Of course, the question of what can be afforded may entail problems of priorities. In any event, social services have to be paid for not only by the higher income groups, but to some extent by the bulk of the citizens, who acquire their services at the cost of lighter pockets, representing a restriction upon their freedom to spend their earnings as they wish.

Nevertheless, the attack on poverty is the cornerstone of the new legislation. Rowntree's Survey of York in 1899 suggested that there are two main causes of acute poverty: interruptions in earning power, and families which are disproportionate to the household income. Mr Prentice's chapter on National Insurance shows how the scheme is designed to guard against as many kinds of interruption in earning power as possible. Social insurance in this country previous to the Beveridge Report had suffered from three main defects. It had been insufficiently comprehensive as to the kinds of persons included; it had failed to guard against many common sources of interruption in earning power; and the rates of benefit were insufficient. The National Insurance Act of 1946 and the National Insurance (Industrial Injuries) Act of the same year, were intended, while retaining the principle of social insurance, to remedy these defects. As for the former two defects, the object has been largely achieved, but the cost of living has constantly outdistanced the rates of benefit. The second source of poverty is attacked by the family allowance scheme, and the system of maternity benefits and cheap supplies of certain foods.

Disease is being attacked by the National Health Service,

while public health legislation seeks to remove its causes. The educational system is tackling the problem of ignorance. Squalor is met by town planning, landlord-and-tenant legislation, and public housing schemes, though the problem is still largely the technical one of building houses more quickly. Idleness may have been checked by the attention paid to industrial relations, while it remains to be seen how far unemployment may be controlled and what price may have to be paid.

But social legislation does not consist in a series of isolated answers to particular problems. However it may be analysed for the purpose of writing books, the scheme stands or falls as a whole, and no one of the Five Giants will be slain while the others flourish. Ideally at least, the recipient of National Assistance should find sympathetic help from a qualified social worker in the general battle against misfortune, and should to that extent be relieved against the worst terrors of ignorance and loneliness. Miss Graham Hall reminds us that the treatment of disease and infirmity requires the alleviation of the other evils to which they frequently give rise. And Mrs Vernon shows how the attack on ignorance entails the removal of poverty and disease, squalor and idleness which, for many, provide insuperable obstacles to scholastic achievements. The law relating to the family and to landlord and tenant is concerned with protection from tyranny, but it cannot ignore the problems of poverty and squalor.

The twentieth century has witnessed a great social revolution in Britain, and its course has been determined chiefly by the law and social legislation set out in this book. But suffering and discontent, like the poor, are always with us, partly because a number of problems remain unsolved and partly because no welfare scheme, however embracing and efficient, can eliminate all the causes of human misery.

In a number of respects there are possibilities of improvement. Economically, there are two converse problems involved. One is the difficulty of making available in practice the benefits which exist in theory. This arises from three sources. First, people are not always aware of the benefits available. It was to help meet the difficulty that this book was undertaken, but it is too much to hope that all those in need will invest in a copy, and if the reader is a believer in Fraternity he (or she) may well ponder over the boundary line between being a busybody and being a good neighbour to the less well informed. An important element in the welfare scheme is provided by the institutions discussed by Mr Payne in his chapter on Aid and Advice. In any event, much remains to be done in advertising welfare schemes and in bringing the unfortunate into touch with social welfare workers, who can point out the provisions which exist.

Secondly, there is still a tendency to 'beware of the Greeks when they come with gifts in their hands'. This is a legacy from recent history, and may be remedied only by time. But much may be achieved within these limits when the Greeks are represented by friendly and easily accessible local officials. Part of the difficulty is the resistance among all free peoples to 'red tape'. Collecting the information necessary to administer welfare services, and minimizing the abuse of them, require an investigation into private business and the completing of complicated forms, both of which are (perhaps understandably) resented. There may be less obtrusive methods of doing so than those normally employed at present, but the problem of acquiring information without asking questions is by its terms insoluble. It may not be too much to hope that, when this is stated clearly to the public, it will meet with a reasonable response.

Thirdly, social welfare still carries the stigma of Poor Law relief, and many are reluctant to claim benefits which they look upon as charity. In this they are encouraged by the ignorant prejudice against welfare legislation on the part of many who, happily for themselves, are not in need of it. This difficulty is a psychological one. One solution is to replace a name which evokes approbrium by a new one (for example, 'National Assistance' for 'Public Assistance') and to administer old forms of relief in a new guise (financial relief to pensioners taking the form of supplementary pensions). But the new names and forms will gradually acquire the old connotation, and there will continue to be a resistance to help on the part of those most in need until the mentality of the workhouse and 'less eligibility' has passed away and the intellectual tyranny of old fallacies is forgotten.

The other and converse problem is to prevent abuse of welfare schemes by the less socially responsible elements. An obvious example is that of 'patient abuse' in the administration of the Health Service. This may (possibly) have been reduced since the introduction of part-payment, but it is widely felt that, at least until poverty has been eliminated, this defeats the very purpose of the scheme and should be used sparingly. The solution is certainly not to be found in a return to the conception of social services as charity, which it is a disgrace to accept. In some cases the difficulty has been attacked by the reintroduction of a 'means test', as in the rent rebate schemes adopted by certain housing authorities. But for many this is still reminiscent of the Poor Law. Clearly, if public resources are to be directed where they are most needed, some method of discovering where they are needed is essential. It may be that in time, when taxation and wages policy have produced more equal incomes, financial relief will be necessary only in the case of sickness, incapacity, or old age, and the existence of these will itself be an adequate guide to needs. But any social service the basis of which is financial need irrespective of the reason (e.g. National Assistance and rent rebates) is itself evidence that some are in greater need of regular help than others. However, there is an urgent call for studies of methods of administration which occasion the least possible embarrassment to the applicants. It may well be that they would prefer to disclose their means to total strangers whom they are not likely to meet in person, if a suitable method of investigation can be devised. And there is always a grave danger of regarding a means test less as a method of redistributing expenditure on the welfare services than as an excuse for reducing it.

A further problem is that of deciding how far the administration of welfare principles may be left to local authorities and how far it should be carried out under central control. The latter course is demanded by considerations of efficiency and uniformity of standards, the former by those of local knowledge, democracy, and the need for 'the personal touch'. A satisfactory mean will no doubt emerge from experiments, but there will always be those who feel that undue weight has been given to one side of the question.

Perhaps the most serious problem is that posed by the third of the Beveridge principles. The protection afforded by welfare schemes should not be allowed to discourage initiative. The danger is that some may be content to foist their problems on to the shoulders of the community. Fraternity is a reciprocal relationship, and the citizen who (quite properly) claims the assistance of the community as his right, and not merely as an act of grace on the part of his benefactors, may equally properly be reminded of his responsibilities. These have not been forgotten in this book, and indeed are the main themes of the chapters on Income Tax, National Service, and The Law and the Motorist. Already considerable thought has been given to preserving a balance between relief in kind (e.g. cheap milk and orange juice for expectant mothers and babies) and making financial grants to be spent at the discretion of the recipient. No doubt these are sometimes mis-spent, but placing the responsibility upon the recipient is a recognition of the third Beveridge principle, and it is to be hoped that as its object is progressively realized, it may be possible to extend still further the trust shown in the public. The truth is that we do not expect our politicians and civil servants to be our nursemaids.

A test of the degree to which this and similar books achieve their purpose is the speed with which they become out of date. Whatever the success of contemporary welfare principles, conceptions of human needs should be constantly developing, and with them ideas of what the community can afford. In a hundred years the social revolution of the mid-twentieth century should be taken as much for granted as are now the reforms of the 1830's.

In any future development, it would be dangerous to lose sight of two factors. First, the individual, however independent in temperament, needs a place in some circle where he is known personally and recognized. And in administering to his needs, the Government would do well to strengthen those connexions and not to detach him from his pattern of life. It is the observance of this principle which distinguishes contemporary residential relief for the aged from the institutions of the nineteenth century. Traditionally the role of providing such a circle has been fulfilled by the family. And the folly of attempting to relieve individual symptoms without reflection upon the family background has been pointed out by a number of social scientists in recent years. Prominent among them has been Mrs Jay, who in her chapter on the Family has developed the theme further.

The second factor is the reflection that no legislation or administrative device can abolish every human problem. No rehabilitation scheme can restore sight to the blind, and no social centre is able to dispel loneliness in those who are too shy to join it. Nor is any administrative system proof against the lazy, inefficient, or tyrannous official. There is no way of abolishing misery. The purpose of the benevolent government is to minimize it.

The complaints of the public do not pass unheeded. Sociologists, economists, and politicians are constantly reminding us that rates of benefit are too low; that harder work more efficiently directed would result in a larger national income available for distribution; that individuals are sometimes prepared to take risks about the future in return for having more to spend now; that human needs do not always fit into the classifications provided by Acts of Parliament; and that the crafty and the thriftless sometimes grab more than their deserts. These matters cannot be discussed in a brief introduction of this kind. Nor do we propose to decide political disputes between those who feel that benefits should be proportional to contributions and those who believe that the less needy should be compelled to share their good fortune.

The task of deciding what to include has proved as difficult as ever. The subject-matter has not been defined with a view to giving a complete picture of the modern welfare state. The subjects chosen have been those which, as experience has shown, are the most constant source of practical difficulty to the citizen. Little is said on university education, youth work, or the provision of housing by local authorities, since the answers to normal inquiries about them are simple and readily accessible. The contributors, for their part, have been selected for their practical experience of the problems which they discuss, and the treatment is very much down to earth. It should be added that there is no collective responsibility for the views expressed.

The purposes of this book are threefold. It is intended to assist the harassed citizen in finding the answers to some of his problems. It is hoped to encourage those good Samaritans who are prepared to help their less fortunate neighbours. And it is desired to provide information for those who take an interest in such matters and have no opportunity of consulting more erudite publications. To these three classes of reader the contributors respectfully dedicate their offerings.

I

Principialities and Powers

PETER ARCHER

THE social services and legislation outlined in these pages have all been introduced because it was felt that in the general interest they were desirable. And if a price had to be paid, in the form of restricted purses or otherwise, it was thought to be worth paying. For increased governmental activity implies certain restrictions, and although no one likes restrictions they are sometimes preferable to situations in which matters are left to take their own course. But social legislation also requires officials whose duty it is to carry it into execution. And they must be entrusted with authority to coerce their fellow-citizens. A democratic system seeks to ensure that this authority is no wider than is necessary for the purpose and that it is not abused.

At the head of all authorities stands Parliament. Within the system of British law, Parliament is supreme. It has power to control every other authority by prescribing what is to be done, and is not itself subject to any control. As a matter of practical politics, it recognizes certain limitations. Its members are chosen by the public, and unless they pursue the policy for which they were elected, they are in danger after the next election of finding themselves with a personal interest in the relief of unemployment. In any event, an Act of Parliament which incurred the hostility of the entire public would have little chance of being observed. Officials would be reluctant to administer it, the police would show little enthusiasm in enforcing it, and the man in the street would pursue a passive, but probably successful, resistance.

Nevertheless, in law (and in practice too, so long as its members retain a modicum of common sense) the commands of Parliament are obeyed. They are made known in two ways. The legal mouthpiece for its wishes is a statute, or Act of Parliament. Officials will carry out the duties imposed upon them by a statute, and any disobedience will be remedied by the courts of law, who will not question its authority. This is not quite so simple as it may sound, since a statute is a document the form of which is determined before its effects are known. It has followed a course prescribed by the rules through the House of Commons and the House of Lords, secured a majority in each House (subject to certain exceptions, equally prescribed by the rules) and has received the Queen's signature. Officials and the courts will then administer the statute in accordance with its precise wording, and it is too late for members of Parliament to protest that what they have said is not quite what they meant to say. Sometimes what they have said is so obscure that no one is quite sure what it means until the courts have given a ruling upon the matter.

The second method by which the commands of Parliament are made known is by a vote of censure upon the Government. If Parliament disapproves of the conduct of certain officials to the extent of censuring the Government, then the Government may feel compelled to resign. Parliament's views upon any matter may therefore take effect more immediately than by the passing of a statute, and the Government, together with the officials whom it controls, is not allowed to lose touch with the wishes of the man in the street.

As a matter of law, Parliament might itself attend to every detail of administration, passing statutes awarding Mr Smith thirty shillings per week because he is unemployed, and sending a plumber to repair the pipe in an old people's home. Such a method of running public affairs would, of course, entail obvious difficulties, and in fact various kinds of officials are appointed to carry out the details of the policies laid down by Parliament. Probably the most important are the departments of civil servants, each department responsible for a particular matter of public welfare. Examples which will be encountered in this book are the Ministry of Pensions and National Insurance, the Ministry of Housing and Local Government, and the Ministry of Education. The department has its headquarters in London, but its offices are found throughout the country.

At the head of each department is a minister, who is a member of the House of Commons or the House of Lords. He is usually assisted by one or more other members, known as parliamentary secretaries (or under-secretaries), and it is the ministers and their parliamentary secretaries who are known collectively as the Government. At their head is the Prime Minister, and they are members of the party or parties who for the moment enjoy the confidence of a majority in the House of Commons. The chief ministers meet from time to time in a committee to discuss the claims to money and resources of their respective departmental interests, and accordingly to decide on the policy which Parliament will be asked to support. This committee is the Cabinet.

There is no reason concerned with efficiency why the public affairs of the country could not be conducted entirely by the staffs of Government departments. But the British people tend to distrust their civil servants. They prefer power in the hands of local officials, who are more readily accessible and over whom they (the public) exercise a more immediate control. For this purpose they have turned to local government authorities. Local government is no modern invention. In Britain it existed before the Central Government and was already an ancient institution when the first Parliament was summoned. But between the twelfth and eighteenth centuries local government authorities lost the greater number of their functions, and it was only in the nineteenth century that they came again into their own. The decline of local government had coincided with the period when it was felt that the community had few obligations towards its members, and the unfortunate were left to fend for themselves. When, in the nineteenth century, it awoke to its responsibilities (or, less misleadingly, raised itself gradually from its slumbers) a separate system of local boards was created to administer each new service. It was only towards the end of the nineteenth century that the present system of multi-purpose authorities was set up.

The smallest units of local government are the parish councils. Their powers are very limited, but not unimportant to the inhabitants of the parish. A number of parishes are together under the control of a rural district council, which provides services beyond the resources of the parish. This system functions quite well in country districts, but in urban areas both parish and rural district councils are replaced by a single authority, the urban district council, the powers of which are more appropriate to the needs of a town. Next in the scale is the borough council, the powers and dignity of which are yet wider. Many boroughs were given their status, either by the Sovereign or by Parliament, many years ago, and their present size would hardly warrant so exalted a position. On the other hand, urban districts of sufficient size and importance still succeed from time to time in persuading Parliament to confer upon them the status of a borough. Above the borough and district councils stand the county councils, providing services which cannot be economically administered over an area smaller than a county (or such at least is the contention). An important modern institution is the county borough council. Many boroughs are of a size which enables them to command great resources. On some of these, Parliament has conferred the status of county boroughs; that is to say, they combine the powers of borough and county authorities and thus become their own county councils. Local government officials being human, there is often considerable jealousy between the various grades of local authority, each anxious (laudably enough) to undertake more responsibility, in return, of course, for the corresponding power.

Local government is a democratic institution. The citizen who takes part in the election of an M.P. may feel that his control over the officials of the ministerial departments is somewhat remote. But if his welfare is partly in the hands of local officials, controlled by councillors representing a smaller electorate, whom he can approach much more easily, he may feel less at the mercy of an impersonal machine. In any event, local men are likely to meet local problems with greater understanding and sympathy. However, not every social service can be effectively administered by the local authorities, and many are the arguments as to their proper sphere. Financially, the Central Government is the upholder (and the burden) of the taxpayer; local government, of the ratepayer; but the two classes are by no means rigidly separate, and there are always new methods of financing a service at the expense of the (usually reluctant) citizen. One such method is represented by National Insurance contributions.

If simplicity were the sole consideration, the administration of the social services would be divided between the ministerial departments and the local authorities. But there are difficulties in control to be considered, professional and political interests to be represented, financial economies to be observed. Consequently, in addition to the departments and local authorities, the subject matter of this book includes many bodies which do not fit into either category – Regional Hospital Boards and Wages Councils, to mention but two.

It might have been possible, having allocated a particular service to a given authority, to leave the authority to administer it at its own discretion. But the British people do not trust their officials so far, and their caution is not without reason. The best-intentioned of officials have their prejudices and their susceptibilities, and they are safer when subject to the control of the public whose lives are affected by their actions. In the nineteenth century it was a habit not uncommon among local authorities to spend ratepayers' money on social festivities, the recipients being the councillors. In consequence of the (not unnatural) protests of the public, the courts evolved the doctrine that any action taken by a public authority might be challenged, unless it could be shown to be clearly within the powers delegated by Parliament to that authority. If the Court was not satisfied of this, the action was declared to be *ultra vires* (beyond the power of) the authority.

The conduct of local authorities is supervised in two ways in order to see that it is within their proper powers. First, the ministerial departments send a number of inspectors to investigate their activities and report back to the minister concerned. Secondly, it is open to any citizen aggrieved by the action of a public authority to challenge it in the courts. And the judges who hear the complaint are not officials of the departments. They are independent authorities, with no axe to grind and subject only to the control of Parliament, a control which by custom is rarely exercised. This independence of the judiciary is an important safeguard of the citizen, and all the more so now that, in the interests of the social services, officials are entrusted with wide powers which might be used oppressively.

In the days when social services were hardly existent and the powers and duties of most officials were correspondingly small, all disputes relating to them could be decided by the courts. In busier days Parliament has created a number of tribunals for the hearing of certain kinds of dispute, as, for example, the Local Appeal Tribunals set up under the National Insurance Act. For the ordinary citizen they usually have the advantages of being quick, cheap, and informal, though there are many who feel that they are not so well qualified as the courts to weigh evidence and apply rules. Those who are dissatisfied with the decision of such a tribunal have sometimes a right of appeal. This will depend upon whether Parliament made provision for it in the statute establishing the particular kind of tribunal in question. But even where the courts are not empowered to hear appeals from a tribunal, they will listen sympathetically to complaints about the procedure which it has followed. The court may not substitute its own conclusions for those of the tribunal, but the tribunal must have carried out its work properly, by hearing and giving due weight to the evidence which each party desires to call.

This, then, is the system designed, after many centuries of experience in public administration and a century of experiments in welfare legislation, to combine the maximum of freedom and efficiency. Volumes have been written on the problems which it raises and on the exceptions to every rule. But this is intended merely as an introduction to the administrative framework for those who are not familiar with its workings, in order to understand the pages which follow.

Much thought has been devoted to the preservation of British democratic government, and rightly so, for it is worth preserving. A welfare state which has adapted old methods of administration to new problems, combining fraternity with liberty and insisting on the best of both worlds, is a great achievement. The technicalities of challenging authority, the limitations on the power of the police, the procedure of the law, are not within our terms of reference, but those in need of advice will discover in later sections where it may be sought.

The best safeguard of liberty is found in the goodwill and common sense of administrators and in the informed interest of the citizen. The spare-time councils of laymen set up to advise the officials responsible for the various welfare services represent the spirit of British administration. For the wearer of the shoe knows where it pinches, and if he fails to complain to the cobbler (politely of course) he has only himself to blame.

2

National Insurance

R. E. PRENTICE

ACCORDING to the Beveridge Report, there were five giants on the road to post-war reconstruction: disease, ignorance, squalor, idleness, and want. It was against the last of these that the Beveridge proposals for social insurance were aimed.

The social insurance legislation passed at the end of the war, and based largely on the Beveridge Report, created the first really comprehensive scheme in our history for relieving want in its common forms. Earlier, piecemeal legislation goes back a long way. The Poor Law, forerunner of National Assistance, dates from 1601. In more recent times, Workmen's Compensation dates from 1897, Old Age Pensions from 1908, and Health and Unemployment Insurance from 1911, but all of these taken together, even by the 1940's, provided only an incomplete patchwork of insurance. Some people were covered for all the main forms of benefit, some for certain benefits only, and some not at all. The Beveridge Report proposed, and Parliament in 1945–8 enacted, the first all-embracing scheme.

Most of this new system of social insurance is laid down in two Acts, the National Insurance Act, 1946, and the National Insurance (Industrial Injuries) Act, 1946, and most of this chapter is devoted to describing them. Some reference will also be made to the Family Allowances Act, 1945, and to the Royal Warrants dealing with war pensions. The related question of National Assistance is dealt with in Chapter 3 and the Health Service, which is another close relation, is described in Chapter 6.

THE NATIONAL INSURANCE ACT, 1946

This Act, which came into force on 5 July 1948, provides for all the main social insurance payments, except those relating to industrial injuries. Broadly speaking, it fulfils Beveridge's object of attacking want by providing for fixed financial benefits to be paid at those times which usually lead people to 'feel the pinch'. There are the occasions when earning power is interrupted by sickness or unemployment. Then there is the time when earning ceases altogether because of retirement. There is the case of the widow who needs help when her husband dies. There are the special burdens of guardianship and the expenses arising from maternity, and there are funeral expenses. All these are the subject of payments under the Act.

The benefits are paid from a Fund built up on the insurance principle, with contributions from all insured persons, from the employers of employed contributors and from the Government. The Act and its 'stable companion', the Industrial Injuries Act, are administered by a special Government Department set up to deal with the new legislation. This was originally called the Ministry of National Insurance and has now become the Ministry of Pensions and National Insurance since it was merged with the old Ministry of Pensions, which had been dealing only with war pensions. In addition to its large headquarters offices in London, Newcastle, and Blackpool (war pensions), the Ministry has local offices all over the country. These are the places where claims are made and decided, and we will nearly all have had contact with them at some time or another.

What we have to pay

Subject to two exceptions only, everyone who is above school-leaving age and below retirement age must now be a contributor to the National Insurance Fund. The upper income limits which existed in the past were abolished by the new Act, and rich and poor were brought into the scheme at the same rates of contribution and with the same entitlement to benefit. The only people not compelled to become insured were those with very low incomes (£102 per year or less), and married women, who can come into the scheme, or stay outside, as they wish. If they stay out they have certain rights derived from their husbands' insurance, but if they come in they are entitled to the full range of benefits in their own right.

For the rest insurance is compulsory, and contributors are divided into three classes. The largest class is that of employed persons, who pay a weekly contribution which now stands at 6s 9d* for men over eighteen. There are smaller contributions for women, and for boys and girls under eighteen. The employer has to pay a contribution for each of his employees, which now stands at 6s 0d* for men. He has the custody of the National Insurance cards of his employees and it is his duty to see that the appropriate stamps are put on each week. Self-employed persons pay a contribution which is larger than that of the employed person, although smaller than the combined contribution of the employed person and his employer, the rate for men now being 8s 5d. The third class of contributors are the non-employed persons, who now pay 6s 6d.

These various rates carry slightly different entitlement to benefits. Unemployment benefit is only payable to employed contributors. Sickness benefit and maternity allowance are only payable to employed or self-employed contributors. All other benefits are payable to people in all three classes.

For each of the benefits paid under the Act a certain minimum number of contributions must have been paid or credited in order to qualify. Contributions are credited, i.e. the card is stamped without payment, during periods of sickness and unemployment and in certain other special circumstances.

Now let us take a closer look at some of these benefits:

Unemployment benefit

This form of benefit has so far been less of a drain on the Fund than was at first thought likely. Although the war-time Government envisaged 'full employment' after the war, they took this to mean that the level of unemployment would be around 3 per cent of the working population. In fact it has always been less than this, except for a few months in the 'cold

* Shortly to be increased respectively to 7s 5½d and 6s 1½d. The other figures quoted may also be increased.

spell' of early 1947, and the average figure has been less than 2 per cent.

All the same, large numbers of claims have been made, particularly for short periods while people have been changing jobs.

To qualify for this benefit a claimant must be undergoing 'a period of interruption of employment.' He must also be 'capable of work' and 'available for employment', which involves registering at the Employment Exchange and being prepared to accept a reasonable offer of a job. The first three days of unemployment do not qualify for benefit unless they form part of a period of at least twelve days' unemployment within thirteen weeks from the first day of the claim.

Some of the more extravagant critics of the Act in its early days painted a picture of idle men who would prefer to live on money from the National Insurance Scheme rather than do an honest job of work. With this in mind it is worth mentioning the ways in which the Fund is protected against improper claims to unemployment benefit.

In making himself 'available for employment' a man must not restrict himself unreasonably in the type of job he will take. What is reasonable will depend on a number of factors, including of course his previous experience, but he could not restrict himself to work not likely to be available in the district. Neither could a claimant make unreasonable provisions as to hours of work, etc. For example, a married woman with domestic responsibilities might reasonably register for part-time work, but only if the hours she specified were in accordance with the requirements of local employers.

Similarly, failure to apply for a vacant job of which he has been notified, or refusal to accept it after applying, may lead to disqualification from benefit for a period of up to six weeks, unless the claimant can show good cause for not taking the job. The same disqualification for up to six weeks applies in the case of dismissal from work for 'misconduct' or for voluntarily leaving a job without just cause.

Another common reason for the refusal of unemployment benefit is that the loss of employment was due to a trade dispute at the claimant's place of work. This disqualification affects not only men who come out on strike. Anyone who loses employment by reason of the dispute is disqualified unless he can show that he is *neither* taking part in the dispute, *nor* financing it, *nor* directly interested in its outcome, and that no-one in his 'grade or class' at the place of employment is taking part in, financing, or directly interested in the outcome.

This is a very wide and rather unfair disqualification. Any-one is 'directly interested' in a dispute if his conditions of work may be affected by the outcome. Again, if a man is not affected in this way but some others of his 'grade or class' strike in sympathy with those who are affected, he is disqualified from benefit. Large numbers of men have been put out of work owing to trade disputes in which they were not participating and have lost benefit because of this section of the Act. The T.U.C. and other bodies have called for an amendment of the section, but so far without success.

Much more could be written about unemployment benefit – about the exhaustion of benefit, when a man is or is not 'on holiday', how people are affected by short-time working – these and many other problems are being disputed and decided constantly. But it is time to move on, reminding the reader that a brief survey cannot cover all the aspects of this complicated Act of Parliament with its host of regulations.

Sickness benefit

This is paid in respect of 'any day of incapacity for work'. The onus of proof is on the claimant to show incapacity, and this is normally done by sending a certificate from the panel doctor, or from the hospital, to the local office of the Ministry of Pensions and National Insurance.

It should be noted that the Act says 'incapacity for work', and this means for any work, not only the claimant's normal work. If a man is unfit for his usual job, but fit for something less arduous, then strictly speaking his doctor should not cer-tify him as unfit for work. Obviously there are many short-term periods of sickness when this is not followed to its logical conclusion, but the proper procedure for a man in this position is to register for lighter work at the Employment Exchange and then claim unemployment benefit if no work is found which is suitable for him.

Although claims are normally dealt with on the basis of the doctor's certificate, this is not necessarily the final authority. If the Insurance Officer (see below) thinks fit, he may arrange for a medical examination by another doctor through the Divisional Medical Office of the Ministry of Health. He can then consider the report of this examination alongside the panel doctor's certificates and decide the claim according to the balance of medical evidence, his decision being subject to the right of appeal as described later. This procedure is a safeguard against the 'lead-swinger' with an over-indulgent doctor, although it would be wrong to suppose that it is only used in such cases.

There are two exceptions to the rule that a claimant must be incapable of work. One is that he is suffering from some disease or disablement which would make it injurious for him to commence work, even though he is not actually incapable of it. The other is that he is a carrier of or has been in contact with an infectious disease.

Certain rules of behaviour are laid down in the regulations, any breach of which may lead to disqualification from benefit for a period of up to six weeks. These include any unreasonable refusal of prescribed treatment (apart from vaccination or inoculation, where conscientious scruples are recognized), and the performance of any paid work, unless this is undertaken on doctor's orders as part of the treatment.

As with unemployment, the first three days of sickness do not count, unless they are part of a longer period, i.e. twelve days or more within the next thirteen weeks. This rules out claims for a host of minor ailments, including, for example, most of the common colds which keep people at home for three days or less.

One further point should be made before leaving the subject of sickness benefit: there is a very strict time limit for applications. A claim should be made within three days of the first day of incapacity. If a claim is late, payment is only made from three days before the date of the claim, unless there is some good cause for lateness. 'Good cause' has been interpreted fairly strictly, and it certainly does not include ignorance of the right to claim or ignorance of the time limit. An example of 'good cause' is an illness so severe that the patient is not capable of thinking about claiming benefit.

Large numbers of claims fail for part if not all of a period of sickness owing to failure to apply in time. While this seems most marked in the case of sickness benefit, with its very short time limit, it also applies to other benefits under both of the National Insurance Acts.

Widows' benefits

It should be made clear that the Act does not provide for an indefinite pension for every widow. After the first thirteen weeks of widowhood an allowance, or pension, is only paid in cases where there are dependent children, *or* the widow is over fifty, *or* she is incapable of self-support.

During the first thirteen weeks following her husband's death a widow is entitled to a *widow's allowance*. This is paid in all cases where the husband's insurance satisfies the contribution conditions.

After this period a *widowed mother's allowance* is paid for so long as she is caring for a child or children who were part of her late husband's family at the time of his death.

If there are no children a *widow's pension* is payable if the widow is over fifty but under sixty at the time of her husband's death. This continues until the age of sixty, which is the retirement age for women. In certain cases the pension is also payable to widows under fifty if they are incapable of self-support by reason of some infirmity.

All of these benefits cease on the death of the widow or her remarriage or her cohabitation with another man as his wife.

Retirement pensions

The pensions payable to retired people under the Act are described in Chapter 9 and need not be restated here in detail.

In considering their place in the scheme it is important to note that they are 'retirement' pensions payable to men over sixty-five and women over sixty who have retired, and they are not 'old age pensions', although they are often called by this name. People who go on working after these ages do not get a pension until they retire or until they reach the age of seventy (men) or sixty-five (women). They can increase the pension they will eventually get by working beyond the normal retirement age.

An important point of which some people are unaware is that a notice of retirement must be lodged with the Ministry four months before the actual date of retirement. Failure to do this may lead to a loss of pension for a time.

These pensions are the heaviest liability on the National Insurance Fund, and this liability is growing every year as the proportion of elderly people in the country increases. Even without any future increase in the current rates of benefit, this factor must lead to higher contributions in the years to come, or alternatively to a much higher payment from the Exchequer into the Fund.

As we have already noted, it was one of the basic principles of the Act to provide for the times when earning power is cut off or interrupted, and the retirement pension was designed to meet the largest common example of this, i.e. the sudden absence of wages when a man retires from his job. Unfortunately, it does nothing, and by its very nature it can do nothing, to bridge the gap between those people who have superannuation pensions and those who have not. An increasing number of retired people now benefit from superannuation schemes in addition to their retirement pensions, and these people by and large do not suffer a catastrophic fall in their living standards on retirement. Some others, of course, have investments or incomes from other sources. On the other hand, people relying on the retirement pension, even when it is supplemented by the National Assistance Board, face a very difficult struggle to make ends meet, and in most cases have to accept much lower standards than they had been accustomed to before retirement.

Whatever satisfaction we are entitled to feel at the working of our National Insurance Scheme as a whole, the problem presented by these two 'classes' of retired people remains unsolved and ought to be tackled in any future reform of the scheme.

Other benefits

A brief note must be made of the other three benefits payable under the Act: maternity benefit, guardian's allowance, and the death grant.

There are two kinds of *maternity benefit*: one kind payable to a woman who is insured in her own right, the other to a woman who is relying on her husband's insurance. In the first case a weekly allowance is paid for at least thirteen weeks, starting with the the sixth week before the expected confinement and continuing for seven weeks afterwards. If the pregnancy continues for longer than expected, the allowance can be claimed for an extra period of up to six weeks without affecting the seven weeks' benefit after the birth of the child. For mothers who are not insured in their own right there is a small lump sum payable when the child is born, followed by an attendance allowance for the next four weeks.

A small *guardian's allowance* is paid in cases where a person is caring for a child as its guardian. It can only be paid when both the parents or step-parents have died and where one of them was an insured person under the Act. The child must be in the guardian's 'family' within the meaning of the Family Allowances Act.

The *death grant* is a small sum, paid on the death of an insured person, which is designed to help pay funeral expenses, etc. It did not exist in any form under the old legislation which preceded the National Insurance Act, and this means that the death of anyone who was over retirement age in 1948 does not lead to the payment of the grant.

Rates of benefit

So far, in order to avoid the constant repetition of figures, no mention has been made of the actual rates of benefit. These are

in any case liable to change and have changed more than once
since the Act came into force.

When the scheme began on 5 July 1948 the basic rate for a
single adult person in receipt of sickness or unemployment
benefit, or of a retirement pension, was 26s a week. The rate at
the time of writing, which came into force in April or May
1955 (the actual date varied according to the type of benefit) is
40s a week. This represents very approximately a 'cost-of-
living increase' designed to maintain the purchasing power of
the rates as originally fixed, but it is fair to add that this increase and the preceding one did not take effect until long after
the old rate had lost a large part of its value owing to rising
prices. The work involved in changing benefit rates, e.g. the
alteration of millions of pension books, is very considerable,
and this is only one of the reasons for the reluctance of successive Governments to raise benefits more quickly. Other reasons
include the unpopular necessity for a rise in contributions, the
inflationary effects of extra spending power, etc. Proposals for
an annual review of benefits have been made and are now the
subject of controversy between the political parties.

The current rate of benefit, then, for a single person is 40s a
week in respect of unemployment or sickness benefit or a retirement pension. For a wife or other adult dependant there is
an extra 25s. If there are children under school-leaving age an
additional 11s 6d is paid for the first child and 3s 6d for each of
the others (these qualify for the family allowance as well).

For example, a retired couple now receive £3 5s a week. A
married man drawing sickness benefit with one child and with
his wife at work would draw £2 11s 6d. A man with his wife at
home and with three children would draw £4 3s 6d, and they
would also be drawing 18s in family allowances.

Widows receive 55s a week for the first thirteen weeks. Those
who then qualify for a widow's pension receive 40s a week,
which is increased in the case of the widowed mother's allowance by a payment for the children on the scale described
above.

How claims are decided

Apart from a few special questions which are determined by the Minister, claims and other questions under the Act are dealt with by an official in each locality known as the Insurance Officer. His duty is to examine each claim, satisfy himself as to the facts, and then decide the issue.

If he rejects a claim, there is an automatic right of appeal to a Local Appeal Tribunal consisting of three members. One of these is taken from a panel of people representing local employers and one from a panel representing organized labour. The chairman is independent and is usually a lawyer. Proceedings at these tribunals are usually rather informal. The claimant and the Insurance Officer state their points of view, and the claimant can be assisted by a trade union representative or some other person, but not by a barrister or solicitor.

From the decision of this tribunal there is a possibility of a further appeal. The Act provides for the appointment of a National Insurance Commissioner and Deputy Commissioners, each of whom must be a barrister of at least ten years' standing. An appeal 'to the Commissioner' can be decided by the Commissioner himself, or by one of his deputies, or by a tribunal of more than one of them.

There is no automatic right of appeal at this level, but leave can be granted by the Local Appeal Tribunal or by the Commissioner himself, and this is usually done if there is any real doubt as to the validity of the Tribunal decision. An appeal can be made not only by the claimant himself, but also by his trade union acting on his behalf. The Insurance Officer also has a right of appeal. This means that a claim could be rejected by the Insurance Officer, allowed by the Local Appeal Tribunal, and then disallowed by the Commissioner as a result of an Insurance Officer's appeal. In this event benefit would normally be paid from the date of the Tribunal's decision and then cease on the date of the Commissioner's decision. The claimant would not have to repay the money unless the Commissioner decided that he had acted 'in bad faith'.

Selected decisions of the Commissioner are published, and

they form a sort of case law on the type of questions often disputed under the Act for the guidance of Insurance Officers, members of Local Tribunals, and others who are concerned in these matters.

Conclusion

This brief sketch of the National Insurance Act can only be taken as giving a general picture of what it is, what the benefits are, and how it works. There is a great deal more to it, as the Act is a very long one and it has spawned a large number of statutory regulations filling in points of detail. These are being added to and amended from time to time.

This means that many of the statements made in this chapter can be qualified in various ways, and some of the rules referred to are liable to be amended by fresh regulations. Anyone wanting the complete up-to-date answer on a point of detail should refer to the Act itself, the regulations, the Commissioner's decisions, or (usually the best approach) should inquire at the local office of the Ministry.

THE NATIONAL INSURANCE (INDUSTRIAL INJURIES) ACT, 1946

This Act, whose title is usually shortened to 'The Industrial Injuries Act', came into force on the same date as the Act we have been discussing, i.e. 5 July 1948, and it is in many ways closely related to it.

Both Acts are administered by the same Ministry, and at the local offices the same people are engaged in dealing with claims under either scheme. Both are financed by an insurance fund built up by contributions from workers, employers, and the Government.

Owing to the relatively small number of claims as compared with the National Insurance Act, the Industrial Injuries Act is able to provide much higher benefits for a very much lower contribution. For example, a single man's rate of injury benefit is now 67s 6d a week, as against 40s for sickness benefit. The contribution only amounts to 5d a week out of the weekly sum of 6s 9d* that an employed man over eighteen has to pay.

In contrast with the other Act, there is no cover for self-employed or non-employed people. Contributors must be employed, i.e. under a contract of service, and all people in this category must contribute. This includes married women, who, as we have seen, can stay outside the main National Insurance Scheme, but who are compelled to contribute to the Industrial Injuries Fund if they are at work and who are, therefore, eligible for all benefits under the Act.

The Act took the place of the old Workmen's Compensation Acts, which were repealed on the day it came into force. These had provided for compensation for injured workmen, but on a very different basis. The employer had been liable to pay compensation in cases of industrial accidents, but only to the extent of paying part of the loss of earnings involved. If an injury did not lead to a loss of earnings, there was no claim under the W.C.A. The compensation was paid weekly, but could be commuted for a lump-sum settlement. Disputed claims were dealt with by the law courts, and this was a slow and expensive procedure for an injured man who might be suffering great hardship. A claim under the W.C.A. ruled out any claim for damages against the employer. All non-manual workers earning over £420 a year were excluded from the Acts.

It is small wonder that the trade unions and other interested parties campaigned for a new deal for the injured workman, and many of their demands have been met by the Industrial Injuries Act. Compensation is no longer paid by the employer, but by the State fund, to which employer and employee contribute. Cases are no longer argued in the courts, but are decided by the quicker and cheaper procedure of an Insurance Officer's decision, subject to appeal to the Local Appeal Tribunal and the Commissioner. The income limit has been abolished and equal compensation is paid to all, irrespective of their income or the loss of earnings due to the accident (apart from the special hardship allowance described below, which is

* See page 25, footnote.

related to loss of earnings). It is not possible to commute compensation rights for a lump sum, and the old difficulty of having to choose between compensation and a claim at common law has now disappeared, as the injured workman can proceed with both.

What injuries are covered?

The main entitlement to benefit arises from 'personal injury by accident arising out of and in the course of employment'. At first sight this may seem a clear enough definition, and it obviously covers the majority of industrial accidents, but there are also a great many borderline cases, and some of these have been the subject of considerable litigation under the old Workmen's Compensation Acts (which used the same words) and of a number of appeals to the Commissioner under the new Act.

The words 'personal injury' have been taken to include internal injuries (e.g. ruptures) as well as external ones and the sudden onset of an illness or of nervous shock. The word 'accident' has also been defined rather more widely than in everyday speech. A germ entering the body has been called an accident. So has the strain through pulling on a stiff lever. So has the handling of frozen sugar-beet which caused a man to suffer from frostbite. But the accident must be a specific event or a series of specific events. A gradual process over a long period (such as the constant use of a vibrating tool, which is liable to injure the hand) is not an accident and is not covered.

The words 'arising out of and in the course of employment' also give rise to some difficulties. The course of employment is usually taken to extend from the time of entering the employer's premises to the time of leaving. If a man slips inside the factory gates he will normally qualify for injury benefit, but if he slips on the pavement outside he will only get sickness benefit. Complications arise in the case of outdoor workers, such as bus drivers, postmen, or travelling salesmen, and there is a lot of case law dealing with the point at which they enter the 'course of employment'.

An accident arising 'in the course of employment' is also

taken to have arisen 'out of' employment unless there is some evidence to the contrary. Exceptions are made in various cases, particularly where the injured person has been doing something for his own purposes rather than his employer's. For example, if he is injured while 'larking about' or while crossing the workshop to borrow some cigarettes, then he would not be covered by the Act. On the other hand, negligence is immaterial. If a man is injured through his own carelessness while doing something which is part of his job, he still has a claim under the act.

Accidents do not form the only basis for a claim. Benefit is also paid to people who suffer from certain prescribed diseases. These are diseases which are associated with certain kinds of employment, so that the risk of getting them is a risk of a particular job rather than a general risk to which everyone is equally exposed. A schedule of these diseases and their related occupations was laid down in regulations at the time of the Act, and there have been one or two additions since.

For example, poisoning by lead, manganese, and several other substances, is covered for people using or handling them or exposed to dust, fumes, or vapour from them. Anthrax is on the list for workers handling wool, hair, bristles, etc., and glanders for 'contact with equine animals or their carcases'. Telegraphist's cramp, writer's cramp, and miner's nystagmus are included, and so is industrial dermatitis for those who are exposed to 'dust, liquid or vapour'. An important addition to the list since the Act came into force is tuberculosis, covered in relation to nurses and other people in close contact with patients. There is a special schedule of occupations relating to pneumoconiosis, which is a fibrosis of the lung due to dust. Silicosis, due to silica dust, is a common form of this disease, and was the dreaded scourge of mining communities for many years. It still occurs, but on a much smaller scale owing to improved ventilation and other preventive measures. In addition to mining, the occupations on the list include sand blasting, the use of a grindstone, the manufacture of china and earthenware, and many others. By an amendment to the regulations, cover for pneumoconiosis has now been extended to any occupation involving substantial exposure to dust, although if it is not in the schedule the claimant must prove the connexion and does not get the same presumption in his favour as if he worked in one of the occupations on the list.

We have now seen that there are two ways in which a claim can arise under the Industrial Injuries Act: from injury by accident or from a prescribed disease. It should be noted that some people may suffer injury owing to their work but fail to get benefit at all. From time to time a case arises of some disability, not a prescribed disease, which is due to a 'process' rather than an accident. For example, a man may suffer deafness owing to prolonged exposure to loud noise, or a lorry driver may suffer some ill effects from a draught coming in through his cabin window. Despite pressure from the trade unions, no amendment has been made to the Act to cover cases of this kind.

What benefits are payable?

As with the National Insurance Act, there have been increases in the various rates of benefit since 1948, and the figures quoted are those which came into force in April and May 1955.

During the first twenty-six weeks following an accident (or following the development of an industrial disease) *industrial injury benefit* is payable for so long as the claimant is incapacitated from work. In other words, it is paid from the date of the accident until the return to work, or until the end of twenty-six weeks, whichever is the earlier. The rate is 67s 6d a week for a single adult person. Additional payments for wife and children are the same as those paid under the National Insurance Act.

At the end of the injury benefit period, if there is any remaining disability, a claim may be made for *disablement benefit*. This is paid in respect of any loss of faculty resulting from the accident, whether or not the claimant is at work. In the case of a permanent disablement the benefit is payable for life.

The rate of disablement benefit depends on an assessment

made by a medical board, who compare the claimant with a normal healthy person of the same age and then assess the extent of his disability as a percentage. For certain injuries the Act lays down the percentages, e.g. the loss of both legs or of both hands is assessed at 100 per cent. So is absolute deafness or very severe facial disfigurement. The complete loss of an arm is measured at 90 per cent or of a hand at 60 per cent. The loss of one eye, the other being normal, is assessed at 40 per cent.

Most disabilities, of course, come outside these categories, and the medical board have to make their own assessment of the degree of disablement. They often make a provisional assessment for a period of perhaps six months or a year, after which the claimant is examined again to see what change, if any, has taken place, and then a new assessment is made. When they are satisfied that the condition has settled down and they can reasonably foresee the future effects of the accident, they make a final assessment, which may be for life or for some shorter period.

For all assessments of 20 per cent or more, disablement benefit takes the form of a pension. A 100 per cent pension is 67s 6d a week, the same rate as injury benefit, and smaller assessments are compensated proportionately. For assessments of less than 20 per cent there are lump sum gratuities varying with the percentage awarded and with the period covered by the assessment.

If an injured person is still incapable of work at the end of the twenty-six-week injury benefit period, he can draw sickness benefit under the National Insurance Act, which is payable in addition to his disablement pension. Certain other additional payments can be claimed by people receiving disablement benefit, as follows:

A payment called a *special hardship allowance* can be claimed when the injury causes a loss of earning power. The claimant must be unable to follow his regular occupation 'or one of equivalent standard'. This inability must have existed since the end of the injury benefit period, or it must be likely to be permanent. If these conditions are fulfilled the amount of the allowance is the actual loss of weekly earnings up to a maximum of 27s 6d.

There is also an *unemployability supplement* for industrial casualties who are likely to be permanently unemployable, a *constant attendance allowance* in cases where the person is so badly disabled as to need constant attendance, and a *hospital treatment allowance* which provides a temporary 100 per cent pension for people in hospital.

Finally, we must mention *industrial death benefit*, which is paid to certain classes of dependants of a person killed in an industrial accident or dying from the effects of an industrial accident or a prescribed disease. In the case of widows, if they are in a category that would qualify for a pension under the National Insurance Act (i.e. aged over fifty, or with dependent children, or incapable of self-support), they get a pension which is 5s higher than the one they would get under that Act. Other widows, who get no pension under the other Act after the first thirteen weeks, get a pension of 20s a week under the Industrial Injuries Act. Provision is also made for other dependants in the following categories: widowers, children, women guardians of the deceased's children, parents and certain other 'prescribed relatives'. It will be seen that the provisions are much wider than those of the National Insurance Act.

How claims are dealt with

We have already examined the procedure under the National Insurance Act, whereby claims are decided by the Insurance Officer with a right of appeal to the Local Appeal Tribunal, and sometimes a further right of appeal to the Commissioner. Substantially the same procedure is followed under the Industrial Injuries Act, and here again a considerable body of case law has been built up in the form of Commissioners' decisions -- more complex on the whole than under the other Act. The definition of an industrial accident, which has been discussed above, gives rise to a number of disputed cases, and so do claims to special hardship allowance.

As with the other Act certain specialized questions are

decided by the Minister outside the normal machinery, and under this Act there is a further category, known as 'medical questions', which also go through different channels. These are mainly concerned with the question whether an accident has resulted in a loss of faculty and, if so, at what percentage this should be assessed. These matters are decided by a medical board consisting of two or more doctors. In most cases there is a right of appeal to a Medical Appeal Tribunal, which has a legal chairman and two medical members.

Claims for damages

Before leaving the question of industrial accidents, it should be mentioned that the rights of an injured person are not necessarily confined to receiving benefit under the Industrial Injuries Act. In certain cases he may also be in a position to claim damages either from his employer or from some other party. Damages, of course, are awarded by a court or are agreed 'out of Court' between the parties involved.

A claim, for instance, could be made against an employer who had failed to carry out his duty under the Factories Acts to provide guards for dangerous machinery, if this failure has caused the accident. In addition to statutory obligations of this kind, every employer owes a duty to his employees at Common Law to take reasonable care for their safety. Failure to provide proper materials, or to organize a 'safe system of work', might provide the basis for a claim.

As we have seen, the old Workmen's Compensation Acts laid down that an injured workman had to choose between a claim under the Acts and a claim for damages. This rule has now been abolished and a damages claim is not prejudiced by the receipt of benefit under the Industrial Injuries Act. The only effect on the claim is the rule that, if damages are recovered, one-half of the benefits received by way of injury benefit, disablement benefit, or sickness benefit for a period of up to five years must be deducted from the total sum of damages.

We have now made a brief survey of the two Acts of Parliament which form the basis of social insurance in this country. Before concluding the chapter there are two other related subjects which should be mentioned – family allowances and the treatment of war pensions. Neither is a question of 'insurance' in the strict sense of the word, but they form part of the financial basis of our Welfare State and they are obviously fairly close relatives of the other benefits we have been describing. The picture given in the preceding pages would not be complete unless they were brought into it.

THE FAMILY ALLOWANCES ACT, 1945

Family allowances came into force earlier than the insurance benefits we have been discussing and, unlike those benefits, they are paid for entirely by taxation. At the same time they are all part of the post-war process by which cash transfers are made from the pockets of all of us to the pockets of those who have some special need of financial help.

The provisions of the Act are very common knowledge. For every child in a family, after the first, the allowance is paid, the original amount being 5s a week for each child and the current amount being 8s for the second child of the family and 10s for every subsequent child.

Each child must be below school-leaving age and must be 'of the family' of the recipient of the allowance. Most cases are quite straightforward, but special rules have been evolved for disputed cases, which may be referred to special referees appointed to decide these matters. Only one allowance can be paid in respect of any one child, and complications arise when children live apart from their parents, or the parents live apart and the child spends some time with each, etc. If the claimant is living apart from the child, he or she must be maintaining it at least to the extent of the value of the allowance.

Allowing for these rare complications, the Act as a whole proceeds very smoothly and is undoubtedly of great benefit, particularly to large families with modest incomes.

WAR PENSIONS

The provisions for war pensions for ex-members of the armed forces are laid down in the various Royal Warrants, and there are also a number of Acts of Parliament dealing with other categories of people, such as merchant seamen and civilian war casualties. Here again the benefits are paid for by taxation, but there are obvious similarities to the other matters we have been discussing. This is illustrated by the fact that the same Ministry now deals with war pensions and the two national insurance schemes. In particular there is a close parallel between the provisions for war casualties and industrial casualties.

The current provisions for war pensions relate to service in the forces since the outbreak of war in 1939 and still apply to servicemen now in the forces. Similar provisions exist for the period of the 1939–45 war for merchant seamen, the Home Guard, Civil Defence Personnel, civilian air-raid casualties, etc. Other provisions, not quite so wide in all respects, are in force for those disabled in the 1914–18 war.

Pensions are paid in respect of disabilities which are either 'attributable' to service or which were 'aggravated' by it – and remain aggravated. The pensions are like those paid under the Industrial Injuries Act, which borrowed its methods from the war pensions arrangements. Assessments are made on the same basis by medical boards and a 100 per cent pension is at the same rate. A slightly different system operates for awards of less than 20 per cent, the lump sum gratuity being preceded by a pension for a limited period.

Another similarity is in the supplementary allowances paid to some categories. There is a *constant attendance allowance* and an *unemployability supplement* on the same lines as those described above in relation to industrial casualties, and there is an '*allowance for lowered standard of occupation*' which is similar to the *special hardship allowance*. There is also a rule providing for the payment of a temporary 100 per cent pension during periods of incapacity due to treatment, which goes a little further than the provisions of the Industrial Injuries Act.

The appeals machinery is a little different. All issues are decided in the first place by the Minister and there is a right of appeal to a Pensions Appeal Tribunal, which is an independent body appointed by the Lord Chancellor. For 'entitlement' appeals (e.g. against the rejection of a claim) the Tribunal has a legal chairman, a medical member, and a 'service' member, who must be an ex-serviceman -- or an ex-servicewoman, or ex-civil defence worker, etc., according to the category of the appellant. For 'assessment' appeals, against the percentage assessment, there are two medical members, one of whom is chairman, and the 'service' member. On a point of law, permission may be given for a further appeal to the High Court, but in most cases the decision of the Tribunal is final.

CONCLUSION

This brief sketch of our national insurance system, with the even more brief references to other closely related matters, is inevitably full of gaps. A proper survey would require a volume, and a large one at that. However, it is hoped that enough has been said to give some idea of the scale and scope of what is being done.

Comprehensive social insurance is still fairly new to us. The Acts and regulations still leave room for criticism at many points. There are anomalies and injustices which should be put right. All the same, Britain has a system which is not only a tremendous advance on our own previous experience, but is also far ahead of the standards of most other countries. It is a proper subject for pride, without complacency.

3

National Assistance

R. E. PRENTICE

IN the chapter on National Insurance we saw how provision is made for the most common forms of hardship. We now have to consider what happens to those people who are in need but who do not fall into any of the categories laid down in the National Insurance Act or the Industrial Injuries Act. And what about people who are drawing benefit under one of these Acts but still cannot make ends meet ? After all, the rates of benefit are quite modest and they take no account of the rent or other commitments of a family, which may be very large. The main purpose of National Assistance is to lay down a sort of 'national minimum' and to provide for those who would otherwise fall below it.

In every community, at almost every stage of development, some recognized procedure has existed to help people who are destitute – if it has only been the toleration of beggars and the recognition of some obligation by more fortunate people to give them alms. In medieval Britain the main burden was carried for centuries by the monasteries, with their tradition of giving food and money to the poor man at the gate. The Elizabethan Poor Law was born out of the social consequences of the dissolution of the monasteries. This law of 1601 established public responsibility for the relief of distress, which has existed in one form or another ever since. The story of the way in which this responsibility has been discharged is a strange mixture of charity and harshness, of genuine compassion and Bumble-dom, of determination to perform a Christian duty and equal determination not to overdo it.

In the nineteenth century the climate of opinion which developed out of the Industrial Revolution produced a harsher attitude than before. The Boards of Guardians and the parish 'workhouse' were among the best-hated institutions in the country, and in most cases this reputation seems to have been well deserved. In the present century the Guardians gave way to the Public Assistance Committees of the local authorities, and these held sway until the National Assistance Act, 1948, came into force.

These local P.A.C's had two main duties. One was to maintain various local institutions – for elderly and infirm people, for orphaned children, etc. The other was to provide relief for people in need, in the form of weekly payments based on a means test. Although many of these committees carried out their work in a progressive and humane fashion, the standard varied between localities and the old spirit of the Poor Law lingered on.

The Act of 1948 took the payment of relief out of the hands of the local authorities. One reason for this was to standardize the system throughout the country. Another was the feeling that the old stigma of 'going on the parish' would more easily disappear. Instead of going almost literally 'cap in hand' before a committee of local people, the claimant now has a private interview with an official of the new National Assistance Board, and it was rightly felt that this was a more dignified proceeding.

Meanwhile the local authority have kept powers for the provision of residential accommodation for elderly people and others. They also have the duty to provide for children who are orphans or otherwise deprived of a normal home, but this is no longer dealt with under the same legislation. A separate Children Act deals with this problem.

Financial help is now administered by a National Assistance Board, which consists of a chairman, vice-chairman, and up to four other members, at least one of whom must be a woman. They have a large staff working under them, not only at headquarters but at area offices throughout the country. The members of the Board are appointed by the Minister of Pensions and National Insurance, but it is important to note that they and their staff are not part of the Ministry. They are a semi-autonomous public body, rather like the Milk Marketing Board or the B.B.C., less independent than a nationalized industry but more independent than a Government department. There is no day-to-day control by the Minister, but an annual report must be submitted to him each year, and this is laid before Parliament.

Assistance grants

It is the duty of the Board 'to assist persons in Great Britain who are without resources to meet their requirements, or whose resources ... must be supplemented in order to meet their requirements.'

An application for assistance can be made by any person aged sixteen or over. Anyone under pensionable age and available for work should apply to the Employment Exchange, and other people should apply direct to the area office of the Board, using a form which can be obtained at any post office. They may present this form at the office or send it by post, in which event they will probably be visited at home by one of the Board's officers. If the claimant has registered for work at the Employment Exchange, payments of assistance are made through that Exchange, and the Board has power to make a grant conditional upon the claimant registering for employment if he has not already done so. In other cases (e.g. sick or elderly people) a book is issued consisting of orders which can be cashed weekly at the post office.

Two disqualifications should be mentioned. A person in full-time work cannot receive assistance. Neither can anyone who is out of work owing to a trade dispute. This latter rule is couched in the same terms as the one we have already examined in relation to unemployment benefit, and it operates against many people who are not actually taking part in a dispute. In the case of assistance, however, this disqualification applies only to the individual put out of work. His wife and children can receive assistance.

The amount of an assistance grant is worked out as follows: first of all, the needs of the applicant are assessed according to the rules which are described below; secondly, his resources are calculated, disregarding those amounts which will be described; then the grant is the sum by which his resources fall short of his needs. The grant is subject to the rule that, after adding to it any part-time earnings, the total must not exceed the amount which the claimant would earn if he were working full-time in his normal occupation.

How, then, are the needs of an applicant worked out? They are the needs of the person making the claim, the wife or husband of that person, and their children under sixteen living with them at the time of the claim. The regulations lay down a scale of allowances providing for these needs, other than rent which is added later. This scale has been amended more than once to bring it in line with changes in the cost of living. The current amounts, which came into force in January 1956, provide 67s a week for a married couple. A person living alone who is a householder and responsible for the housekeeping, etc., is said to need 40s a week. For all other persons the scale varies from 36s for an adult over twenty-one to 13s for a child under five.

There is a separate scale at higher rates for people who are blind or who are the victims of tuberculosis. For example, the normal figure of 67s a week for a married couple is increased to 87s if one of them is blind or tubercular, or 101s if they both are.

An allowance for rent is then added to the needs of the family as determined by the scale. For this purpose rent is taken to include rates. If the applicant is a householder or is living alone, the allowance is usually the net rent that he pays, although there is a procedure whereby the figure is reduced for an abnormally high rent. If the applicant is living as a member of someone else's household, the rent allowance will be a reasonable share of the rent that the householder is paying.

In cases where the house is owned by the person applying for assistance or by his wife and there is a mortgage, the interest payments are treated as rent, but not the capital repayments. If part of the house is let or sub-let, the proceeds are taken as reducing the rent, and if they exceed the rent, the excess is regarded as an income to be taken into account when assessing the resources of the family.

Now that we have seen how the needs are worked out we must turn to the question of calculating the resources which are set off against them. In the main these resources are any income or property on which the family would have to rely if the Board did not make a grant. The income would include any part-time earnings (full-time work, as we have seen, disqualifies the applicant altogether), most classes of National Insurance benefit, any rent or interest on investments, etc. The income of the applicant, the wife or husband, and any dependants are all taken into account. In considering property no account is taken of furniture, household effects, and personal belongings.

The regulations allow some forms of income and property to be disregarded within limits. Income can be disregarded in the following categories: sick pay from a friendly society or a trade union up to 10s 6d a week; superannuation up to the same limit; Workmen's Compensation payments, disability pensions (military or industrial), or maternity allowances, up to 20s a week. The total amount that can be disregarded if there is more than one source of relief is 20s a week. Maternity grants and death grants are disregarded altogether.

If the applicant is in part-time work, then the first 20s of his net earnings are disregarded, unless he was compelled to register for work at the Employment Exchange by the National Assistance Board, in which case only the first 10s is disregarded. The first 10s 6d a week from any charitable grant is also ignored as a rule.

Two forms of capital are not taken into account: the value of the house in which the applicant lives and the first £375 of war savings, which includes Defence Bonds, National Savings Certificates, and deposits in the Post Office Savings Bank or Trustee Savings Bank.

If the remaining capital is worth less than £75 it is ignored. If it is above £75 but not more than £400, a sum of 6d a week is added to the income for the first £75, and a further 6d for each complete £25 after that. Normally, no assistance grant can be made if the capital is worth more than £400. It has been found in practice that only a very small proportion of applicants have much capital over the value of £75 which is not in the form of war savings.

One further adjustment may have to be made in considering the resources of an applicant. If the person is a householder, or the husband or wife of a householder, any member of the household not dependent on him is considered as supporting him up to the value of 7s a week – less if the income of this non-dependant is very low. For instance, a grown-up son or daughter living at home would normally be considered as contributing 7s a week to a parent applying for assistance. This rule is not effective if the non-dependent member has dependants of his own. In that case he is only regarded as paying a share of the rent.

After all these adjustments have been made, the assistance grant emerges as the amount by which the resources fall short of the needs. If there are any special circumstances which lead to exceptional needs which cannot be covered by these rules the Board has power to make payments to meet them.

The Report of the National Assistance Board for the year 1954 showed that in December of that year a total of 1,796,000 assistance grants were being paid. Allowing for dependants, it was reckoned that about $2\frac{1}{2}$ million people were being helped by the Board. More than two-thirds of these were retired people who were being paid a grant to supplement their retirement or old age pensions. A large proportion of the others were receiving benefit under the National Insurance Scheme because of sickness, unemployment, or widowhood.

The Act established Appeal Tribunals to hear appeals in each locality, although without the further right of appeal which exists under the National Insurance Scheme. In practice most of these appeals deal with the amount of the assistance grant, and it was found during 1954, according to the Board's report, that about a fifth of these appeals succeeded.

OTHER ASPECTS OF NATIONAL ASSISTANCE

Part III of the National Assistance Act lays certain duties on local authorities, and these are described in detail in some other sections of this book. They include the provision of homes for aged or infirm people in need of care or attention; temporary accommodation for people in urgent need of it for reasons 'which could not reasonably have been foreseen'; and welfare arrangements for blind, deaf, dumb, and crippled people, which can be made by the authority itself or through the agency of voluntary organizations.

Meanwhile the National Assistance Board has certain other duties apart from the payment of grants. Some of these are derived from the Act of 1948 and some from other legislation.

One of these duties is the administration of non-contributory old age pensions payable under the Old Age Pensions Act, 1936. These are small pensions, based on a means test, paid to people who have not qualified for a retirement pension under the 1946 Act, or for a contributory old age pension under the legislation which preceded it. In practice many of the people who qualify are also entitled to an assistance grant, and the Board's officers arrange for the payment of both simultaneously.

Through visiting these elderly people and the large number of retirement pensioners who are getting assistance grants, the Board's officers are in touch with a large proportion of the retired population of the country, particularly those in poorer circumstances. It is part of their duty to make discreet inquiries in order to see whether any other help is needed and can be provided. In one case there might be need for a home help. In another, a new member can be introduced to the local Darby and Joan Club. Many of these officers are doing invaluable work in putting elderly people in touch with statutory or voluntary services which they badly need.

Another duty of the Board is to provide reception centres for 'casuals', that is people without a settled way of living. The demand for these centres has been falling. In December 1954 the nightly average of those accommodated throughout Great Britain was 1,784, as compared with 2,368 in December 1948. There are now just over 100 of these centres, and at many of them an average of fewer than ten people stay each night. Care is taken to see that they are not used by people who are able to afford a night's lodging, and efforts are made to rehabilitate those who become persistent users of the centres. Casuals who persistently refuse to maintain themselves can be prosecuted under the Act, and this power is used as a last resort. Those convicted are usually sent to prison.

The provision of temporary housing accommodation for the large number of Polish people who have settled in Britain since the war was another duty placed on the Board. Several hostels were provided for this purpose, but the numbers have been declining as the inhabitants have become absorbed into the community and have made their own housing arrangements on a more permanent basis.

The Board was given a further duty in 1949 when the Legal Aid and Advice Act came into force. As there is a means test before aid can be given, the Board was considered the appropriate body to investigate the income and capital resources of those applying for legal aid.

OUR ATTITUDE TO NATIONAL ASSISTANCE

Unfortunately the old feelings about the stigma of the Poor Law have not completely disappeared. This is a great pity, and it is incumbent on people who are interested in these matters to try to remove the misconceptions which still persist.

The means test still exists, and this is surely inevitable. It has been humanized and the procedure has been made more private, but the fact remains that no one can reasonably expect to claim assistance without having to prove his need. This is the main distinction between assistance and the various benefits discussed in the last chapter. Those benefits are paid in certain given circumstances irrespective of need; national assistance is paid if the need is there irrespective of the cause. This need must be proved by some kind of means test.

Another inevitable facet of this question is that the thoroughly lazy and irresponsible person is often attracted to the idea of living off national assistance. The Board has the power to deal with him, and uses it. It can and does prosecute people who refuse to maintain their dependants. It can and does prosecute the 'casual' who makes no effort to maintain himself. It can and does make assistance conditional upon people registering for employment if they are fit to do so.

When all this has been said there remains a large number of people who have a genuine need of national assistance. They satisfy the means test and they do not come remotely near the sort of people mentioned in the last paragraph. Their claim is just and there is absolutely nothing degrading or undignified about the receipt of assistance in these cases.

Unfortunately old attitudes die very hard. There are many people, especially elderly people, who are too proud to apply. They have probably contributed for years towards paying assistance grants to many other people by means of their taxes. Their hardships may be very real. But they will not apply or, if they are finally driven to it, they do so with a sense of guilt.

This is an attitude we should all try to discourage. As a community we recognize our duty to care for those who are undergoing hardship. Our National Insurance scheme is bound to leave some gaps. Having provided for the means test, having guarded against the odd 'scrounger', we do not be-grudge -- or we should not -- the payment of assistance to those who really need it. Neither should anyone who needs it have any hesitation in applying.

4

Income Tax

J. R. B. PRICE

ORIGINALLY instituted at the end of the nineteenth century, the British Income Tax system quickly expanded so that it has now become the prime producer of annual revenue in Great Britain, its incidence affecting the vast majority of us to a greater or lesser extent.

It will, of course, be appreciated that it is impossible to do more than merely touch upon the principal features of the system in the limited space available in this chapter, for the law of Income Tax is not only highly complex, but has over the years attained vast proportions, being now contained in no less than 532 sections and 25 schedules of the Income Tax Act, 1952, as amended each year by the Finance Acts, which translate into law the Budget Resolutions. It should also be pointed out that the rates and allowances mentioned in this chapter are those in force when the book was printed in February 1957, and that these may be changed in the future. None the less, it is hoped that the pages which follow will give the reader some idea of the basic structure of the system so that he or she can appreciate not only the duties but also the rights of a taxpayer.

As a general rule income tax will be payable in respect of all income that is received by a person resident in the United Kingdom (which includes England, Wales, Scotland, Northern Ireland, and the Scilly Isles) whether that income arose in the United Kingdom or not, and on all income that arises within the United Kingdom wherever the recipient resides, and each year all such income must be declared on the taxpayer's return form which he or she will normally receive in April of each year.

As the late Lord Macnaghten once remarked, however, in a case then under appeal to the House of Lords, 'Income tax, if

I may be pardoned for saying so, is a tax on income', so that no profit that can properly be described as a capital profit will fall within the charge to tax, it often being a matter of considerable difficulty to decide whether any particular profit falls under capital or income. For example, if I purchased a house in 1955 and lived in it for a year, reselling it at a profit in 1956, the profit arising from that transaction would almost certainly be regarded as an addition to capital and thus not taxable, but if I had purchased three or four houses in 1955 and resold them all in 1956 at a profit the likelihood is that I would be held taxable on the profit on the ground that I had been carrying on a trade, namely that of property dealing, trading profits being assessable to Income Tax under Case I of Schedule 'D' of the Act.

It will be seen therefore that before any profits or gains accruing to an individual can be held to be taxable they must be shown not only to be of the nature of income but also to fall within the scope of one of the charging schedules of the Act, and it will be convenient at this stage to describe briefly the various types of income that fall within these charging schedules, which are five in number.

Schedule 'A' charges income which arises (or is deemed to arise) by virtue of the taxpayer's ownership of land or buildings situated within the United Kingdom.

Schedule 'B' charges income which is deemed to arise by virtue of the taxpayer's occupation of certain amenity lands, such as parklands.

Schedule 'C' charges income arising to a taxpayer which has been paid out of public revenue, and normally in this case tax has been deducted before payment is made, the taxpayer receiving a net sum.

Schedule 'D' is the most comprehensive of the five schedules and is subdivided into six separate sections known as 'Cases';

Case I concerns profits arising from the carrying on of a trade.

Case II concerns profits arising from the carrying on of a profession or vocation.

Case III concerns payments of interest, annuities, and other annual payments not falling within Schedule 'C'; here again tax is normally deducted at source.

Case IV concerns income arising to a person resident in this country from securities situated outside it, such as a mortgage on a foreign property.

Case V concerns income arising to a person resident here from possessions situated abroad, such as foreign stocks and shares. In addition, income earned abroad through a trade or profession by a person resident here is charged under this Case, but only to the extent that the earned income is remitted to this country.

Case VI is a residual case which affects any income arising in any year which is not chargeable under any other Schedule or Case.

Schedule 'E' concerns income arising from the holding of an office or employment and also charges pensions, certain National Insurance benefits, and family allowances. Tax is deducted at source under the Pay-as-You-Earn system (P.A.Y.E.) which is discussed in more detail later in the chapter.

Once it has been established therefore that any profit or gain is to be held as income and falls within the scope of one of these five charging schedules, it will become income assessable to income tax, and an assessment will be made on the taxpayer in respect of it, either directly, the taxpayer receiving a Notice of Assessment informing him of the extent of his liability, or indirectly, tax being collected by means of its deduction at source (as in the case of wages or salaries, where the appropriate tax is retained by the employer and then remitted by him to the Revenue).

The Assessment is normally made on the income that arises in an Income Tax Year, as opposed to a calendar year, the Income Tax Year running from 6 April in one year to 5 April in the following year. Thus the assessment for 1957–8 would normally concern the income that the taxpayer received during the period 6 April 1957 to 5 April 1958, this basis of assessment being known as the 'current year basis'. In certain cases, however, the assessment to income tax is based on the income arising in the previous year, and this is known as the 'preceding year basis' of assessment.

Income chargeable under Schedules 'A', 'B', 'C', and 'E' and under Case VI of Schedule 'D' is assessable on the current year basis, but income arising under all the cases of Schedule 'D', save Case VI, is assessable on the preceding year basis. Thus, in the case of a person assessable under Schedule 'E' the assessment for 1957–8 will be on the salary he receives between 6 April 1957 and 5 April 1958, whilst a person who is receiving income chargeable under, say, Case III of Schedule 'D' will be assessed for that year on the income arising to him over the period 6 April 1956 to 5 April 1957.

Under both Cases I and II of Schedule 'D', however (which concern trading and professional income) the assessment is not based precisely on the income arising in the preceding Income Tax Year but on the income arising in the taxpayer's accounting year (whatever dates he may choose for the purpose) ended in that preceding Income Tax Year. There are also special provisions as to the assessment of trading and professional income in the first three and last two years that the trade or profession is carried on.

Example 1

Assume that a trader, who has been in business for some years, makes up his business accounts to 31 December each year. His trading profits liable to tax were as follows:

Profits for year ended			31.12.54	£1,800
,,	,,	,,	31.12.55	£1,650
,,	,,	,,	31.12.56	£2,100

The Income Tax assessments on his business profits, made under Case I of Schedule 'D' will therefore be:

1955–6	£1,800
1956–7	£1,650
1957–8	£2,100

Although all profits or gains of an income nature that are

chargeable under one of the five schedules fall within the liability to tax and go to make up a person's total income, an individual is entitled to various reliefs from income tax, and it is only the residue of his total income remaining after such reliefs have been deducted (known as his taxable income) that will be liable to tax. Furthermore, as will be seen later, a certain amount of this taxable income will not be liable to the full rate of income tax, known as the 'standard rate' (at present 8s 6d in the pound). It should always be remembered, however, that, in the case of a married man, any income that his wife may be entitled to is treated as his income, so that it is the total annual income of them both that will fall to be computed each year, any reliefs applicable being granted against that total, the husband being primarily liable for the payment of tax on the joint taxable income, save in exceptional circumstances, where a separate assessment is claimed.

The reliefs at present available are as follows:

Personal relief. A married man whose wife is living with him or, alternatively, is wholly maintained by him, is entitled to relief from tax on £240 of the joint family income. Any other individual is entitled to relief on £140.

Child relief. Relief is given in respect of any child under sixteen years of age or who, if over sixteen, is studying full-time at some educational establishment or is undergoing a course of full-time training which lasts at least two years. The relief is on the sum of £100 in respect of each such child, but it will be withdrawn if the child is entitled to more than £85 as annual income in its own right.

Dependent relative relief. Any taxpayer who maintains a relative of himself or of his wife is entitled to relief on the sum of £60 if that relative is so incapacitated as to be unable to support him or herself; if the relative is the widowed mother or mother-in-law of the claimant, however, it is not necessary to show incapacity. The relief will be reduced, however, by £1 for every pound of income that the relative is entitled to in excess of £105 per annum. Thus a taxpayer maintaining a relative in receipt of £135 per annum would only be entitled to claim £30 relief under this head.

Relief for daughter's services. A taxpayer who, by reason of incapacity, is compelled to rely upon the services of a daughter is entitled to relief on the sum of £40 if the daughter is resident with, and maintained by, the taxpayer.

Housekeeper relief. Relief on the sum of £60 is claimable by a widower or widow who either employs a female person, or alternatively has living with him a female relative, who is looking after the claimant's children. Even if the female person does not look after the claimant's children the relief will still be granted if that person is acting as a housekeeper, provided she is employed as such and resides in the same house as the claimant.

It will be seen that it may be advantageous in certain circumstances to claim this relief instead of relief for a daughter's services.

In addition to widowers and widows the relief may be claimed under certain circumstances by both single and married individuals who have female persons resident with and maintained by them for the purpose of looking after children; normally, however, a married man cannot claim unless his wife is incapacitated.

Life assurance relief. Relief is given in respect of premiums paid on life assurance policies if the life assured is that of the claimant or his wife. The rate of relief will, however, vary according to whether the policy was effected before or after 22 June 1916, the policies being generally known as 'pre-1916' or 'post-1916' policies accordingly.

In the case of pre-1916 policies the amount of relief depends on the total income of the claimant. Thus for individuals whose income does not exceed £1,000 per annum relief is given at the rate of 3s 6d in the pound on the amount of the premium, at 5s 3d in the pound for those with incomes of between £1,000 and £2,000, and at 7s in the pound for those whose incomes exceed £2,000. There are also special provisions to deal with the case where a person's income falls only just below one of these income limits.

In the case of post-1916 policies however the relief is at a fixed rate, being given on the sum of two-fifths of the premium, unless the premium is itself under £25 per annum, in which case relief is given on the sum of £10; if the premium is under £10 relief is given on the whole amount of the premium.

In all cases however the premiums that qualify for relief (known as the allowable premiums) cannot exceed 7 per cent of the capital sum assured by each policy, and furthermore the total amount of premiums qualifying cannot exceed one-sixth of the claimant's total income.

Example 2

A taxpayer, whose total income amounts to £1,200, effected two policies of assurance on his own life in 1940; the sum assured under the first policy was £1,000, the premium payable annually being £80, and the sum assured under the second was £300, the annual premium being £20.

Policy 1. The premium exceeds 7 per cent of the sum assured, so that the allowable premium will be £70. Relief will be given in the sum of $\frac{2}{5} \times £70 = £28$.

Policy 2. The premium payable is under £25; therefore relief will be £10.

Now assume that a taxpayer with a total income of £1,200 effected a policy on 20 June 1916, the sum assured being £1,500 and the annual premium payable being £27. The full premium will be allowable, and relief will therefore be given in the sum of 27 × 5s 3d = £7 1s 9d, which will be deducted from the tax payable on an income of £1,200 (all other relevant reliefs having been granted).

Earned income relief and additional personal relief. A taxpayer is entitled to relief on two-ninths of his earned income, with a maximum relief under this head of £450. It will be seen, therefore, that a taxpayer will qualify for earned income relief on earned income up to an annual figure of £2,025, for $\frac{2}{9} \times £2,025 = £450$. In the case of a married man, however, it is the total earned income of himself and his wife that must be considered, the relief being given on the joint figure and the maximum remaining at £450.

Example 3

(*a*) A single man receives a salary of £900 per annum. His earned income relief will be $\frac{2}{9} \times £900 = £200$.

(*b*) A single man receives £2,500 annually in the form of director's fees. His earned income relief will be at the maximum figure of £450.

(*c*) A married man receives a salary of £1,250 and his wife earns £550 per annum. Earned income relief will be $\frac{2}{9} \times £1,800 = £400$.

Quite apart from this relief, however, a wife is entitled to claim additional personal relief on her separate earned income, and this relief is given at the rate of seven-ninths of her earned income, with a maximum relief of £140.

Example 4

A married man receives an annual salary of £900 and his wife earns £270. Earned income relief will be given on the total earned incomes (i.e. $\frac{2}{9} \times £1,170 = £260$) and the wife may claim relief at the rate of seven-ninths of £270 with a maximum relief of £140; in this example the maximum figure applies, the total reliefs on the joint earned incomes therefore amounting to £400.

Small incomes relief. This relief is given to those persons who are in receipt of an annual income (whether it be earned or unearned) which does not exceed £300. The relief is given at the rate of two-ninths of their total income, but earned income relief cannot also be claimed. Thus an individual who earns £150 per annum and receives a further £120 unearned income will be entitled to relief under this head at two-ninths of £270 = £60. There are special provisions dealing with persons in receipt of annual incomes of between £300 and £400.

Age relief. Any taxpayer who, or whose wife, has attained the age of sixty-five, and whose total annual income (whether earned or unearned) does not exceed £600, will be entitled to relief under this head at the rate of two-ninths of his total income, but earned income relief cannot also be claimed. Here again there are special provisions to deal with persons over sixty-five whose income does not exceed £600 by a very wide margin.

Reduced rate relief. After all the reliefs available to the taxpayer (according to the circumstances) have been claimed against his or her total income, a figure of taxable income is reached, and were it not for reduced rate relief the whole of this taxable income would bear tax at the standard rate of 8s 6d in the pound. As it is, a certain amount of this taxable income is taxed at reduced rates, those rates at present being as follows:

The first £60 of taxable income is taxed at 2s 3d in the pound
The next £150   ,,   ,,   ,,   4s 9d   ,,   ,,
The next £150   ,,   ,,   ,,   6s 9d   ,,   ,,

The balance of taxable income over the first £360 will then be taxed at the standard rate of 8s 6d in the pound.

In the case of a married man reduced rate relief will be given on the joint taxable income, but if his wife is earning she will be entitled to separate reduced rate relief on so much of her earned income as remains after any earned income relief and additional personal relief have been deducted from it. She is not, however, entitled to separate reduced rate relief on her unearned income.

It should be noted that no reliefs are taken into account in computing total income for surtax purposes, surtax being payable on the excess of an individual's income over £2,000.

Example 5. Typical computation of a married man's Income Tax liability

H is a married man, aged forty-five, with two children, one of whom is nine years of age and the other eighteen; neither child has any income of his own and the elder is taking a degree course at a university. H receives a salary of £1,150 per annum and his wife, W, is earning £650 per annum. In addition H receives each year £150 income from investments, He pays an annual premium of £40 on an endowment policy with life cover for £500 which he took out in 1954. He maintains his widowed mother who is in receipt of an annual income of £145. H's income tax liability will be calculated as follows (Note 1):

Incomes

Husband's salary	£1,150	
Wife's salary	£650	
Husband's unearned income	£150	
Total Income	£1,950	

Reliefs

Personal Relief	£240		
Child Relief	£200		
Dependent Relative Relief	£ 20	(Note 2)	
Life Assurance Relief	£ 14	(Note 3)	
Earned Income Relief	£400		
Additional Personal Relief	£140 =		£1,014
Taxable Income			£ 936

Tax payable

On joint income		On wife's earned income (Note 4)	
£60 at 2s 3d = £6 15s od		£60 at 2s 3d = £6 15s od	
£150 at 4s 9d = £35 12s 6d		£150 at 4s 9d = £35 12s 6d	
£150 at 6s 9d = £50 12s 6d		£150 at 6s 9d = £50 12s 6d	
£360	£93 os od	£360	£93 os od
			£93 os od

Balance of taxable income

(936 — 720) = 216 at 8s 6d =		£91 16s od
TOTAL TAX PAYABLE =		£277 16s od

Notes

1. In this example no account has been taken of National Insurance contributions payable or family allowances receivable.

2. Restricted owing to relative's own income of £145.

3. Allowable premium £35.

4. She would be entitled to reduced rate relief on £650 less $\frac{2}{9}$ earned income relief and $\frac{7}{9}$ additional personal relief (maximum £140). £650 − (£144 + £140) = £366, with a maximum, of course, of £360 reduced rate relief.

Whilst these examples illustrate the principles on which an individual's tax liability is determined, many taxpayers whose income is derived wholly from their employment may not have received a direct assessment, tax already having been deducted from their salaries or wages by their employers under the P.A.Y.E. system. It is emphasized that the principles on which the liability of any individual is measured are precisely the same whether the P.A.Y.E. system is applicable or not, for the system is no more than the machinery by means of which tax is collected, and all reliefs that a person may be entitled to are taken into account. In other words, instead of the taxpayer receiving the full amount of his salary or wages, claiming all the reliefs he is entitled to, and then receiving a direct assessment for the eventual tax payable, a proportion of that tax (approximately one fifty-second if the individual is paid weekly) will be deducted from each payment of salary or wages and then remitted to the Inland Revenue by his employers.

In order to arrive at a correct figure of tax to be paid over the year, any reliefs that the taxpayer is entitled to must, of course, be taken into account, and once these are known the taxpayer will be allotted a Code Number corresponding to the reliefs he is entitled to. Once this Code Number has been ascertained all the employer has to do is to consult the weekly Tax Tables issued by the Revenue and he will be able to see the appropriate tax to be deducted from the total of the weekly payments to the employee as they accrue.

Thus a single man with no reliefs save for personal relief of £140 (plus any earned income relief and reduced rate relief to which he may be entitled) might be allotted a Code Number of 35, and if Table A of the Tax Tables were to be consulted it would be found that in Week 1 of the current year (running from 6 to 12 April) he would be allowed 'free pay' (that is to say pay on which no tax is payable) of £3 14s. Any remuneration received in that week in excess of that figure will therefore be 'taxable pay' and the figure of tax payable thereon will be found in Table B of the Tables. Thus if X received in that first week wages of £10 his taxable pay would be £6 6s and the tax payable on that figure by a person with a coding of 35 is stated in Table B to be £1 1s. Each of the tables is cumulative so that each week there will appear a figure of total free pay to date and a figure of tax payable on the total taxable pay to date. At the end of the year, therefore, in the normal case, the correct amount of tax on the employee's income should have been deducted. If for some reason this should not be so an adjustment will be made, either by a further direct repayment or by additional assessment. Furthermore, if any change of circumstances occurs during the year which will affect the total amount of reliefs claimable by the taxpayer (such as marriage or the birth of a child) this fact should be notified to the local Inspector so that it may be taken into account in the revision of the taxpayer's Code Number.

Whilst Income Tax is payable on a person's total income (after the relevant reliefs have been taken into account) the figure of total income may be reduced for the purposes of assessment in a number of further ways. Thus in the case of a person carrying on a trade or profession, or deriving income from employment, it is only the net profits of the trade, profession, or employment – that is to say the total profits less those expenses that are allowable for Income Tax purposes – that will be assessable.

With trades and professions, any normal commercial expenditure wholly and exclusively laid out or expended for the purpose of that trade or profession may be set against the profits; in the case of expenses incurred by those chargeable under Schedule 'E' the expense must have been incurred wholly, exclusively, and necessarily in the performance of the employee's duties in order to be deductible, and it will be seen that this latter rule is somewhat stricter than the former. A trader or professional man may also be able to get relief in the form of capital allowances in respect of certain capital expenditure that he may incur in the provision of various types of assets he uses in his business (such as machinery or plant), and if he should qualify for these allowances they will go in reduction of his assessment made upon his trading profits. Again, if a person sustains a loss in his trade or profession, there are provisions in the Act permitting him to set off the amount of that loss against either his other income or against subsequent trading profits. Finally, an individual's income may be reduced by the amount of any annual charges that he or she may be obliged to meet.

These are annual payments out of income, and in the majority of cases they are to be paid under deduction of tax. The payer of the interest (which might, for example, be mortgage interest) when making the payment will deduct from it Income Tax at the standard rate and send to the payee only the net amount, the payee being able to make a claim for repayment of the tax deducted, or a part of it, if his income is so small as either not to be taxable at all or to be taxable at one of the reduced rates. Certain annual payments, in particular mortgage interest paid to a Building Society, however, are payable gross, but whether the charge is payable gross or net it will still reduce the total income of the payer for tax purposes. If paid gross it will merely be deducted from the total income of the payer in the following manner:

Assume that X has income from employment of £1,200, investment income of £50, and owns a house the income from which is deemed to amount to £50 (chargeable under Schedule 'A'). He pays annual interest on a Building Society mortgage of £60. His total income would in such a case be considered as (£1,200 + £50 + £50) − £60 = £1,240.

Should the payment be made under deduction of tax the charge will still reduce the total income of the payer, but in a somewhat different manner. It is not deducted from a figure of total income as is the case if the charge is payable gross, for the payer has, in effect, already received relief from tax on the amount of the charge by virtue of the fact that he has only paid to the payee the net amount instead of the full amount of the debt. Thus, if we take the figures used in the above example, the payer will be assessed on £1,300 (leaving aside for the moment the question of reliefs) but the tax on £60 of that £1,300 that he will have to bear will not be his tax but that of the payee; in the end the same result is reached, but by different methods.

It will be seen from the example given above that an individual may be deemed to receive a certain amount of income by virtue of his ownership of a house, and the amount of such income is determined by a valuation which is based on what is known as the 'rack-rent' of the property in question, the rack-rent being the rent at which the house could be let to a tenant over a number of years on the assumption that the landlord was bearing the cost of repairs but the tenant was paying the rates. Once this valuation figure has been reached it is known as the gross annual value (or G.A.V.), but the owner will not pay tax on the amount of the G.A.V. but on a figure representing the G.A.V. less the amount of a statutory repairs allowance, the resultant being known as the net annual value (or N.A.V.) of the premises. The rates of this allowance vary according to the figure of the gross annual value of the property. They are as follows.

G.A.V. of not more than £40 — ¼ G.A.V.
G.A.V. of £40 to £50 — £10
G.A.V. of £50 to £100 — one-fifth G.A.V.
G.A.V. of more than £100 — £20, plus one-sixth of excess of G.A.V. over £100.

Thus each house owner is deemed to receive the amount of the N.A.V. as part of his annual income, and this must be included therefore in the figure of total income that he returns each year to the Inspector of Taxes. It may happen, however, that the owner has expended sums on repairs in excess of the statutory repairs allowance already granted to him in reaching the figure of N.A.V., and in these circumstances he will, if certain conditions are fulfilled, be entitled to make a claim to have the tax payable on that N.A.V. reduced. In order to sustain such a claim, known as a maintenance claim, the owner must show that the average expenditure on repairs over the preceding five years exceeds the repairs allowance for the year of claim, in which case tax may be reclaimed on such excess.

Example 6

Assume that a house-owner has a house, the G.A.V. of which has been set at £40. The statutory repairs allowance will be £10, giving a N.A.V. of £30, and tax would normally be charged on this figure. If, however, it can be shown that the owner has expended, over the previous five years, more than £50 on repairs (say £75) he will be entitled to repayment of tax on the excess of one-fifth of £75 over £10, i.e. £5. The result is that instead of bearing tax on £30 he will only bear tax on £25.

It only remains to say that each taxpayer may give Notice of Appeal within the prescribed time limit against any assessment made upon him, the appeal being made initially to one of two bodies of Commissioners, known as the General or Special Commissioners, according to the subject-matter of the appeal. In the case of Income Tax the time limit is normally twenty-one days from the receipt of the Notice of Assessment.

Whichever tribunal hears the appeal the taxpayer is entitled to conduct his case in person or alternatively to instruct a qualified accountant, solicitor, or counsel to argue the case on his behalf. There is a further right of appeal from a decision of these Commissioners, but only on a point of law, to the High Court, the Court of Appeal, and eventually to the House of Lords. In many cases, however, an aggrieved taxpayer may well find that he will be able to resolve his differences by a talk with his local Inspector of Taxes, who will be found ready and willing at any time to discuss any problems that arise and explain any technicalities that have not been discussed within the short compass of this chapter.

5

Public Health

J. E. SIDDALL

Historical background

The concentration of the community into urban units at the beginning of the nineteenth century, combining as it did with an amazingly rapid growth in population, started to force the pace of sanitary legislation and administration in Britain. It was typical of English local government that the extensions and innovations were produced locally, usually by private Act of Parliament, a system still in use to-day, and gradually extended both by a copying of precedent and by adoption in public general Acts. It was also typical that, although in certain areas where they did not exist special sanitary authorities were created, within the space of a very few years these new powers were absorbed and administered by the oldest forms of local government, namely the boroughs, some of which had many centuries of continuous existence behind them when the nineteenth century opened. Where there were not boroughs, there gradually emerged, from the sanitary authorities thus formed in the middle of the nineteenth century and later, the urban and rural district councils, whose powers to-day are very similar to those of the non-county borough. Boroughs generally, together with these district councils, will be known as 'the local authority' throughout this chapter.

The other authority of a localized nature with whom the public comes primarily into contact is, of course, except in a county borough, the county council. This is an authority responsible for the administration of many important functions, such as education, ambulances, fire brigade, police, etc., but it is the local authority – or the local council as it is often called – to whom the ratepayer pays his money, although it often only spends a minor share of that money. One of the most important functions of the local authority is public health, and in this respect it has not merely powers but duties as well. Whereas the local councillor or alderman is often the first line of approach either with regard to a claim or with regard to an improvement in existing conditions, it is obvious that the council normally works through its staff. It is legally compelled to appoint a Medical Officer of Health, who must be a duly qualified medical practitioner. It must also appoint a sanitary inspector or inspectors. The Sanitary Inspector (now Public Health Inspector) should be the first person to be approached in regard to any matter affecting public health.

Food and Drink

The term 'public health' is a wide one, and the standard legal textbook (Lumley's *Public Health*) aggregates eight volumes of approximately 1,000 closely-printed pages each. The main source of the legislation is the Public Health Act, 1936. It is obvious that, to maintain health in a community, water sources must be kept pure, and waste products hygienically disposed of. To begin therefore with water. An abundance of pure water is a necessary prerequisite, and it is, generally speaking, the duty of the local authority to see that this is available. In most cases the local authority is actually the supplier of the water and maintains a special staff in connexion with it. If for some reason there is not a supply available, or the existing supply is polluted or inadequate or not at a reasonable distance, the matter should be taken up with the authority.

Food and drugs come primarily under the provisions of the Food and Drugs Act, 1955, and the Food Hygiene Regulations, 1955, but other Acts are also involved. Thus it is an offence for anyone to add or to permit any other person to add substances to food so as to render that food injurious to health if they intend to sell it; similarly, to abstract from any food any constituent of it so as to affect injuriously its nature, substance, or quality, unless notice is given to the purchaser of the alteration. Furthermore, if a person sells to the prejudice of the purchaser a food or drug which is not of the nature, not of the substance, or not of the quality which is demanded, it is an offence, unless,

not being fraudulent or injurious to health, a wrapper or notice
gave proper warning of the abstraction or addition. There are
special provisions relating to drugs and to spirits. Incorrect
labelling of food and drugs can be an offence. Similarly, the
law prohibits the selling, or offering for sale, or consignment for
sale, of food which is intended for but is unfit for human consumption, and this includes food given as prizes, and unsound
food can be seized by an authorized officer of a local authority.
Apart from the question of the careless or fraudulent addition
of injurious substances to food, some commodities, such as
milk, have to be protected throughout their course, and for this
reason the manufacture of foods or the pickling or preserving
of them can only be carried out in premises which comply with
certain standards of hygiene, and in the case of some foodstuffs, for example ice-cream, conditions are very strict and
premises have to be registered. There are often by-laws in
connexion with the wrapping and handling of food; personal
cleanliness in handling food is required, including refraining
from the use of tobacco where the food is open; food-poisoning
cases must be notified, and with some kinds of food and drugs
the actual constituents are based upon regulations or a commonly accepted basis of manufacture, as, for example, the
British Pharmacopoeia.

Not strictly allied with actual public health, but usually enforced by the local authority, are tests as to quantity; and
Weights and Measures Inspectors, who are sometimes also
Public Health Inspectors, test weights and ascertain whether
the quantities sold of foodstuffs, coal, or other commodities are
of full weight, and measure that a pint bottle contains a pint,
or that a glass contains a half-pint. It seems useful that these
tests are available as well as tests merely for dirt, bad quality,
or an injurious addition.

Prevention of nuisances

Another category of duties aimed at keeping sources pure, or
stopping trouble when it has started, can be vaguely classed as
the prevention of nuisances. The term 'nuisance' under the

Public Health Acts has a technical meaning, which is both wider in some respects than the ordinarily accepted sense of the word and yet narrower in that the actionable nuisance must generally be in some way prejudicial to health – 'or a nuisance'. Thus, for example, barking dogs can be a nuisance and can possibly be dealt with under by-laws relating to good rule and government, but they would not be dealt with by a Public Health Inspector. If, however, animals are kept in such a state that they are prejudicial to health or a nuisance (in the statutory sense), it is a matter with which a Public Health Inspector would deal.

To give a complete list of nuisances is difficult, but the following are technical examples:

(*a*) Any premises in such a state as to be prejudicial to health or a nuisance. This would seem to apply to premises which are a nuisance by reason of their condition and not because of the purpose to which they are put. Thus, disrepair can be a nuisance, as, for example, a dangerous chimney or area grating, a defective roof or ceiling, or a defective kitchen range, or likewise an accumulation of soil causing damp to an adjoining house.

(*b*) Any animal kept in such a place or manner as to be prejudicial to health or a nuisance.

(*c*) Any accumulation or deposit which is prejudicial to health or a nuisance; for example, where a stableman kept dung accumulating so that neighbours had to keep their windows closed, or a deposit of refuse causing a smell and an accumulation of flies.

(*d*) Any dust or effluvia caused unnecessarily by any trade, business, manufacture, or process, and prejudicial to the health of or a nuisance to neighbouring inhabitants. In this connexion it should be realized that the effluvia need not necessarily be proved to cause an injury to health. In fact, the proof of injury to health from a smell is not at all easy. It might be that the smell caused windows to be kept closed and thereby reduced a person's resistance to disease, but the existence of a smell is not always indicative of a decline in or threat to health.

(e) Any workplace not provided with sufficient means of ventilation, or in which sufficient ventilation is not maintained, or which is not kept clean or free from obnoxious effluvia, or is so overcrowded while work is carried on as to be prejudicial to the health of those employed therein. This provision does not include a factory or workshop, but, apart from that, includes any place in which persons are employed otherwise than in domestic service – presumably an office.

(f) Any other matter declared by the Public Health Act, 1936, to be a statutory nuisance.

It must be realized that once the local authority is satisfied of the existence of a statutory nuisance it is under an obligation to serve what is known as an Abatement Notice on the person by whose act, default, or sufferance the nuisance arises or continues, and if that person cannot be found, on the owner or occupier of the premises on which the nuisance arises. The notice will require the owner or occupier to take such steps as may be necessary to abate the nuisance, and if the nuisance arises from the defect of a structural character the notice is to be served on the owner of the premises. The local authority has powers, in default, of remedying and of recovering the cost. If, however, the person on whom the notice has been served fails to carry out any of the requirements of the notice, the local authority is under an obligation to apply to a justice of the peace for the issue of a summons to require the person on whom the notice was served to appear before a magistrates' court, and the Court, if it is proved that the alleged nuisance exists, or that although abated it is likely to recur on the same premises, is to make an order requiring compliance with the Abatement Notice and prohibiting a recurrence. Non-compliance with a nuisance order can involve a fine not exceeding £5 or, in the case of a continuing offence, 40s for each day. It will thus be seen that the procedure for dealing with nuisances is complete and obligatory throughout all its course.

Whilst on the subject of nuisances we should not forget the damage and trouble which can be caused by pests, and the Prevention of Damage by Pests Act, 1949, makes it the duty of every local authority to take such steps as may be necessary to secure that its district is kept free from rats and mice; this involves not merely destroying the rats and mice on land which the local authority itself occupies, but also enforcing on owners and occupiers of land their duty to carry out the destruction themselves. The occupier of any land, and this includes a building, is to give notice in writing to the local authority if he knows that rats and mice are living on or are resorting to his property in substantial numbers. A farmer is excused from doing this. Again, just as in dealing with a nuisance, the local authority may compel the owner or occupier to take steps to destroy these pests, and if he fails so to do the expenses incurred by the local authority in carrying out the notice may be recovered, and again there is the penalty of a fine. Where food is infested, every person whose business consists of or includes the manufacture, storage, transport, or sale of food is to give to the Minister of Agriculture and Fisheries notice in writing that infestation is present in his premises, vehicle, etc., and the Minister may give directions to such business proprietor prohibiting or restricting his business and requiring him to carry out such general or structural works as will be necessary to control the infestation. It will be realized that many of these matters normally classed as nuisances are also the subject of local by-laws.

Dangerous buildings

Dangerous or dilapidated buildings or structures come under the special provision of section 58 of the Public Health Act, 1936. A dangerous building could be dealt with under the Towns Improvement Clauses Act of 1847 by the Surveyor, but the Public Health Act provisions are much wider. Primarily the 1847 Act dealt with dangers to passengers in the street. But the 1936 Act can deal with a building which is in such a condition or is used to carry such loads as to be dangerous to persons in the building or in adjoining buildings or premises on which the building stands. Again, it enables the local authority to apply to a magistrates' court where any building or structure or part of a building or structure is by reason of its ruinous or dilapidated condition seriously detrimental to the amenities of the neighbourhood. The remedy again here is that the magistrates may make an order requiring the owner of the building or structure to execute such work of repair or restoration as may be necessary, or at his option to demolish the building or structure and remove any rubbish resulting from the demolition.

It will be remembered that earlier it was stated that in addition to the general list there was a number of cases which were deemed to be statutory nuisances. A small example could be barbed wire adjoining a highway, but far more in character are many of the statutory nuisances under the Public Health Act, 1936.

Movable dwellings

Thus a tent, van, shed, or similar structure used for human habitation which is in such a state or so overcrowded as to be prejudicial to the health of the inmates, or the use of which (by reason of the absence of proper sanitary accommodation or otherwise) gives rise (whether on the site or on other land) to a nuisance or to conditions prejudicial to health, is a statutory nuisance, and in this case the term 'occupier' includes any person who is for the time being in charge of such tent, etc. In this case, unless the occupier of the land on which the tent, etc., stands did not authorize it, the Abatement Notice can be served on him as well as on the person in charge of the tent, etc.

In any event, movable dwellings are subject to special control by local authorities apart from town-planning restrictions. A person is not permitted to allow any land occupied by him to be used for camping purposes on more than forty-two consecutive days or more than sixty days in any twelve consecutive months, unless he holds in respect of the land so used a licence from the local authority, or each person using the land as a site for a movable dwelling holds a local authority licence. A short move is also obviated, because, if the land on to which the person moves is within a hundred yards of a site on which there is, during any part of any day, a movable dwelling, it is to be regarded as being used for camping purposes on that day, provided it is within the occupation of the same person. There are one or two exceptions to this; for example, a movable dwelling which is kept by its owner, on land occupied by him, in connexion with his dwelling-house and used by his household, or one kept by its owner on agricultural land occupied by him, and used for habitation only at certain seasons and only by persons employed in farming on that land. Again, where the movable dwelling is used as part of the business, and in the course of the travels, of the proprietor of a roundabout, amusement fair, or travelling circus. Again, if it is not used for human habitation. There are also special clauses with regard to organizations which satisfy the Minister of Housing and Local Government on proper management, etc. and can obtain a general certificate of exemption.

In default of a licence held either by the occupier of the land or by the person keeping it, to have the movable dwelling on the site is an offence in the same way as breach of any condition attached to a licence, and involves the person responsible in the usual fine not exceeding £5 and a daily penalty not exceeding 40s. It is therefore necessary to consider the question of these licences. If an application is made to a local authority and the local authority does not grant the licence, it must inform the applicant of the refusal, or he is deemed to have been granted a licence. If the licence is refused, or conditions are attached by which the applicant feels aggrieved, he may appeal to a magistrates' court against the decision of the local authority.

The licences issued by the local authority will normally be restricted in time, probably to twelve months, and the local authority may attach to any such licence such conditions as it thinks fit. It may restrict the number and classes of movable dwellings, specify the space to be kept free between any two such dwellings – for in these cases fire risks must be taken into consideration – and impose conditions with respect to water supply, for here sanitary conditions are most important and, as was pointed out earlier, the supply of abundant pure water is a preliminary requisite of good conditions of public health.

With regard to the case of a licence authorizing the use of a movable dwelling, the question of space comes in, and, again, its removal at the end of a specified period, as well as clauses for securing proper sanitary conditions, not the least of which might well be the proper provision of sanitary dustbins, for the collection and disposal of house refuse do present a problem, and if proper conditions are not observed it will produce breeding grounds for flies and attractions to rats.

Removal of refuse

The problem of the dustbin is a not inconsiderable one. The first problem to be decided is who is to supply. This is to be decided by the local authority, who may by notice, require the owner or occupier of any building within the district, or, if the whole of the district is not covered by a refuse collection scheme, in the part served, to provide such number of covered dustbins of an approved material, size, and construction as are required. Then, if either the owner or the occupier feels aggrieved by any such notice within the prescribed time, he may appeal to a magistrates' court, and this court may either uphold or reject the finding of the local authority. Pursuant to the Local Government (Miscellaneous Provisions) Act, 1953, the appellant may serve a copy of his notice of appeal on the other party -- for example, if the owner is served with the notice he may appeal and call upon the occupier; then the Court may on the hearing of the appeal make such order as it thinks fit with respect to compliance with the first-mentioned notice, either by the appellant or the other person. Meanwhile, as an alternative, the local authority may itself supply the bin and may make an annual charge not exceeding 5s in respect of each dustbin so supplied, and this can be recovered as part of the general rate. There may be by-laws in connexion with dustbins prohibiting the deposit in them of liquid matter and imposing duties on the occupiers of premises to facilitate the work of refuse removal. To place an explosive in a dustbin is an offence in the same way as to place in it articles which have been in contact with infectious disease. It should be realized that, where the local authority has undertaken the removal of house refuse in the whole or any part of its district, the occupier of any premises within the district may require it to remove his house refuse, and if without reasonable excuse the local authority fails to comply with the notice within seven days, the occupier may recover the sum of 5s for every day during which the default continues. It should be observed that the liability is on the local authority to remove house refuse. Trade refuse it is under no such obligation to remove, and for this the local authority may charge. House refuse is refuse of the nature normally emanating from a private house. Whereas it is an offence for any person to sort over or disturb the contents of any dustbin when placed in any street or forecourt for the purpose of removal or to sort over or disturb the material deposited in any place provided by the authority for the deposit of refuse, this may be done by employees of the local authority in connexion with the disposal, for the local authority may sell any refuse removed by them from any premises.

Similar provisions with regard to cleansing operate in the case of cesspools, pits, and the like, although many local authorities who collect house refuse free maintain a system of charges for this type of work. There are powers to the local authority to secure that provision is made for the adequacy of sanitary accommodation to dwelling-houses and elsewhere, and that, subject to the provisions of the Act, separate water closets are provided throughout and maintained. Section 52 of the Public Health Act, 1936, makes it an offence to injure or improperly foul a convenience used in common by members of two or more families, and if for want of proper cleansing or attention the convenience becomes insanitary, those persons having the use thereof who are in default are to be liable to a fine not exceeding 10s, again with a continuing liability. The occupier is also liable to cause the flushing apparatus to be kept supplied with water sufficient for flushing, and also where necessary to cause it to be properly protected against frost.

Sewers and drains

The disposal of waste water is again a matter of public health law. Section 48 of the same Act permits the local authority to open up drains or private sewers which connect with the public sewer and to carry out tests. Where under section 39 it appears to the local authority that satisfactory provision has not been and ought to be made for drainage; or that a drain or private sewer connecting with a public sewer is so defective as to admit subsoil water; or any drain, soil pipe, rainwater pipe, spout, sink, or other necessary appliance provided for a building is insufficient; or any cesspool, private sewer, or drain is prejudicial to health or a nuisance; the local authority is under an obligation by notice to require the owner, or sometimes the occupier, to make good these defects.

On the other hand, subject to the provisions of section 34, the owner or occupier of any premises is entitled to have his drains or private sewer made to communicate with the public sewers of the authority and to discharge foul water and surface water from those premises into the sewer. He cannot, of course, connect a foul water sewer to a surface water sewer or the reverse, and before connecting with the sewer or opening any street necessary to that end he must give the appropriate notice to the local authority. Similarly, notice must be given under section 41 where, except in case of emergency, underground drains which communicate with a sewer or with a cesspool shall be neither repaired, reconstructed, altered, nor covered in until the appropriate notice has been given to the local authority. The local authority is responsible for the main sewers and for the eventual disposal of the waste water as part of its general duties, and this liability to dispose includes also trade effluents, but these are subject, although with special circumstances prior to 1937, to notice and liability for payments. It is an offence to permit to pass into a public sewer or into a drain communicating with a public sewer any matter likely to injure the sewer or drain, to interfere with the sewer or flow of its contents, or to affect prejudicially the treatment and disposal of its contents. Similarly it is an offence to throw or cause to be emitted any chemical refuse or waste steam or any liquid at a higher temperature than 110° F. or any liquid which, when so heated, is either alone or in combination with the contents of the sewer or drain dangerous or the cause of a nuisance or prejudicial to health, or any petroleum spirit or carbide of calcium.

Health in factories

The general health provisions with regard to factories are regulated by the Factories Act, 1937, and a factory inspector who finds any act or default in relation to any drain, sanitary convenience, water supply, nuisance, or other matter which is liable to be dealt with by the local authority under Part 1 of the 1937 Act, or under the law relating to public health, has to give notice thereof to the local authority, and it is the duty of the local authority to make such inquiry into the subject of the notice and to take such action thereon as seems to that authority proper for the purpose of enforcing the law, and to inform the inspector of the proceedings taken in consequence of the notice. If the Secretary of State is satisfied that the local authority has failed to enforce any of the provisions of Part 1 of the Act he may authorize an inspector to take such steps as appear necessary or proper for enforcing those provisions. The general health provisions with regard to the factory state that it shall be kept in a clean state and free from effluvia arising from any drain, sanitary convenience, or nuisance. Accumulations of dirt and refuse are to be removed daily by a suitable method from the floors and benches of workrooms and from staircases and passages, and the floor of every workroom is to be cleaned at least once in every week. Inside walls and partitions are to be cleaned once in every period of fourteen months if they are smooth and impervious, and painted or varnished if appropriate once in every period of seven years. Overcrowding is not to take place so as to cause risk of injury to the health of the person employed, and standards are laid down, and also standards of temperature, lighting, ventilation, and drainage of floors. Sufficient and suitable sanitary conveniences for the persons employed in the factory are to be provided, maintained, kept clean, and lighted.

Prevention of pollution

In addition to the production of waste material which is disposed of via the sewers, there is also what is commonly known as a smoke nuisance. Any installation for the combustion of fuel which is used in any manufacture or trade process or for working engines by steam, and which does not so far as practicable prevent the emission of smoke to the atmosphere, is a statutory nuisance, and is known in the Public Health Act, 1936, as a smoke nuisance. A similar statutory nuisance is any chimney (not being the chimney of a private house) emitting smoke in such quantity as to be a nuisance. Black smoke is the most difficult to defend, for if the smoke is any colour but black it will be a defence in proceedings that the best practicable means for preventing the nuisance have been adopted. It will be remembered, too, that 'smoke' includes soot, ash, grit, and gritty particles, and that 'chimney' includes structures and openings of any kind from or through which smoke may be emitted. The local authority officer, where he forms the opinion that a smoke nuisance exists, must notify the occupier of the premises on which the nuisance exists, and an abatement notice may be served and followed up with a procedure similar to that available in the case of other statutory nuisances.

There are several further points in this connexion. The 'best practicable means' has reference not only to the provision and efficient maintenance of adequate and proper plant for preventing the creation and emission of smoke, but also to the manner in which that plant is used. By-laws may be made regulating the emission of smoke, the colour, density, or content as required, and building by-laws may require in new buildings other than private houses such arrangements for heating or cooking as are calculated to prevent or reduce the emission of smoke. It has, of course, been recently realized that the domestic chimney can similarly contribute its quota to atmospheric pollution, and the imposition of smokeless zones by local authorities, initiated under local Acts, is being tried out. Certain trades are of themselves deemed offensive, and if one is established without the consent of the appropriate local authority the person who does so is liable to a fine not exceeding £50. Offensive trades are those of a blood boiler, blood dryer, bone boiler, fat melter, glue maker, rag and bone dealer, soap boiler, tripe boiler, etc., or any other trade, business, or manufacture which was declared to be such under section 51 of the Public Health Acts (Amendment) Act, 1907, in the particular borough, or where the local authority has made and has confirmed an order declaring a certain trade to be an offensive trade.

Just as public health prohibits the pollution of the atmosphere, similarly the pollution of rivers and streams can be prevented. Not merely the considerable pollution of a river, where the River Board or Conservancy Board would take action under the Rivers (Prevention of Pollution) Act, 1951, but ponds, pools, ditches, gutters, or watercourses which are so foul as to be prejudicial to health or a nuisance, or any non-navigable watercourse which is choked or silted up so as to obstruct or impede the proper flow of water and thereby to cause a nuisance or give rise to conditions prejudicial to health, are statutory nuisances. The liability with regard to the watercourse which is silted up falls only on the person by whose act or default the nuisance arises or continues. To throw or deposit cinders, ashes, bricks, stone, rubbish, dust, filth, or other matter into a river, stream, or watercourse incurs a fine not exceeding 40s; and the local authority may require a watercourse to be culverted where building operations are in prospect; and culverts may be required by urban local authorities to be repaired and cleansed.

Infectious diseases

There are many other special provisions, aimed at lodging-houses, shops, and boats, and for enforcement, but sometimes all these attempts at preventive medicine fail and disease breaks out. Then it is essential to secure not merely that the sufferer is restored to health but that the outbreak is confined to a minimum. Certain diseases have been made notifiable, and further diseases under the Public Health Act, 1936, are smallpox, to the local authority so that it may be aware of their existence and may take appropriate steps to deal with them. Notifiable diseases under the Public Health Act, 1936, are smallpox, cholera, diphtheria, membraneous croup, erysipelas, scarlatina or scarlet fever, typhus fever, typhoid fever, enteric fever, and relapsing fever, and to these diseases have also been added measles, whooping-cough, and chickenpox. There are certain other diseases which, whilst not notifiable within the meaning of the Act, are infectious diseases. The duty of notification falls upon the head of the family to which the patient belongs or other responsible person in the house and upon the medical practitioner, and a failure to notify renders the defaulter liable to a fine. In the last resort this liability can fall upon the occupier, who should send notice to the medical officer of health of the district in which the building is situated; and this term 'occupier' can include the person having charge of a building let out in tenements or of a lodging-house. Where these infectious diseases occur special steps are to be taken; special procedure both for tracing the cause of the outbreak and for prevention of contamination are the responsibility of the local authority and of its Medical Officer of Health and Public Health Inspector. For instance, where there is enteric fever and dysentery, which would include typhoid and paratyphoid, the local authority can require that until further notice persons specified are to discontinue any occupation connected with the preparation or handling of food or drink for human consumption, and can specify steps to be taken with regard to cleansing, disinfection, decontamination, and disposal. A medical officer of health who suspects that any person employed in any trade or business concerned with the preparation or handling of food or drink for human consumption is a carrier, must report to the local authority, who can require medical examination and can similarly, if such examination proves such tendency or there is other evidence of it, prevent such a person handling such food or drink until the contrary is proved. Food poisoning similarly calls for investigation to be made, and a medical officer can, until investigations are complete, give notice to the person in charge of the food suspected that it is not to be removed or used for human consumption.

Other provisions for preventing this spread of infection are most important. It is an offence liable to a fine of £5 if any person knows he is suffering from a notifiable disease and exposes other persons to the risk of infection by his presence or conduct in any street, public place, place of entertainment or assembly, club, hotel, inn, or shop. There is a similar liability on a person who has care of one whom he knows to be so suffering. Similarly liable is one who gives, lends, sells, transmits, or exposes without disinfection clothing, bedding, or rags which he knows to have been liable to infection. By section 150 of the Public Health Act, 1936, a penalty is imposed on any person who, having the care of a child who is or has been suffering from or has been exposed to infection of a notifiable disease, and after receiving notice from the medical officer that the child is not to be sent to school, permits the child to attend school before he has obtained a certificate that the child may attend without undue risk of communicating the disease to others. Infected articles may not be sent to laundries, and outwork of altering, washing, or making of clothing apparel in the home may be prohibited. The sale or exchange of articles by rag and bone dealers is mostly prohibited; and library books should not be returned when they have been in contact with infectious disease, except after notification to the local authority, who will take any necessary steps. The use of public conveyances by persons suffering from notifiable diseases is prohibited, and precautions must be taken by persons letting houses or rooms in hotels to such persons, to secure that they have been disinfected to the satisfaction of the Medical Officer of Health before they are let or re-let to any other person.

As always, there are special provisions with regard to certain more than usually vulnerable places, as, for example, dairies, cowsheds and milk shops, ice-cream premises, catering establishments, slaughterhouses, and meat shops. In all these cases there should be immediate notification and the necessary disinfection of persons and premises to the standards required by the Public Health Department of the local authority.

6

The National Health Service

JEAN GRAHAM HALL

THE National Health Service Acts, 1946–52, aimed at promoting the establishment of a comprehensive health service which was (*a*) available to all civilians in England and Wales, (*b*) capable of covering all necessary forms of health care. They were designed to secure improvement in the physical and mental health of the people and at the same time to foster the prevention, diagnosis, and treatment of illness. In a White Paper issued before the passing of the 1946 Act the Government of the day stated that they wanted to ensure that in the future every man, woman, and child could rely on getting all the advice and care which they might need, irrespective of their ability to pay. The Act came into force on 5 July 1948. There are separate Acts making corresponding provisions for Scotland.

The Minister of Health was entrusted with this duty, and the final responsibility remains with him. He is advised by a Central Health Services Council upon general matters relating to the services provided under the Acts.

The scope of the Acts includes hospital services (both in- and out-patient treatment); the services of specialists, who can visit the patients' homes if needed; general medical and dental services; the provision of medicines and appliances; services administered by the Local Health Authorities (county and county borough councils), such as maternity and child welfare, ambulance services, home nursing, and health visitors; and other preventive measures, such as immunization.

At the very core of the scheme remains the family doctor. The duty generally falls on him to advise on the need for the various forms of treatment. The general practitioner is kept informed by Medical Officers of Health, Regional Hospital Boards, Hospital Management Committees, and Boards of

Governors of teaching hospitals of all arrangements in his area for carrying out the services available to the public.

GENERAL MEDICAL CARE

The arrangements for general medical care are under the authority of Local Executive Councils, of which there is one for each administrative county and county borough, except in a few cases where there is one Council for two areas. Each Council consists of twenty-five members. Five of these are appointed by the Minister of Health. Representatives of the local Health Authority, local medical committee, dental committee, and local pharmaceutical committee also sit on the Council.

The family doctor

Each Local Executive Council prepares and publishes a list, which is kept up to date, of doctors providing general medical services in its area. This may be divided into districts if the area is large. Copies of this list are available in the local post office.

In theory everyone is permitted to choose his own general practitioner. A full choice is not always possible, because if the doctor's list has reached the permitted maximum he cannot accept the would-be patient. A doctor in single-handed practice may not have more than 3,500 patients on his list. If there is a partnership, one of the partners may have up to 4,500 on his list, but the combined total must not exceed 3,500 per partner. If a doctor has an assistant, he is allowed to add an additional 2,000 patients to his list.

The family doctor service is free to everyone who chooses to make use of it, whether or not he or she is paying National Insurance. If someone decides not to use the service, he may choose to be a paying and private patient. In this case, the provision of drugs under the service cannot be claimed. Any drugs prescribed for a private patient must be paid for by the patient.

The parent or guardian, or person in charge of a child under sixteen or an invalid or other person who cannot choose for himself, has the same right of choice. A special form is provided for persons leaving H.M. Forces, to make application to be placed on a doctor's list.

Where a person cannot obtain the consent of any doctor in his area to take him on his list, such a person will be allocated to a doctor on the list with or without the consent of the doctor. Application should be made to the Executive Council in this matter. The Local Executive Council also operates an allocation scheme (*a*) to deal with requests from people to find them a doctor, and (*b*) to arrange temporary treatment where necessary, as in the case of visitors from abroad.

Should a patient wish to remove himself from a doctor's list, he may do this by giving fourteen days' notice to the Local Executive Council, whether or not he decides to put himself on the list of some other doctor. The doctor may also ask that the patient should be removed from his list, unless the patient is actually under treatment by him, on giving seven days' notice to the Local Executive Council.

The name of a person is deleted from his doctor's list after three months' absence if he leaves the United Kingdom. It is also deleted if he enters H.M. Forces. If a person dies, his name is removed from the doctor's list from the date of death.

The family doctor retains his traditional right to treat his patient as he thinks fit, and no regulations operate concerning what drugs the doctor may or may not prescribe. Doctors are exhorted, however, not to prescribe proprietary drugs where a standard one is available. From time to time one hears how a minority of doctors prescribe fantastic and expensive drugs in order to keep patients, but special regulations govern improper or excessive prescribing by doctors.

It is a doctor's responsibility to provide his own accommodation in the area of his practice. This must include proper and sufficient surgery and waiting-rooms for his patients. These vary in the standard of comfort. A layman might sometimes wonder whether toilet facilities might not be more appreciated than out-of-date magazines during the inevitable period spent in waiting-rooms.

Where several doctors band together in a group practice it is very much easier to afford better facilities, including perhaps a receptionist. Each doctor sees and visits his own patients. The greatest advantage lies in the spreading over of emergency calls which have to be answered at all hours.

The Act makes provision for health centres equipped and maintained by county councils and county borough councils acting as Local Health Authorities, at which facilities shall be available for the provision of general medical, dental, and pharmaceutical services as well as specialist and any other services which a Local Health Authority is empowered to provide. The advantages of having all these services under one roof are obvious. As yet, however, only a very few such health centres are in existence, on the official plea that scarcity of resources prevents the building of new centres.

Another very real difficulty lies in the watertight divisions between the general medical services, the hospital services, and the services provided by local authorities. In order that health centres should function well, a very real degree of co-operation would be required.

Where the family doctor considers that his patient requires the services of a consultant, or needs hospital treatment, the doctor is empowered to arrange this on his own initiative.

Drug, dental, and supplementary ophthalmic services

Everyone who receives the services of the family doctor is entitled to drugs and medicine, and certain appliances, prescribed by his doctor as part of the treatment. Chemists, while undertaking other work, may dispense drugs and medicine under the National Health Act. They are required to remain open at reasonable times in order that patients can obtain their medicines. Late hours of opening are usually arranged on a rota basis by chemists in a local area. At present a charge is made of 1s per item on each prescription form. This is payable to the chemist by the patient on handing over the prescription made out by his doctor, although it may in certain cases be refunded upon application. For diseases which require several items to be used simultaneously, the prescription is called a 'pack', and the total charge is 1s per prescription form. When prescribed appliances are needed, a charge is made depending on the material cost of the article.

The average cost of a prescription has risen from 3s 1d in 1949–50 to an estimate of 5s in 1956–7. The Minister of Health stated that the increase was due to several factors, including an increase in the proportion of proprietary prescriptions, which rose from 16 per cent in 1949 to 36 per cent in 1956. The Minister hoped soon to be in a position to do something more about investigating the costs of drug firms, explaining that it ought to be possible to set up a central testing laboratory for this purpose.

Dental services also are available under the Act. At present examination is free, but on the undertaking by the dentist of any treatment, a payment of £1, or the full cost of treatment if less than £1, must be made by the patient. This will cover the whole period of treatment. Freedom of choice exists between dentist and patient, and dentists may take private patients as well as those under the National Health Act. One of the current difficulties is a shortage of dentists, and appointments, for other than very urgent and emergency treatment, have often to be made some months ahead. A list of dentists undertaking National Health work can be obtained from the Local Executive Council, the address of which can be obtained from the town hall or county hall.

The Hospital Eye Service is part of the services provided by the hospitals, and staffed by specialists. The family doctor can refer any patient in need of such service to the appropriate hospital or centre. Under the Supplementary Ophthalmic Services Scheme provision is made for the testing of sight and supplying of glasses on the recommendation of a doctor. A list of ophthalmic medical practitioners and ophthalmic opticians can be obtained from the Executive Council office or at a post office.

Hospital and specialist services

Under the Act, it is the duty of the Minister of Health to meet all reasonable requirements for accommodation and services, including:

(a) Hospital accommodation;

(b) Medical, nursing, and other services of the hospitals; and

(c) The services of specialists, whether at a hospital, a health centre, or a clinic.

Hospital services are available to everyone, and no insurance qualification is required. The arrangements are usually made in the first place through the family doctor. The Act allows for payment by the Minister of Health, in certain cases, of travelling expenses (including the travelling expenses of a companion) incurred by persons for the purpose of availing themselves of hospital and specialist services. In cases of need, application should be made to the Almoner of the hospital.

The Act further provides that, in any hospital, accommodation in single rooms or small wards, which is not for the time being needed by any patient on medical grounds, shall be available for patients who undertake to pay for this accommodation. Such 'amenity beds', where available, are obtainable at charges designed to cover part of the cost.

Where there exists an excess of accommodation over urgent needs, room may also be made available by the Minister of Health for patients who undertake to pay the whole of the cost of accommodation and services provided. Thus we have, in hospitals, both National Health patients and private patients.

In each case, these and other important decisions are made, on behalf of the Minister, by the Hospital Management Committees, who concern themselves with the internal administrative work of the non-teaching hospitals; Boards of Governors make decisions on behalf of the teaching hospitals.

Fourteen Regional Hospital Boards were set up under the Act, to administer hospital and specialist services in their areas. Both professional men and laymen are members of the Boards. The teaching hospitals are exempt from the supervision of the

Boards, but all others have their governing bodies appointed by the Boards. Hospital Management Committees are made up of both professional men and laymen, the latter being in the majority.

Whether the best interests of medicine and of patients generally are served when the teaching hospitals are divorced from the others will remain a matter of controversy. Certainly it can be seen that a barrier between the two kinds continues to exist. In the London area many ambulances needed for local work have spent much time taking up to the London teaching hospitals patients who could, in some cases, equally well be treated locally.

The whole question of hospital administration and management is now an important one. There are at least some arguments for returning to Local Health Authorities the management of some hospitals, particularly if the teaching hospitals are to remain outside the general system.

Many and varied are the services provided by hospitals, for both in-patients and out-patients, of a specialized and a general nature. Great care is now taken to ensure that patients do not, through worry about family and personal matters, fail to gain every benefit from attending hospital. The social worker in each hospital is the Almoner, and she should be consulted on all matters of this kind.

Most hospitals have long waiting lists for in-patient treatment. At the same time, some have closed wards owing to lack of staff. In Chapter 9 the question of a long stay by elderly patients is discussed. Nursing remains a career which attracts girls with a vocation. As well as the provision of sufficient domestic help, one would suggest that to demand a higher standard of education from would-be entrants would accord to the nurses a higher professional status *vis-à-vis* other professions, thus improving the chances in competition with teaching, and social and secretarial work, for the same type of entrant.

The hospitals have been among the sadder casualties of economy drives since the war. There is an urgent need in many parts of the country for new buildings to replace the present often antiquated ones. One of the benefits of the Act has been the provision of an adequate hospital administration service. Alas, while this service is being built up, many Hospital Management Committees continue to cut down their vital and irreplaceable medical staff.

One of the interesting features of the Act is that the provision of specialists (whether at a hospital, a health centre, a clinic, or, if necessary on medical grounds, at the home of the patient) comes within the general heading of 'Hospital and Specialist Services'. This bias of interest towards the hospitals is a possible explanation why one rarely hears of specialists visiting the homes of patients.

HEALTH SERVICES PROVIDED BY LOCAL HEALTH AUTHORITIES

The Local Health Authorities, i.e. the county and county borough councils, are responsible under the Act for providing certain services:

Maternity and child welfare services

It is the duty of every Local Health Authority to make arrangements for the care, including in particular the dental care, of expectant and nursing mothers and of children who have not attained the age of five years and are not attending primary schools maintained by a Local Education Authority. Clinics for ante-natal and post-natal care, with specially trained doctors and nurses in attendance, have proved very popular. The addresses of these clinics and the times of attendance can be obtained from the local town hall or county hall.

Health Visitors attend the clinics, and also visit the homes of all children under two years of age. They are able to anticipate difficulty and can often thus help to avoid it. Health visitors, in addition to their highly specialized nursing training, also undergo a general training in social work, and thus maintain a valuable link with other, non-medical, social services.

An expectant mother is entitled to the services of a doctor who undertakes maternity work (whether he is her usual doctor or not) and of a midwife, as well as general care before and after the confinement. The doctor will advise whether there is need for the confinement to take place in hospital. If this is unnecessary on medical grounds, the expectant mother can make her own choice as to whether or not she has her baby at home. However, hospital accommodation for other than priority cases is in short supply.

Home nursing and home helps

For those people who require nursing in their own homes a duty lies on every Local Health Authority to make provision for such care. This can be done directly under the Local Health Authority itself, or in conjunction with an organization of nurses, such as the District Nursing Association.

In addition to this, the Local Health Authority may (and nearly all do use these permissive powers) make arrangements to provide domestic help for households where such help is required owing to the presence of any person who is ill, lying-in, an expectant mother, mentally defective, aged, or a child not over compulsory school age. This is not a free service, and the Local Health Authority can recover from a person assisted by the service such charges as the authority consider reasonable, having regard to the person's means.

Vaccination and immunization

An obligation rests upon the Local Health Authority to make arrangements with medical practitioners for the vaccination of those who live within its area against smallpox and also for immunization against diphtheria. The provision of such services is compulsory, but not their use. A low death rate from these two diseases should not lull parents into thinking that protection against them is unnecessary; it provides proof that the universal use of protective measures can defeat the disease.

The authorities, with the approval of the Minister of Health, can, and if so directed by him shall, make similar arrangements for vaccination or immunization against any other disease.

Ambulance services

The provision of ambulances and other means of transport (i.e. 'sitting-case cars') is another duty of every Local Health Authority. Transport may either be within the area of the Local Health Authority or to places outside. The authorities may carry out this duty either by themselves providing the necessary ambulances and other means of transport, or they may make arrangements with voluntary organizations such as the Red Cross, or the St. John's Ambulance Brigade, to supply or supplement these.

Because the Ambulance Service and the Hospital Service are not under the same authority there is room for possible friction and misunderstanding between them. Delay and frustration to patients sometimes result.

Other services

In another chapter of this book other services, such as the Mental Health and Mental Deficiency Services, are described. They too are part of the National Health Service.

THE COST OF HEALTH

It is impossible to divorce the National Health Service, with an annual expenditure in the region of £515 million per annum, from Parliamentary control. From time to time it becomes the subject of political controversy. Is the country getting full value for the vast sum now being spent on the service ?

Many people, both inside and outside the medical profession, are disturbed at the present cost of the service. The Health Service costs £10 per year for every man, woman and child in the country. The Hospital Service alone costs over £280 million a year. This works out at a little over £5 per head of the population. The average cost per bed each year is £555. In some hospitals the cost comes to nearly £1,200 per year.

The three-part system

At the beginning of 1956, the Committee of Inquiry into the cost of the National Health Service, set up by the Minister of Health, reported that 'The service's record since the appointed day has been one of real and constructive achievement'. This encourages enthusiasts for the scheme to press for conditions a little nearer perfection, and to say that this country lags behind in the provision of adequate industrial medical services and an all-embracing occupational health service.

Not all the available doctors are used to their full professional capacity. In April 1956, thirty-five doctors were receiving unemployment benefit. This figure is symptomatic of a considerably larger number of young and competent doctors unable to find places in any branch of the National Health Service.

The architect of the service made a fundamental mistake in dividing it, for administrative purposes, into three watertight compartments. This division has kept the Local Health Authority apart from the rest of the services, left the general practitioner isolated, and prevented integration of the hospital and domiciliary branches. No liaison committee can bridge these gaps. The reorganization and expansion of the hospital services, with the addition of new specialist and technical staff, has resulted in much less effective liaison than existed previously between hospital doctors and general practitioners.

However, with all the faults of the present service, one must recognize that very great improvements have been made in the health of the people. A very high standard of clinical medicine can be foreseen within the service. The National Health Service could be moulded into the finest in the world.

7

Mental Deficiency and Mental Illness

JEAN GRAHAM HALL

AT the present time over one-third of all beds provided under the National Health Service are occupied by patients suffering from mental disability or mental disorder. This shows the importance and the magnitude of the problem.

Whenever we speak of 'mental trouble' it is necessary to differentiate between mental deficiency and mental illness, and to recognize clearly to which of these we are referring. Each presents quite separate social and medical problems, and needs quite different provisions.

Mental deficiency is a disability which is recognizable by the time a person is eighteen years of age and is a retardation of the development of the mind. Mental illness, whether or not amounting to insanity, may be cured or alleviated, depending upon its degree and type.

In 1954, a Royal Commission was set up to consider the law relating to both mental deficiency and mental illness. The Ministry of Health and the Board of Control gave evidence to the Royal Commission suggesting several changes in the law. It is likely that the Royal Commission will advise certain changes requiring legislation by Parliament.

The duty to promote the establishment of a comprehensive health service now rests with the Ministry of Health. Certain functions under the Mental Deficiency Acts rest with the Board of Control. In the House of Commons, the Minister of Health answers any parliamentary questions which arise relating to the Board of Control. The county councils and the county borough councils are the Local Health Authorities.

Mental Deficiency and Mental Illness

MENTAL DEFICIENCY

The legal definition of mental deficiency is 'a condition of arrested or incomplete development of mind, existing before the age of eighteen years, whether from inherent causes or induced by disease'. Mental defectives are not capable of normal development. They cannot be treated and cured in the same way as mentally ill people.

At present the law divides mental defectives into four categories, dependent upon the degree of social awareness and social capability which is present. On the borders, of course, these categories merge into one another.

1. *Idiots* – those who are unable to guard themselves against common physical dangers. They are incapable of benefiting from training and need constant care and attention.

2. *Imbeciles* – those whose mental defectiveness does not amount to idiocy but who are incapable of managing themselves or their affairs. Children who are imbeciles are incapable of being taught these things at school.

3. *Feeble-minded persons* – those in whom mental defectiveness does not amount to imbecility, yet who require care, supervision, and control for their own protection or for the protection of others. In the case of children, their incapacity involves a disability of mind of such a nature and extent that it makes them incapable of receiving and benefiting from education at school. Given a high degree of patient training, many of the feeble-minded can overcome some of their deficiencies and look after themselves quite well. The extent to which this is possible depends entirely upon the degree of development of each individual. The difference between a high-grade feeble-minded defective and a normal person is not at first always easily discernible.

4. *Moral defectives* – those whose mental defectiveness is coupled with strongly vicious or criminal tendencies. They require care, supervision, and control for the protection of others. This category arouses great controversy among would-be reformers who wish to see it abolished. It could fairly be

said that the other three categories are quite sufficient to cover anyone who at present could be termed a moral defective.

Marriage of a mental defective

By the Matrimonial Causes Act, 1937, if either party to a marriage at the time of the ceremony is a mental defective, the marriage can be annulled, provided that the petitioner was ignorant of the fact. Proceedings must be instituted within a year from the date of the marriage, and the petitioner must not have consented to marital intercourse since the discovery of the existence of the mental deficiency.

Should a mental defective contract a marriage without freely consenting or understanding the nature of the ceremony, the marriage is void. The test is whether there is real consent, not only to marry, but to marry the particular person. If the defective is incapable of physically consummating the marriage, the marriage can be annulled.

Civil and criminal responsibility

The Will of a mental defective is valid if when he makes it he clearly understands (*a*) the nature and extent of his property, (*b*) the persons who have claims upon his bounty, and (*c*) the relative strength of their claims.

Any contract which a mental defective makes is valid and binding upon both the defective and the other party unless, at the time of making the agreement, the mental defective was incapable of understanding the terms therein and the other party knew this.

A mental defective is liable to be found guilty and punished like any other person if he commits a crime. However, his mental state should be considered when the Court determines responsibility and considers treatment.

Care of defectives

The duty of the Ministry of Health to promote the establishment of a comprehensive health service includes care and supervision of, and provision for, mental defectives, either directly through the Ministry or through various agencies.

Under the Mental Deficiency Act, 1913, and the National Health Act, 1946, the Local Health Authorities, functioning through their Mental Health Sub-Committees, are assigned the following duties:

1. Ascertaining what persons within their area are defectives subject to be dealt with under the Acts.

2. Providing suitable supervision for such defectives. If this affords insufficient protection, taking steps to ensure that they are sent to institutions or placed under guardianship.

3. Making provision for the guardianship of defectives placed under guardianship by order under the Acts.

4. To the extent that the Minister of Health directs, of making arrangements for the care and after-care of persons suffering from mental defectiveness.

In practice, the Medical Officer of Health makes a report to the Mental Health Sub-Committee on each case known to the Local Health Authority. The sub-committee then decides whether the defective should (*a*) remain at home under statutory supervision, (*b*) be recommended for guardianship, or (*c*) be recommended for institutional care.

(*a*) *At home under statutory supervision.* If a defective's parents can look after him at home and give him the care he requires so that he is not a nuisance to himself or to other persons, he can be placed under statutory supervision. He is not then certified as a mental defective. A 'duly authorized officer' of the local Health Authority will visit regularly to ensure that the conditions at home are satisfactory and that the care is adequate. Alternatively, a voluntary association of mental welfare, acting for the Local Health Authority, undertakes the visiting.

This visiting is of great value. The officer gives friendly and useful advice, assists in an emergency, and generally takes any steps necessary in the particular case. Not all officers have any, or sufficient, training in social welfare for this skilled task. Plenty of room exists for the increased employment of well-trained and qualified social workers in this field, visiting more frequently than hitherto.

Defectives under statutory supervision can be admitted to short-stay institutional accommodation, without certification, for a maximum period of eight weeks at a time. Alternatively, they can obtain temporary admission to a mental deficiency institution. Such arrangements, made by the Local Health Authority with the Hospital Management Committee, assist the family of the defective to overcome temporary domestic crises or illness and relieve it of impossible burdens. Temporary care should be more widely used and the period of possible stay more widely extended.

(*b*) *Guardianship*. This is a half-way house between statutory supervision and institutional care. An order is made in the same way as if a defective required institutional care, and then the Local Health Authority boards the defective out in a private family, paying the full cost of his maintenance. Guardianship is vested in the person with whom the defective is boarded. An officer of the Local Health Authority must visit at intervals of not more than six months. A medical practitioner with experience in mental deficiency must visit on behalf of the authority at intervals of not more than twelve months. If the Authority decides, at any time, that the defective under guardianship needs institutional care, the guardianship order can be varied.

Mental institutions are overcrowded and understaffed. Guardianship relieves the pressure upon them in suitable cases. It has worked very well where high-grade or medium-grade defectives have ability enough to benefit from a stable, homely background.

(*c*) *Institutional care*. A defective in need of more care than he can receive in his home, or who is a danger to himself or others, may be placed in an institution. The usual procedure originates with the presentation of a petition by the duly authorized officer to a magistrate. The consent of his parents is necessary, and in addition two medical practitioners must certify that the person is a mental defective. The order for detention in the institution is made in the first instance for one year, then for a second year, followed by five-year periods, with a special examination at the age of twenty-one.

Most institutions suffer from overcrowding, the number of places available being totally inadequate to meet the long waiting lists. Acute shortage of staff presents an ever-increasing problem. Institutions vary greatly in suitability, but craft training is a feature of most of them. Some defectives, able to undertake menial work under supervision, assist with the daily chores and help in the gardens or farms. Others need constant care and close supervision. From time to time conditions in mental hospitals cause public uneasiness, but little action results from the spasmodic agitation.

Shortage of staff and accommodation has forced mental hospital authorities to consider whether more of the higher-grade defectives could not be licensed out.

A defective in an institution who has responded to training, and improved sufficiently, may be sent out on daily licence, working in the community but returning to the institution every evening. Farm work, domestic work, or employment in carefully selected factories often proves highly successful. This can be a preliminary to full licence, whereby the defective both resides and works outside the institution but continues to receive visits from the Hospital Management Committee. Authority to grant such a licence rests with the medical superintendent of the institution. In the first instance it is usually issued for six months. Some institutions provide hostels for their licence cases.

The Disabled Persons (Employment) Act, 1944, defines disease as 'a physical or mental condition arising from imperfect development of any organ'. Defectives capable of undertaking remunerative work are therefore entitled to place their names on the Register of the Disabled and obtain help from the Disablement Resettlement Officer at the Labour Exchange.

Where an order exists, the only way for a defective to obtain complete freedom from supervision is for the order to be discharged. If there is any doubt as to the validity of the order, legal advice should be sought through a solicitor. At present, ultimate authority in the matter of discharge rests with the Board of Control. The Hospital Management Committee of the institution reviews the question of discharge in relation to each patient every two years and makes its recommendation to the Board of Control. Any patient can himself make direct application for discharge to the Board.

Provisions for children

Defective children of school age are the responsibility of the county councils and borough councils in their capacity as Local Education Authority. Some Education Authorities organize special classes in the ordinary primary and secondary schools, under the care of sympathetic and encouraging teachers, for retarded children in need of special educative treatment not amounting to attendance at a special school.

Special schools, which educationally sub-normal children attend daily, are also the responsibility of the Education Authority. The curriculum of these schools places strong emphasis on activity, crafts, gardening, and useful everyday knowledge to enable the pupils to cope with their daily needs. Many children who would benefit considerably from such specialized training still flounder unhappily along in the ordinary schools owing to lack of accommodation.

The Education Act, 1944, states that where the Education Authority finds that a child is suffering from a disability of mind of such a nature and to such an extent as (a) to make him incapable of receiving education at school, or (b) to make it inexpedient that he should be educated in association with other children, either in his own interests or those of other children, or (c) to require supervision after leaving school, then the matter must be reported by the Education Authority to the Local Health Authority. Although this sounds somewhat complicated, in effect it only means that one department at the county hall or town hall reports the matter to another department.

By providing occupation centres and home teaching the Local Health Authority seeks to provide for the ineducable mentally defective children thus reported. At occupation centres most of those attending continue to do so after attaining their sixteenth birthday. Teaching in the formal sense does not constitute part of the daily programme. The emphasis is upon habit training and occupation, helping at the same time to re-move some of the strain from the family of the defective for a definite period each day. Trained and devoted supervisors wel-come voluntary helpers where they are available.

In scattered areas without occupation centres, or where through physical disability the defective is unable to attend a centre, the Local Health Authority is empowered to arrange for a home teacher to visit the homes of defectives, giving simple instruction in handicrafts and general training.

In the field of mental deficiency, voluntary associations play an important role, supplementing the work of the Local Health Authority and sometimes undertaking some of it for them. The national co-ordinating body is the National Association for Mental Health.

MENTAL ILLNESS

As a nation we have become much more enlightened on the subject of mental health in recent years. Many temporarily mentally sick people have sought the haven of a mental hospital as a temporary measure rather than bear the worry and burden of their illness without specialist aid. The stigma of entering an 'asylum' has now been erased by Act of Parliament. Many of our mental hospitals are well-equipped, well-managed com-munities, with villas, farms, workshops, and recreational facili-ties attached to the therapeutic centre. Of every ten patients entering mental hospitals to-day, seven go as voluntary patients.

Early advice in cases of mental disturbance is very im-portant. This can be obtained from the family doctor, the duly authorized officer at the county hall or the town hall, or the police.

The law differentiates very clearly between certified patients on the one hand and, on the other, voluntary patients suffering from mental ill-health who seek advice, and frequently insti-tutional care, on their own initiative.

Certified patients

The Mental Treatment Act, 1930, repealed the use of the word 'lunatic' for a certified patient and substituted the phrase 'person of unsound mind'. Institutional care of such a person is the responsibility of the Regional Hospital Board, acting on behalf of the Minister of Health. Arrangements for admission to the institution remain with the county borough councils and county councils as Local Health Authorities.

Where the duly authorized officer of the Local Health Authority is satisfied (i) that the case is one in which he has a duty to perform under the Act, and (ii) that it is necessary for the safety of the public or the welfare of the patient that he should forthwith be placed under care and control, he removes the patient to a hospital for observation, for a period of three days.

During this three-day period the Medical Superintendent of the hospital may certify that the person is of unsound mind and for his own welfare should remain for a further period of not more than fourteen days. During that further fourteen days the Medical Superintendent can discharge the certificate. But if he is satisfied that the patient should be sent to a mental hospital, he advises the duly authorized officer to obtain a reception order to the mental hospital.

A useful procedure in an emergency is that by which a police constable can take to a place of safety a person wandering at large, whom he has reasonable grounds for believing is of unsound mind, and then call a justice of the peace. If the justice is satisfied that the person is of unsound mind and a proper person to be detained, and a medical practitioner, whom the justice must call in, signs a medical certificate to that effect, the justice may then order that the patient shall be received and detained in an institution for persons of unsound mind.

Relatives of the person of unsound mind may prefer to make their own arrangements, particularly where removal is not an immediate necessity. A husband, wife, or other relative can present a petition to a specially appointed justice (whose name can be obtained from the magistrates' court). The petition must be accompanied by two recent medical certificates. One of the certificates should be signed by the patient's usual doctor. The petitioner must give an undertaking that he, or someone appointed by him, will visit the patient at least every six months.

At the present time persons of unsound mind who have been certified can be received into:

(i) *A mental hospital*, i.e. one of the hospitals which the Regional Hospital Board, and under it the Hospital Management Committee of the actual hospital, manage for and on behalf of the Minister of Health. Treatment in such a hospital is free, regardless of the means of the patient.

(ii) *A registered hospital*, i.e. a hospital kept up either by charitable institutions and/or contributions made on behalf of the patients, and recognized by the Minister of Health.

(iii) *A licensed house* run for profit for private mental patients. Justices of county and quarter-sessions appoint three or more of their number and a medical practitioner to visit such institutions within their district.

Reception orders must be renewed at the end of twelve months, again after the lapse of a second twelve months, and then at the end of periods of two, three, and five years. At those times the Medical Superintendent of the institution must certify, for the information of the Board of Control, that the patient is still of unsound mind and continues to need care and treatment.

Discharge

Three members of the Hospital Management Committee, or two members with the written advice of the Medical Superintendent, may order the discharge of a patient, whether or not application by a relative or friend of the patient has been made.

On the recovery of a private patient in a registered hospital or licensed house a notice must be sent to the petitioner, or the person responsible for the patient's maintenance, stating that unless the patient is removed within seven days he will be discharged.

A patient detained under a reception order made by petition, may also be discharged on the direction of the petitioner or, if the petitioner is dead, on the signed direction of the husband, wife, or relative, or the person responsible for the payment of maintenance of the patient.

Sometimes certified patients escape from institutional care. If they are found and brought back within fourteen days the original order remains valid. If, however, the patient remains at large for more than fourteen days, fresh proceedings for detention must be taken.

Temporary patients

Under the Mental Treatment Act, 1930, a patient who is suffering from mental illness and would benefit from temporary treatment but is incapable of expressing himself as willing or unwilling to receive treatment, may be admitted to institutional care as a temporary patient. The relative or, at the relative's request, the duly authorized officer, makes application to the Medical Superintendent of the mental hospital. This application must be signed by two doctors, one of whom must be the patient's usual doctor, and the other a doctor approved by the Minister of Health for this purpose. The medical examination by each of the doctors must be made within five days previous to the making of the application.

Six months is the limit of time during which a temporary patient may be detained, unless the time is extended by the Board of Control. The total time of detention, including any extension, must not exceed twelve months.

Voluntary patients

Voluntary treatment in mental hospitals, registered hospitals, and licensed houses may be obtained on the written application of the intending patient to the Medical Superintendent. For a patient under sixteen, the application must be made by his parent or guardian and accompanied by medical recommendation. The patient's usual doctor should be approached on this matter.

A voluntary patient cannot be detained against his will. He need only give seventy-two hours' notice in writing to the Medical Superintendent of his intention to discharge himself. The patient can do this in spite of the fact that he is in the middle of a course of therapeutic treatment likely to benefit him considerably. Many voluntary patients get 'fed up' with something quite trivial and discharge themselves all too soon. Where the patient is under sixteen the notice must be given by the parent or guardian.

Worries about domestic affairs often reach such large proportions that they almost overwhelm voluntary patients. Trained psychiatric social workers try to help patients to face these difficulties and assist in smoothing them out where this is possible. Psychiatrists treating patients want to know their home background, and the psychiatric social worker collects and collates this information.

On discharge many voluntary patients attend at an out-patients' clinic to continue treatment and receive advice and encouragement. Some clinics run therapeutic clubs with great success.

Any medical practioner can refer a patient to the mental health clinic, where one exists. Inquiries about such clinics should be made at the county hall or town hall. Advice and treatment at such a clinic in the early stages of a mental illness will often prevent the necessity of entering an institution at all.

Information about child guidance clinics for problem or maladjusted children is also available at the county hall or town hall. At such clinics teams consisting of a psychiatrist, a psychologist to deal with educational matters, and a psychiatric social worker, interview both parents and children.

Through giving wise counsel and advice to the parents, and by skilled therapeutics and play treatment of the child, much can be achieved. If the home background is suitable, the child can remain there. Some hostels are available for seriously maladjusted children. Waiting lists are discouragingly long both for appointments at the clinics and admission to the hostels.

Marriage and civil and criminal responsibility

If at the time of the ceremony of marriage either party is of unsound mind or subject to recurrent fits of insanity or epilepsy, the marriage can be annulled. If one spouse is incurably of unsound mind and has been under care and treatment for at least five years immediately preceding the presentation of the petition, the other spouse may sue for a divorce.

A testator making a Will must clearly understand (a) the nature and extent of his property; (b) the persons who have claims upon his bounty; and (c) the relative strength of their claims. Where the testator is subject to delusions with regard to the persons who would be the natural objects of his bounty, e.g. relations or close friends, his Will made under the influence of such delusions is invalid. On the other hand, where the testator is subject to delusions which leave the general power of understanding unaffected and are wholly unconnected with his Will, such delusions do not affect his capacity to make a Will.

Any contract made by a person who by reason of mental disease is incapable of knowing what he is doing can be avoided by him, provided that his state of mind was known to the other party to the contract. However, a contract is binding if the person afterwards confirms it when his state of mind is such that he understands what he is doing. Where necessaries are sold and delivered to a person incompetent to contract, he or his guardian is bound to pay a reasonable price for the necessaries.

In criminal law every person is presumed to be sane until the contrary is proved. If an accused person is too insane to stand trial, he is detained during Her Majesty's pleasure pending recovery. It is a defence to a criminal prosecution for the accused to show that he was labouring under such a defect of reason due to a disease of the mind as either (a) not to know the nature and quality of his act, or (b) if he did know this, not to know that he was doing wrong. If such a defence succeeds, the verdict is 'Guilty but insane'. The defence of insanity is rarely pleaded in answer to any charge other than that of murder.

Where difficulty arises in connection with the management

and administration of property and estates of persons of unsound mind, advice may be sought from the Master in Lunacy,
appointed by the Lord Chancellor, at the Royal Courts of
Justice, London, WC2.

8

The Handicapped

JEAN GRAHAM HALL

THE Welfare State offers protective provisions of a specialized nature for its mentally and physically handicapped citizens. Each type of handicap needs different help, and each disabled person requires individual attention.

The facilities provided for those handicapped with either mental illness or mental deficiency are described in Chapter 7.

THE CRIPPLED

Under the National Health Service, hospitals and specialist facilities for the physically disabled are provided free of charge. In the first instance the family doctor should be consulted. He can make arrangements for the patient to be seen by an orthopaedic specialist at the clinic or out-patients' department of one of the main hospitals. Such hospitals have rehabilitation departments where physiotherapists and remedial gymnasts assist the patient to regain, by remedial exercises, the fullest possible use of his faculties. The treatment also includes occupational therapy. Crafts and new skills are taught on a remedial basis. The entire treatment, devised to meet the needs of each patient, remains very individualistic.

Appliances to meet the individual need can be fitted at the clinic or out-patients' department. Certain charges are now made for these, e.g. £1 for surgical abdominal supports, £3 for surgical appliances, with extra charges for repairs. Anyone in receipt of National Assistance can obtain repayment or exemption. This also applies to war pensioners in respect of their pensionable disabilities.

Training and placing in employment is the responsibility of the Ministry of Labour. By the Disabled Persons (Employment) Act, 1944, the expression 'disabled person' means a person who, on account of injury, disease, or congenital deformity, is substantially handicapped in obtaining or keeping employment, or in undertaking work on his own account, of a kind which, apart from that injury, disease, or deformity, would be suitable to his age, experience, or qualifications. The Act empowers the Minister of Labour to provide or make suitable arrangements for the training of disabled persons, over sixteen years of age, who need such training to make them competent to undertake suitable work.

The Disablement Resettlement Officer at the local Labour Exchange makes the necessary arrangements for attendance at one of the training centres, which are of both a residential and non-residential nature.

The Disablement Resettlement Officer also assists in placing the disabled person in suitable employment. This will either be in the open market or in a Remploy factory, where registered disabled persons with severe handicaps work under sheltered conditions, undertaking tasks within the scope of their abilities, at the same time covering a wide range of products and skills. These factories were set up by the Government under the Disabled Persons Employment Corporation. In addition, the Ministry of Labour maintains a register of disabled persons, and every employer who has a substantial number of employees must give employment to a quota of registered disabled persons.

County councils and county borough councils, the local welfare authorities, have power to make arrangements for promoting instruction of handicapped people in their own homes, or for providing special workshops where they can engage in suitable work. This is a permissive power, and inquiries should be made at the county hall or town hall to see if the local welfare authority has implemented it.

Financial grants available to disabled persons under the National Insurance Scheme, the Industrial Injuries Act, and from the Assistance Board are all dealt with in other chapters of this book.

Special clubs for the physically handicapped, run by voluntary organizations, give fellowship and cheer to many. They help members to realize that they are not alone in facing what sometimes seem insuperable difficulties. The local Citizens' Advice Bureau (the address of which can be obtained at a post office) would know of any such clubs in a given area.

Responsibility for medical treatment and education of disabled children rests with the Local Education Authority, at the county hall or town hall.

BLINDNESS

The National Assistance Act, 1948, places a duty upon county and county borough councils to make arrangements for promoting the welfare of blind persons within their areas. Ever since 1920, when a specialized department of the Ministry of Health was set up, these local welfare authorities have had this duty of caring for the blind.

Responsibility may be delegated to a registered voluntary organization, and many local authorities have done this. As a result it is impossible to say, between one area and another, whether the facilities and information will be provided at the county hall or town hall, or whether welfare has become the responsibility of one of the voluntary societies. Co-operation between the public and voluntary bodies remains very close and has existed for many years.

Either the local authority itself or the voluntary organization to which it delegates its powers makes arrangements:

(*a*) To inform people of the available services.

(*b*) To give blind people instruction, in their own homes or elsewhere, in methods of overcoming the effects of their disabilities. This is done by the Home Teachers – a devoted body of women who form the backbone of the blind welfare services. They teach Braille and handicrafts and, in addition, give help and advice on a remarkably wide plane.

(*c*) To provide special workshops where blind people may be engaged in suitable work. This normally consists of such trades as mat and basket making, shoe repairing, and both machine and hand knitting.

(d) To provide work which blind people can carry on in their own homes. Much of the same type of work is undertaken as in the workshops. The home workers are supplied with suitable materials and helped to dispose of their finished work.

(e) To provide blind people with recreational facilities. Sometimes a grant is given to a voluntary body to assist in running a club on suitable premises. In more remote areas facilities such as the radio are made available in the home.

(f) To compile and maintain a voluntary register of blind people. They are encouraged to register in order to obtain the benefits of the many services, which can thus be more easily and effectively planned.

(g) To provide accommodation in the form of homes and hostels where these are required. The elderly blind need particular and specialized care. Most of the homes reach a particularly high standard, but they are inadequate to meet the growing need. The hostels, fewer in number, cater for blind workers without homes of their own.

Under the National Assistance Act special provision is made for blind persons in need of financial assistance above the ordinary scale. Rent is allowed in addition to the following:

For husband and wife:	
Of whom one is blind	82s od
Of whom both are blind	95s od
For other persons:	
Aged twenty-one or over	56s 6d
Aged eighteen to twenty-one	43s 6d
Aged sixteen to eighteen	35s 6d

In December 1955, the latest date for which figures are available, 57,000 blind persons were receiving these special-scale allowances.

Blind persons qualify for the non-contributory old age pension, under the Old Age Pensions Act, 1936, at the age of fifty years instead of the usual seventy. This meets the need of those people who become blind with the onset of old age.

The newly-blinded active adult finds the adjustment to his or her newly-restricted life very difficult to make. The Royal National Institute for the Blind runs two social rehabilitation centres to assist in this process. On learning how to make the necessary personal and social adaptations, the next step is to attend at one of the Ministry of Labour's employment training centres and enter, perhaps, new and wider fields with a skill which only needs careful placing in employment. This is done through the Disablement Resettlement Officer at the local Labour Exchange, who is assisted by the specialized service given by the Placement Officers of the R.N.I.B.

Education for blind children between the ages of five and sixteen is compulsory and remains the responsibility of the Local Education Authority. All schools for blind children are residential. The children learn to read and write Braille in addition to the usual school subjects, taught by specially trained and devoted teachers. They also learn social adaptability, independence of outlook and movement, and a development of their latent skills. Very great difficulty arises when children have some other handicap in addition to their blindness. Some special schools are provided for mentally backward blind children, and great care is taken to ensure that every child capable of benefiting from education is given that opportunity.

Whether a blind child should go into residential care before the age of five years is a matter which can only be decided when the individual circumstances are considered. Some parents find it more difficult than others to cope with the specialized needs of blind children. Following the pattern of co-operation between public and voluntary bodies, the R.N.I.B., in their Sunshine Homes for the under-sevens and in other schools for older children, provide the facilities for early adaptation and training. The local authorities pay for the children from their areas at these homes and make the necessary arrangements with the R.N.I.B. for entry to them. For under-fives the local Medical Officer, and for over-fives the local Education Officer, should be consulted in the first instance. Arrangements about Braille books and the Talking Book Library, or for getting in touch with the local welfare association, are undertaken by the R.N.I.B. St Dunstan's deals with the war blinded.

DEAFNESS

Deafness is a handicap which may exist from birth, or it may come on the sufferer gradually in adult life.

Deaf children need an unusual amount of individual love and attention to help them penetrate their lonely world. Oral communication is difficult, because the deaf child cannot learn to speak by imitation, and what only amounts to deafness is sometimes mistaken for mental backwardness because of the absence of response to usual stimuli.

Under the Education Act, 1944, education in special residential schools is compulsory for all deaf children between the ages of five and sixteen years. Particular attention is paid to lip-reading and speech training. Teachers at the schools devote endless patience to their work, and the results can be gratifying. The Local Education Authority makes the necessary arrangements for entry to such a school.

Because the deaf child must contend with so many handicaps, the earlier he starts training the better. Speech for him is artificial and laboriously learned. Although lip-reading is assiduously taught, this must be implemented by other methods of communication, such as sign language. Unfortunately, lip-reading needs a high degree of intelligence and ability on the part of the child. Its recent success must not mask the fact that only one deaf child in four becomes sufficiently master of it.

Medical facilities are provided under the National Health Service. So far as deaf children are concerned, if mothers attend the ordinary clinics, the Health Visitor there will make any necessary appointments for consultation with a specialist.

Adults who begin to fear they are becoming hard of hearing should consult their family doctor. He can refer patients to an ear clinic where consultation with a specialist will be possible, free of charge. Hearing aids of the 'Medresco' type are supplied to patients referred from the clinics to a distribution centre. These very effective aids are supplied and serviced free of charge.

Sometimes a worker who has become deaf will need to change his employment. If necessary, he can learn a new skill at one of the Ministry of Labour's training centres, during which time he will receive a maintenance allowance. The Disablement Resettlement Officer at the local Labour Exchange helps in placing the deaf person in suitable employment; he should apply for inclusion in the register of disabled persons and gain the benefits which arise from doing this.

Voluntary organizations concerned with the welfare of deaf persons, and their addresses, and any further help and information can be obtained from the National Institute for the Deaf.

TUBERCULOSIS

Tuberculosis breeds in bad housing conditions, where overcrowding is rife. Fresh air, cleanliness, good food, and a high standard of living are its enemies. Responsibility for measures designed to ensure the prevention of tuberculosis rests with the Local Health Authorities, at the county hall or town hall. They are also responsible for the removal of the causes of infection.

Mass radiography is one very effective means of detecting tuberculosis in its earliest stages. Units operating under the Regional Hospital Boards, in co-operation with local authorities, visit particular areas from time to time. The process is quick, efficient, and effective, and one cannot over-emphasize the importance of voluntary submission to the X-ray by all citizens. Notices are inserted in local papers and all possible means of publicity are used to ensure that people know when a unit is visiting their area.

If anyone suspects that he, or a member of his family, might have contracted tuberculosis, he should not wait until the unit visits his area, but instead should immediately consult his family doctor. The doctor can arrange that the patient attends a chest clinic for diagnosis without delay. This, like mass radiography, is free under the National Health Service. Hospitals and sanatoria for treatment are provided in all parts of the country. In suitable cases arrangements can be made for the patient to go abroad for special treatment. There are also village settlements in England run by voluntary organizations to which suitable patients can go and stay for a considerable period.

After-care of patients who have undergone a course of treatment is very important. The Local Health Authorities employ a specialist tuberculosis officer, working from the local chest clinic, with a staff of nurses and welfare officers, to ensure that this is effectively undertaken.

Through co-operation of its various departments the local authority can often provide more suitable and spacious housing accommodation, make arrangements for the boarding-out of the children of infected parents, offer the services of a home help while a convalescent mother is not yet strong enough to carry out her household duties, and supply extra bedding and clothing where this is needed.

The National Assistance Act makes special provision for persons who have suffered a loss of income in order to undergo treatment for tuberculosis. In December 1955, the last date for which the relevant figures are available, 28,000 persons were in receipt of such an allowance – calculated on the same favourable scale as that which applies to blind persons.

Sometimes after contracting tuberculosis the former mode of employment is too arduous or in some other way unsuitable. Training for openings in new fields and suitable placement remain the responsibility of the Ministry of Labour. The arrangements are made by the Disablement Resettlement Officer at the local Labour Exchange.

EPILEPSY

Epilepsy remains a much misunderstood handicap. To see someone lose consciousness, fall down, shaking and rolling, appearing to turn a strange bluish colour, is not a pleasant sight. The mistaken idea has unfortunately spread that all epileptics are mentally subnormal, difficult in temperament, and unemployable. Thus people tend to shun known epileptics, and the helping hand of friendship remains unproffered. According to medical opinion, the full causes of epilepsy are little understood, and difficult to detect if the sufferer is not having a fit at the time of examination. Epileptics often remain silent about their handicaps and fail to make full use of the medical and social services available to them.

We know that one out of every 1,000 children is epileptic. Some only have very mild attacks and can manage schooling in the ordinary class. Others must be sent to special residential schools, which are unfortunately too few in number, with the consequent long waiting lists. The Local Education Authority at the county hall or town hall may be approached to arrange home tuition for such a child until a residential vacancy becomes available.

Medical treatment, with the constant use of drugs, can greatly alleviate the condition. The family doctor should be consulted, and he can arrange specialist treatment free of charge.

If the fits are not too serious, there is no reason why adult epileptics should not undertake carefully-chosen employment in work which does not involve such hazards as heights and complicated machinery. If the epileptic registers as a disabled person, he can avail himself of the helpful services of the Disablement Resettlement Officer at the local Labour Exchange and become part of the quota of disabled persons which every employer must take into his employ.

One should warn epileptics, however mild their attacks, that under the Road Traffic Act, 1930, any person who suffers from epilepsy or sudden attacks of disabling giddiness and fainting is prohibited from holding a driving licence. A false statement on such a matter renders the applicant liable to a criminal prosecution.

SUMMARY

This chapter seeks to offer guidance to the layman concerning the possible sources of help which can be called in aid to overcome or alleviate various handicaps. It does not claim to be either detailed or comprehensive.

Contact the Medical Officer of Health at the county hall or town hall in connexion with preventive measures. To obtain specialist medical services, go first to the family doctor.

Many other voluntary societies in addition to those mentioned exist to give sufferers from specific handicaps all the help and information which is at present available. Such societies also try, when a need arises which is not covered by legislation or present sources of help, to press for new and more adequate measures. The local Citizens' Advice Bureau would know of such a society.

9

Provisions for Old Age

JEAN GRAHAM HALL

WHEN a man reaches the age of sixty-five, and a woman the age of sixty, they qualify for many provisions made for old age. The need for the provisions is most uneven. There is no single homogeneous group with common or uniform needs. Some people do not use the available services for a very long time; perhaps never. Others find they cannot manage at all on the inadequate minima offered. Financial troubles, incapacity, sickness, bad housing, lack of family help, and loneliness all strike in a variety of ways at different times.

MONETARY INCOME

On reaching retiring age, one of the first hurdles to overcome is the sharp fall in income. Personal savings, annuities, or endowment policies are a matter for each individual.

In general, the size of the retirement pension under the National Insurance Act, 1946, up to the present weekly standard of £2, varies with the length of the working life during which contributions are paid. The contributor's earnings during that period in no way affect the amount paid on retirement. Between the ages of sixty-five and seventy (men) or sixty and sixty-five (women) the pension is only payable if the recipient has retired from work – except for permitted occasional earnings not exceeding at the present time £2 10s per week. The pension is taxable.

Only by continuing in work after the age of sixty-five (men) or sixty (women) can a worker increase this pension. In spite of this inducement of higher retirement allowance, up to the present time few people have been willing to stay at work after sixty-five years. However, the incidence of full employment has caused a sprinkling of employers to lead the way in promoting schemes for older workers to remain at work, or even induce them to be specially recruited. The older workers undertake lighter work, such as clerical work with less responsibility, viewing, inspecting, sweeping, messengering, and the less heavy and arduous jobs connected with production. Less responsibility and shorter hours naturally mean less pay. The movement is likely to spread, especially when people realize that enforced leisure is not always preferable to suitable employment. The Labour Exchange will be able to assist inquirers. A possible solution to the dilemma is that the retirement pension should be limited initially to six months or a year, made permanent on the application of the pensioner. Each pensioner would thus be compelled to consider, after a six-month trial, whether he would prefer work for a further period or retirement, and freely opt accordingly.

In work such as teaching, the police force, or local government employment, and also with an increasing number of private firms, there are pension schemes in addition to the retirement pension. The difficulty so far as the worker with the private firm is concerned arises from the non-transferability of pension rights between one employer and another, so that this kind of pension scheme is in fact an inducement to the worker to remain in the one employment until his pension rights mature.

A person of seventy or over, not in receipt of either a retirement pension or a widow's pension, may qualify for an old age pension towards which he or she has made no contribution, payable under the Old Age Pensions Act, 1936. A means test is attached to this non-contributory pension. The pension rate is 26s per week, paid on cash orders at the nearest post office. If a pensioner is too old or too infirm to go there himself, arrangements can be made for someone else to do this on his behalf.

Where a person has no independent financial means and no pension, or the pension or other resources are insufficient for his individual needs, it is the duty of the Assistance Board, under the National Assistance Act, 1948, to help him. Application forms, together with explanatory leaflets, are available at any post office. If assistance is given, this is drawn on an order form book at the nearest post office to the applicant's home. Under the present scale the ordinary allowance for a married couple for needs other than rent (for which a special allowance can be made) is 63s per week. The applicant's means are taken into account, but certain resources of income are disregarded in computing the allowance, e.g. the first 10s 6d per week of any payment made in superannuation, earnings, or charitable grant, and the first £375 capital assets held in Savings Certificates.

ACCOMMODATION

'Suitable accommodation' for older people depends entirely on their state of health. Therefore this can best be considered under three heads:

1. In hospitals,
2. In welfare homes, and
3. Living in one's own home.

1. *Hospitals*

The elderly patient living in suitable housing, with a family or close friends to give any necessary domestic help, can quite easily get all the medical care he needs from his general practitioner unless acute sickness overtakes him. Then he must have recourse to a hospital. Hospitals are now under the management of the Regional Hospital Board, but admission to them is obtained through general practitioners.

Hospitals, with their specialized services, should have a turn-over of acutely ill patients in need of full nursing care. They are not, and never have been, intended as permanent accommodation. All too often when the elderly patient could be discharged, his relations, if they exist, do not feel able to cope with him at home. This standstill position means that to-day there is a blocking of beds used for those elderly patients, often very infirm, in need of considerable but not full nursing care. They have recovered from the ailment for which they went into hospital, but no one wishes to take responsibility for their convalescence and constant care. It follows that many other, acutely sick, elderly patients experience great difficulty in getting a hospital bed in their turn.

Many hospitals now have a special geriatric unit where, in fact, the only ailment is that of old age. The best modern units have hospital beds for the acutely sick, a long-stay annexe for the chronic sick, and an out-patient and after-care department.

2. *Welfare homes*

Under Part III of the National Assistance Act, 1948, a duty devolves on every county and county borough to provide residential accommodation for persons ordinarily resident in its area, who by reason of age, infirmity, or any other circumstance are in need of care and attention which is not otherwise available to them. The local authority, in lieu of or to supplement its own provision of residential accommodation for old people, may make suitable arrangements, including financial ones, with a voluntary organization. Information about admission to a home can be obtained from the county hall or town hall.

A well-run residential home or hostel, whether under the auspices of the local authority or a voluntary society, is a joy to visit. Warm, comfortable, specially built or (more often) converted houses, meet all the reasonable needs of the residents. Amenities such as newspapers, periodicals, and concert parties are provided. Usually special arrangements are made for religious worship. Visitors are allowed and welcomed. Residents are free to go out and come in as they choose, and expected only to observe the times set for meals and to return at a reasonable time in the evening. The accommodation and way of life in the welfare homes is intended to provide an acceptable substitute for normal home life. One might sometimes sigh and hope for the availability in the not too distant future of more individual accommodation and smaller homes.

Accommodation in local authority homes is available to those in need, irrespective of their means, but residents are required to pay for their accommodation according to their resources. However small his or her income, every resident keeps at least 6s 6d per week for personal requirements. In many homes, up to a maximum of 10s 6d per week payment to the resident may be made by the governing body if he gives assistance in running the home. Much of the lighter general work and housework of the homes is done in this way by the able-bodied residents. The need on the one hand to run the establishment efficiently is matched on the other by the need for many active and willing residents to find congenial and useful occupations.

The position *vis-à-vis* the hospitals and the welfare homes is that, for official purposes, old people are either ill or well. Upon this artificial division depends which statutory body is responsible. With all its advances, the post-war legislation has led to what has been termed a 'tragic no-man's-land' for old people, in which the half-sick, half-well, find it difficult to obtain adequate provision.

A crying need exists for more residential homes for old people where they can get some supervision and some, but not full, nursing care as they gradually become more frail and more infirm. Sick people are not admitted to the welfare homes, but if residents succumb to illnesses for which they would normally be nursed at home, they receive at least equal care in the welfare homes. As much as anything, it is within the discretion of the matron in charge, bearing in mind the type of home, whether the elderly sick are allowed to remain or have to be found other accommodation.

Various methods could be adopted to remedy the present unsatisfactory position. At the present time, as we have already seen, long-stay annexes for those in need of nursing care are attached to hospitals. It might conceivably work very much better if, instead of the present arrangement, hospital annexes were attached to welfare homes, thus allowing for an easy and two-way traffic from one to the other. Alternatively, a slight alteration in outlook of those bodies setting up homes would mean that by having suitable nursing staff and some night supervision, not necessarily by trained staff, coupled with better-laid-out accommodation, the homes could deal with the ever-increasing proportion of semi-incapacitated residents.

In order to achieve this, it might be provident to establish a joint committee of the hospital management committees and the local authority, with an over-all responsibility for the health and welfare of old people. One could go further and say that the present state of affairs shows a lack of wisdom in divorcing hospital management from local government.

3. *Living at home*

Many an old couple live in a house which was once the family home. Now, the children having married and gone away, it is inhabited only by the elderly couple or the surviving spouse alone. The problem of old people living alone is one peculiar to our age. In former times there were fewer old people. The various generations of a family lived more communally as a unit, and it consisted of many more young people. The modern desire of young married couples to have a place of their own has meant that the older generation no longer potters about the family home, helping with the babies and young children. Loneliness and lack of personal care for the older people result.

A recent survey carried out by the National Assistance Board shows that the great majority of old people are overhoused rather than underhoused, although the accommodation, water facilities, and toilet arrangements are often far from satisfactory. Hardly any of those with spare accommodation would consider sub-letting rooms. They have never sub-let and are 'afraid of getting in the wrong type of people'. Older people become very attached to familiar surroundings, however inconvenient or unsuitable.

Some local authorities make special provision for older people in their housing programmes. On the best estates one finds a diversity of housing for varying needs. Much-sought-after one-room accommodation, with alcoves providing space in the warmth for the bed, are an excellent idea; particularly if placed on the ground floor or accessible by lifts.

The Housing Act, 1936, gives a local authority power to

recognize or promote the extension or formation of voluntary housing associations. Furthermore, the local authority can make arrangements with such housing associations for them: (1) to provide any type of housing which the local authority is itself empowered under the Act to provide; and (2) to alter, repair, or improve houses or buildings in which the local authority has an interest, with a view to the provision or improvement of housing accommodation. Voluntary housing societies usually build or convert property with imagination and skill. The major contribution made by them lies in the field of experimentation, for they have been eager to try new ways of dealing with problems.

I would like to see the possibilities of transfer and exchange developed between (1) the local authority's own available property, and also (2) the local authority's and privately owned property.

1. The transfer of elderly tenants of a local authority to other vacant accommodation in the same ownership is a simple administrative measure. This would set free the under-occupied accommodation much needed for families, at the same time giving the older tenants more suitable dwellings. In such cases the local authority can contribute towards the expenses of moving. Very tactful persuasion by the housing manager may be necessary to coax the reluctant. Although a local authority would not wish to use them, there are residuary powers to compel the move.

2. Exchange involves tenants of different landlords. This is more complicated, because four parties must come to an agreement. However, the encouragement of moves of this nature would obviously assist in solving what sometimes seems an insuperable problem. A progressive local authority could achieve much by negotiations undertaken in an open-minded and helpful spirit.

Transferring older tenants to smaller accommodation would logically result in their paying less rent. But, because the smaller accommodation may carry less subsidy from the government to the local housing authority, and may have been built at a later date than the old, in times of higher prices, that property may actually carry a higher rent. The coming of old age usually means a shrinkage of income. There is much to be said for the adoption by more local authorities of a differential rent scheme. Under such a scheme, the actual rent paid varies above or below the former basic rent of the dwelling, according to the tenant's income. The net rent is reckoned at between one-eighth and one-fifth of the household income. In addition to this sum, rates must be added. Opponents of the scheme tend to concentrate on the actual working out of the scheme, afraid that some local government busybody will probe too much into one's personal affairs. However, where the scheme is initiated with tact, discretion, and fairness, it answers more problems than the one with which we are now concerned, i.e. older people left in unsuitable dwellings. It provides for the possibility of a family house when children are young, expensive, and their need for space is not necessarily matched to the family income.

SERVICES IN THE HOME

Numerous auxiliary services are now available to elderly people living at home, although the extent of them varies from district to district. The local authorities provide some of the services, voluntary bodies provide the others. Many local Old Peoples' Welfare Committees have been set up to give individual advice. The National Old Peoples' Welfare Council, in association with the National Council of Social Service, co-ordinates the work of these local committees. If these services were universally provided, and used to the full, many elderly people could remain much longer in their own homes instead of entering welfare homes because they cannot cope with an increasingly complex life without amenities.

When illness overtakes someone, and home nursing is required, the services of a nurse in the home can be arranged through the Public Health Department at the county hall or town hall. A duty rests on these Health Authorities to make provision in their area, whether by arrangement with voluntary organizations, or by themselves employing nurses, for those persons who require nursing in their own homes. This service, part of the National Health Service, is provided free of charge. Most people, whether elderly or not, appreciate tremendously the services of the district nurse.

Where, owing to illness, domestic help is required with the housework, home helps may be obtained, through the local authority at either the county hall or town hall. The Home Help service consists of women able and willing to undertake all the chores of housework, including cooking and shopping if necessary. They are organized and paid by the local authority and work either full- or part-time, doing housework in several homes, for a few hours a day at each, as an emergency measure.

The National Health Act lays down that the help must be required 'owing to the presence of any person who is ill'. That the interpretation of the phrase shows signs of elasticity is entirely due to the goodwill of some local authorities, in stretching the meaning of 'illness'. The service is not uniform in standard. The other difficulty which arises, so far as elderly people are concerned, is that when using the Home Help service, in contrast to the home nursing service, charges which the local authority regard as reasonable may be recovered. These charges, if made, are related to income, and are often very low. Nevertheless, elderly people on a fixed income, and not in the habit of paying for domestic help, are frequently loth to use the service because of expense. Dwellings can thus easily become neglected, falling below accepted standards. The local authority may be forced in the end to offer accommodation in welfare homes, at far greater cost to themselves. The provision of a greater number of home-helps would often deal with the problem before it reaches such dimensions.

Some local authorities provide such useful services as 'meals on wheels', whereby a hot mid-day meal, at reasonable cost, is brought to the home. Instead of providing the service themselves, other local authorities contribute towards the funds of a voluntary organization such as the Red Cross or Women's Voluntary Services who undertake the work on their behalf.

A great deal more could be done in the direction of making elderly people more active in their own homes, if a leaf were taken out of the books of some progressive Local Health Authorities who make available physiotherapy and chiropody services. These services if brought to the doorstep become very wasteful in terms of equipment and expert's time. Arrangements by which mobile units tour country districts, stopping at suitable places such as village halls, should be multiplied. Protests on the grounds of the expense of this or any comparable scheme can always be met with the reminder that to put elderly people into homes with a capital 'H' is a far more costly venture.

Particularly since the war, we have seen the development and expansion of the club movement among the over-sixty-fives. Some clubs remain purely social affairs, with darts, billiards, cards, concerts, chat, and cups of tea. Others provide facilities of a much more ambitious nature, and cater for a demand for pursuits such as photography, weaving, rug-making, and gardening. Most clubs are under the auspices of a religious or social body. By the National Assistance Act, a local authority is empowered to make contributions to the funds of any voluntary organization whose activities consist of or include the provision of recreation for old people.

To the question 'Can the Welfare State improve the provisions made for old age?' the answer is obviously 'Yes'. To the supplementary 'Can these provisions help to make life more bearable and pleasant in old age?' the answer is again 'Yes'. The pursuit of happiness and a worthwhile life is a matter for each individual, but the community should try to assist each one in his hour of need.

10

The Child and his Family

PEGGY JAY

THE social service provisions which impinge on the home and the family are extensive, complex, and widely variegated. These services have grown up piecemeal during the last hundred years. They came into being as a result of growing public concern over the material evils suffered by certain sections of the community. The miseries caused by poverty, disease, and ignorance were seen at their most intense in the case of helpless young children and their equally defenceless mothers. The domiciliary Health Service; the welfare services run by the Education Authorities; the preventive and residential help offered by the Children's Departments; the help for the poor and the homeless and the aged provided by local Welfare Committees – all these services, and many others, are the State's answer to the challenge of these age-old human tragedies. The essential problem, however, remains. How in the maze of provisions, and the multiplicity of authorities, can the ordinary family seek the help they need, at the time they need it?

THE YOUNG CHILD IN THE FAMILY

When the birth of a baby is expected there are various avenues through which advice and assistance will be forthcoming. Under the National Health Service the mother will have registered with the family doctor of her choice. He will direct her to the local ante-natal clinic. Alternatively the Health Visitor can be contacted through the Health Department at the town hall or county hall. She will pay a home visit, and be a mine of information and a tower of strength in the months of waiting and the bewildering early days after the baby's arrival. Health Visitors are required to be State Registered Nurses and Midwives, but they do not themselves assist at confinements, except in an emergency. The Health Visitor's special function is to be the health educator of mothers of young families. This she does as the officer responsible to the local authority for carrying out the duties imposed on them by the National Health Service Acts, and making 'arrangements for the care of children who have not attained the age of five years, and are not attending primary schools'.

The local Health Committees organize home help schemes. Where there has been a confinement or illness in the home the local council may supply a competent person to give some hours of daily help in domestic work. Payment is assessed on the family means. Where the mother has to be away from home for a short period of illness, some councils are now able to send a daily child help into the home, the father caring for the home at night, or, very rarely, a resident help. Where a young mother is forced to go out to work for financial reasons the Day Nursery service may take care of young children from birth to five years. This provision is now very limited, and various conditions have to be fulfilled before an application can be considered. The costs are assessed on the family income. The physical conditions of these nurseries are generally excellent, but it is being increasingly realized that a whole day separation for the little child from its mother is emotionally damaging. These day nurseries are useful as a last resort in order to avoid the complete breakdown of the family and the entry of the child into a residential nursery.

Perhaps the most generally known and used of all the local health services is the infant welfare centre. These clinics, apart from giving invaluable advice on feeding, health, clothing, and general baby management, now often provide mothers' social clubs, discussion groups, and toddlers' play sessions. It is impossible to exaggerate the value of this provision to the lonely young parent in a new housing estate or new town. Finally, there are the child guidance clinics. There is no doubt of the help these clinics can bring to unhappy children and their anxious parents. It is to be hoped that parents will increasingly seek this help and advice (through the doctor or otherwise) at an early stage, and not wait for doctor, teacher, or Health Visitor to suggest it at a later date, when things may be more difficult to deal with.

There are various links between the school and the home, based on the child's 'non-educational' or 'welfare' needs. These are in addition to the basic link of the personal contact between the head, the school, and the parent. The Education Service employs School Nurses, who take over, when the child's fifth birthday is reached, the functions of health supervisor previously undertaken by the Health Visitor. In many areas these jobs are combined in the same person, so that valuable continuity is maintained. The old School Attendance Officer, now known as the School Welfare Officer or School Enquiry Officer, will call on a home when attendance at school has been sparse or irregular. London has its own unique School Care Committee organization. Here voluntary social workers, based on the school and directed by professional people, visit the home and assist in carrying out medical advice, assessing for various payments and discussing problems of behaviour, school meals, and uniform.

THE CHILDREN'S DEPARTMENT

We come then to the services performed by the Children's Departments of the local authorities. Here is the youngest of the services, born only in 1948, dealing with the oldest of human problems – the child in need of the love and shelter and comfort of his own home and family. The Children Act of 1948 set up the framework of the present-day services. This Act co-ordinated, through a new Home Office Department and new local authority Children's Committees, the work which had originally been carried out by the old Boards of Guardians, working under the Poor Law, and later, at local authority level, by a mixed bag of Health, Education, and Welfare authorities.

The spirit behind the work of Children's Departments to-day is increasingly that of preventive work within the still extant family, and rehabilitation work for the return of the child to its own family. This work, however, is carried out despite, rather than because of, the letter of the law. The two main operational clauses of the Children Act describe ways in which children may 'come into care'. Section 1 states that it is the duty of a local authority to receive a child into its care 'where it appears that he has neither parents nor guardian or has been and remains abandoned by his parents or guardian or is lost; or that his parents are, for the time being or permanently, prevented by reason of mental or bodily disease or infirmity or other incapacity or any other circumstances from providing for his proper accommodation, maintenance and upbringing, and the intervention of the local authority is necessary in the interests of welfare of the child.' Section 5 of the Act lays down the duty of the local authority to accept children committed to them by the courts as a 'Fit Person'. The need of the children for a person other than their parents to care for them arises, under this clause, from their own, or their parents', actual or potential delinquency. In other words section 1 children are 'received into care' on the initiative of their parents who are 'prevented' from caring for them. These circumstances do not of course apply in the case of abandoned and deserted children. Whereas section 5 or 'Fit Person' children come into care on the initiative of the courts who take them from their home and 'commit' them to the local authority or other suitable body or person.

The field workers or home visitors of the Children's Service are known as Child Welfare Officers. They are usually graduates trained in social science who work from the local office of the Children's Officer. A home visit will be paid on the request of a parent, foster parent, or guardian who feels in need of help and advice. Alternatively one will call as a result of some person or organization outside the home feeling that advice or help may in fact be needed. If a child is received into care, whether on the request of his parents whose circumstances are such that they positively *cannot* care for him, or on the initiative of the courts because his home conditions are judged undesirable, he will, if under five, be placed in a residential nursery, unless a suitable foster home can be found at once. These nurseries are often converted country houses and are first class in the material conditions they offer. The standards of staffing, furnishing, diet, clothes, and play opportunities are very high indeed. They often cost the public purse ten guineas a week for each child. The contribution of parents to this cost is assessed on their income. It is a sobering thought that while so many young parents are aware of the material advantages of these nurseries, so few understand the depth of unhappiness and emotional shock for the young child suddenly separated from his own familiar mother.

Other forms of residential care are found in small family group homes, where seven or nine children live with a House-mother – often in a modern purpose-built house. Cottage homes in large residential homes contain fifteen or twenty children with a House-mother. These House-mothers are often married, their husbands following their own occupations. Remand homes are used for children awaiting an appearance before a juvenile court. Approved schools are run by the local authorities' Children's Committees or by voluntary organizations, for the Home Office. They give education, vocational training, and above all personal advice and help to children committed to their care. Reception centres, where children newly taken into care are sorted out and assessed, are often also used as 'places of safety' for children admitted in an emergency.

Whether a child's stay away from his own home is for a long or short period, his own Child Welfare Officer will keep in contact with him and his family. Her work will be to make plans for his future, always hoping for, and working for, his return to his own home. Just under half the 65,000 children who are in care in the United Kingdom to-day are boarded out in foster homes. These foster homes are sought for by the Child Welfare Officers. Very careful inquiries are made before a home is approved for taking a foster child, with a view to matching the needs of the individual child, and the demand for these homes always exceeds their supply. A boarding-out allowance, on scales laid down nationally, is paid by the local authority, on whom responsibility for the child ultimately rests. The Child Welfare Officers visit regularly and keep a friendly and helpful eye on the child's progress.

The powers which local Children's Departments have to arrange adoption are perhaps the least known, but to those whose work it is, are the most satisfying part of their efforts to help children in need. There is no doubt that adoption is far the most satisfactory solution for the child who is actually, or for all practical purposes, without parents of his own. Adoption became a recognized legal process in 1926. Since the 1948 Children Act the proportion of annual adoptions arranged by local authorities, as opposed to voluntary societies, has risen steadily. There are, however, a considerably larger number of people wanting to adopt babies than there are babies available for adoption. In London it is said there are ten approved couples waiting for every available baby. The tragedy is, however, that the proportion of certain religious groups of children in care do not match up with the proportion of those groups in the community at large. The Children Act lays down that children must be brought up in their own religious faith. In practice this means that they are only placed for adoption in a home of people professing that faith. The effect of this disparity, and of the legislative position, is that many Roman Catholic children in care, who are available for adoption or boarding out, wait indefinitely for a home suited to them.

OTHER STATUTORY SERVICES

There are two statutory social services which help the family at home, and which are not run by the local authority. The National Assistance Board, working through local advisory sub-committees and visiting officers, exists to help families in danger of want through financial hardship. These visiting officers often become the means of setting a family on its feet. Their work is of a constructive and long term kind, and not just devoted to patching up an immediate financial crisis. Where failure to find a suitable job is the root of the trouble, the N.A.B. officers often have a very fruitful working arrangement with the local offices of the Ministry of Labour.

The other main statutory, but non-local-authority, service is the Probation Service. Probation officers are servants of the local magistrates' court. They visit homes where individuals may be awaiting trial, or where someone has been 'put on probation' by the Court after conviction of an offence. Where applications are made to the Court for Maintenance or Separation Orders, the case is often referred to a Probation Officer, especially if there is any hope of reconciliation between husband and wife. Probation officers can become of help to the whole family, as a result of their knowledge of one of its members.

THE VOLUNTARY SERVICES

Perhaps the most widely known of all the voluntary organizations which work for the child and his family is the National Society for the Prevention of Cruelty to Children. The N.S.P.C.C. has local offices all over the country, and its inspectors, often familiarly known as the 'Cruelty-man', are well known among social workers dealing with families in difficulty. Over the three years 1951–4, the society had an average of 99,000 children under its notice. These cases are brought to the society's attention by any of a number of people who are in touch with children in the course of their daily work. The focus of the inspector's work is to help the child within its own home, and only as a last resort to bring the case to court, with the possible result of the child being removed from its home. If this fact were more widely understood there might be less cause for the reluctance of neighbours and others, who know that cruelty or neglect is being suffered by a child, yet fail to bring the case to light. In a recent three-year inquiry into cruelty and neglect suffered by children, a committee of the British Medical Association and the Magistrates' Association stated:

'Evidence was brought to show that in many cases children

have been the subject of neglect or cruelty over a considerable period before it is brought to notice.'

The other main voluntary organization in the field of family help is the Family Service Units. These units are doing pioneering work with families in trouble in some half-dozen of the largest towns. They are remarkable for the quality rather than the extent of their work. The essence of their success lies in the approach of the individual worker to the family as a friend 'on the level'. A report on their work, quoted by Donald Ford in his classic work *The Deprived Child and the Community*, describes how 'Friendship was made the basis of their work; a friendship without condescension or professional aloofness; not forced or superficial but a relationship of mutual trust and respect as between equals'. Donald Ford portrays their work as that of an 'ambassador from the community, to prove that the community still cares about the family'. Local authorities are recognizing increasingly the unique and invaluable work which these units perform. Public money spent in supporting them is public money saved in maintaining intact a family group. Two other voluntary organizations doing invaluable work for the well-being of the family are the Marriage Guidance Council and the Family Planning Association. Their central address will be found in the appendix.

TOO MANY COOKS

There is no doubt, then, that both at the statutory and the voluntary level, numerous and complex services are provided to help the child and his family. The recently published B.M.A. report on Cruelty and Neglect stated that 'in any given area no fewer than forty people may have the right, and in some cases the duty, to visit the home on some aspect of family welfare'. Donald Ford describes a case where thirty-two visitors were calling on a family. We have then a picture of duplication and delay. The cry has gone up for more and better co-ordination. As a result of the Joint Circular issued by the Ministries of Health and Education and the Home Office in

July 1950, 'Co-ordinating Officers' have been appointed in 123 local authorities, of whom the majority are children's officers. These officers, working through various kinds of co-ordinating committees, function with a remarkable disparity of efficiency and enthusiasm. The basic need, it appears, is for a concentration of responsibility rather than an increase of co-ordination. Many families are to-day slipping through the net of social service provision. The first need, if the meshes of the net are to be tightened, is for a Royal Commission or high-level Committee of Enquiry into the impact of the Social Services on the Family Group. This demand has recently been voiced by a group led by Mrs Geoffrey Fisher, by the Magistrates' Association, and by the joint committee of the British Medical Association and the Magistrates' Association. The Committee of Enquiry announced by the Home Secretary in February 1956 into the working of the Children and Young Persons Act of 1953 and the Children Act of 1948, will go some way to meet this demand. The terms of reference are sufficiently wide to allow proper consideration of the prevention of suffering of children neglected in their own homes. The Chairman is to be Lord Ingleby.

What then is the essential quality needed for an effective family service in the future? Dr John Bowlby has pointed the way when he states:

'In a society where death-rates are low, the rate of employment high, and social welfare schemes adequate, it is emotional instability, and inability of parents to make effective relationships, which are the outstanding cause of children becoming deprived of normal home life.' The Social Services have largely overcome the natural evils of hunger, disease, poverty, and ignorance. The hydra-headed problems of the future are those centring on the intangibles of human happiness and personal relationships.

The essential quality of a family social service must then be that it is personal, continuous, and centred on the relationship between the family and the one individual worker. As this need becomes increasingly recognized the training of many professional visitors to the home will need fundamental revision. The sense of inadequacy which many workers now feel was vividly illustrated by the evidence given by Health Visitors in the Working Party's recent report on their work, training, and recruitment. 'When we asked them what sort of problems they felt least able to cope with, and where their training was inadequate, there was an almost unanimous agreement that they did not know enough about human behaviour – they wanted 'more psychology', 'more on child development', 'something to help us with marital problems'.

United and secure family groups are the essential components of a happy and effective community. A community will ignore at its peril the need to nurture and protect these family groups.

Education – a National Responsibility

BETTY D. VERNON

INTRODUCTION

EDUCATION is the foundation on which the superstructure of our social services, indeed of our whole community, is built. Yet less than 150 years ago a motion proposed in Parliament by J. A. Roebuck that 'This House proceed to devise a means for the universal and national education of the whole people' proved premature and had to be withdrawn. By way of salving its conscience Parliament voted, in 1833, the first education grant. A sum of £30,000 was set aside for 'the erection of school houses'. This was an historic gesture, though a beggarly one, since in the same year the same Parliament voted £50,000 to improve the royal stables!

As with most social services, education has developed haphazardly. The zeal of humanitarians and of nonconformists, the tenacity of religious bodies, the initiative of individuals, the drive of politicians – and sheer historical accident – evolved a dual system of education for England and Wales: a system which offers one type of education for the fee-paying minority and one for the non-fee-paying majority; a system which certainly until 1944 was complex, wasteful of ability, and inequitable, and which in no sense could be called a unified social service.

TERMS OF THE ACT

The 1944 Act aimed to change much of this. It laid the responsibility for education, from nursery schooling to advanced study, fairly and squarely on the shoulders of the State and of local authorities. It recognized the need for a co-ordinated national policy, and sought to make available free, to every citizen in England and Wales, suitable educational opportunities. Education was to become a full social service, administered by the Local Education Authority (the L.E.A.), which was the county council or the county borough council, operating through its Education Committee, in conjunction with the Ministry. A Minister of Education was created to supersede the phantom President of the mythical Board of Education. It became his duty, under section 1 of the Act, to 'promote the education of the people of England and Wales, and the progressive development of institutions devoted to that purpose, and to secure the effective execution by local authorities under his control and direction, of the national policy for providing a varied and comprehensive educational service in every area.' The Act recognized in effect that the poorest he that is in England hath as much a life to live as the greatest he.

The span and purpose of education in the public (non-fee-paying) sector was clearly stated. 'Public education', says section 7 of the Act, 'shall be organized in three progressive stages, to be known as primary education, secondary education, and further education, and it shall be the duty of the local education authority for every area ... to contribute towards the spiritual, moral, mental, and physical development of the community, by securing that efficient education throughout those stages shall be available to meet the needs of the population of their area.'

In every area of the country there must, therefore, be sufficient schools for primary and secondary education. But these schools shall not be deemed sufficient 'unless they are sufficient in number, character, and equipment to afford all pupils opportunities for education offering such variety of instruction and training as may be desirable in view of their different ages, abilities and aptitudes ... including practical instruction and training appropriate to their respective needs'.

The equality of educational opportunity to which protagonists of the Act aspired was not readily achieved. Two factors operated against this. Local authorities were unequally equipped. The vision and initiative displayed, the financial resources expended, had varied so widely in the past that by

1944 different areas had educational facilities of widely divergent standards. Moreover, since the private fee-paying sector was left intact, money could buy education. The social prestige attached to the independent schools, plus their high staffing ratio and the good academic attainments of the best schools, created a scarcity value which the Education Act augmented rather than diminished.

General obligations

Education is compulsory for all children between the ages of five and fifteen. The policy of raising the school-leaving age to sixteen, which had been regarded as an inevitable outcome of the 1944 Act, has up till now been pigeon-holed. The Minister has not yet satisfied himself that it has become practicable to raise to sixteen the upper limit of compulsory school age.

Every parent must ensure that his child receives 'suitable education', and every L.E.A. must make suitable provision for this to be possible. Schooling is free to the 6·6 million youngsters in schools maintained by the local authorities, and regular attendance is compulsory. Truancy and absenteeism are investigated by School Welfare Officers (or School Enquiry Officers), and legal action may be, and is, taken against uncooperative parents. L.E.A.s must also see that children are educated according to the wishes of their parents '... so far as is compatible with the provision of efficient instruction and training and avoidance of unreasonable public expenditure.'

RANGE OF EDUCATION

In January 1954 there were over 7 million young people receiving primary, secondary, or special education in the public (non-fee-paying) and private (fee-paying) sectors. Almost 6·6 million children attended schools maintained by L.E.A.s, 101,000 were in direct-grant schools (which have fee-payers and non-fee-payers), and some 258,000 were in private (fee-paying) schools recognized as efficient. It is estimated that perhaps 200,000 children are being educated in schools that are not recognized as efficient.

Education under the Act is regarded as a continuous process, having three clearly defined stages: (*a*) Primary, which covers nursery, infants, and junior children; (*b*) Secondary, which is broadly tripartite and includes grammar schools, secondary selective or secondary technical schools, and secondary modern schools; and (*c*) Further Education, for all citizens, young or old, over compulsory school age. And these are the stages for which L.E.A.s must provide.

Primary

Primary provision includes nursery, infant, and junior schools, and covers theoretically the two- to ten-and-a-half-year olds. In practice it means usually the five- to eleven-year-olds. Children attend infant schools until they are seven or over; thence they move to junior schools until they are about eleven. Both groups are usually housed in one building and, unless the schools are small, under separate heads. All-age schools, where youngsters aged five to fifteen are under one roof in one unit, still exist, but their reorganization has lately been speeded up.

Nursery schooling, protagonists hold, should begin early. If separate nursery units are not possible, nursery classes should be planned in primary schools. These needs are recognized within the Act, but to-day nursery schools are the exception rather than the rule. Only 3 per cent of all children between the ages of two and five receive such schooling. Of these one child in three is in an L.E.A. nursery; two in three are in nursery classes. Up till now the Minister has not generally allowed new nursery accommodation to be built until he has been satisfied that the local provision could meet adequately the needs of children of statutory school age.

In much infant teaching to-day the emphasis lies on flexibility and innovation. Modern infants' schools stimulate, at their best, not only the beginnings of the basic skills of reading, writing, and arithmetic, but also a much wider pattern of growing interests, developing activity, and creative achievement. The primary classroom should be a lively place with an informal friendly atmosphere prevailing and busy, purposeful activity fostered by the teacher. In the junior school there comes, or should come, a period of consolidation and growing fluency in skills. The child enters a phase in which, according to the 'London Education Service', his interests begin to range widely, with 'an avidity for experience and information'.

Eleven-plus transfer

The Education Act stipulates that every child must receive education suitable to his abilities and aptitudes. Around the age of ten or eleven all children in primary schools, and some in fee-paying schools, face the problem of transfer to secondary schools. The method of diagnosing what type of secondary school is most suitable varies from one L.E.A. to another.

Until recently all authorities utilized some form of eleven-plus examination. It comprised papers in Arithmetic and English and an Intelligence Test. Gradually examinations are being superseded by less formal testing, and greater emphasis is now being placed on personal assessment made by the heads. These assessments are closely linked with the school record card which is kept for every child in primary school. This card notes, through the years, details of scholastic achievements, potential ability, social behaviour, and general personality. Whatever machinery L.E.A.s employ, and the eleven-plus examination is constantly under criticism, some assessment has at present to be made to fit children into available secondary schools.

Secondary schooling

The extension of secondary education for all has been described as the most important single reform introduced by the 1944 Act. It was indeed a great step forward. But facilities vary so widely between areas, that the range of choice is often inadequate to meet the differing abilities of young people at secondary stage.

No precise mention of the tripartite system (grammar, technical, and secondary modern schooling) occurs in the Act. The Ministry, however, uses this terminology in its regulations, stating that '... it would be wrong to suppose that these three types will necessarily remain separate ... different types (of schools) may be combined in one building or on one site as considerations of convenience and efficiency may suggest.'

Within the tripartite system grammar schools are those most keenly sought after. In fact, no more than 20 per cent of all children of secondary school age attending L.E.A. schools in England and Wales attain this goal. But between different areas there are startling variations; over 69 per cent receive grammar schooling in Merionethshire, only 9·3 per cent in Gateshead.*

The essentially academic curricula of grammar schools are planned to enable youngsters to take their General Certificate of Education (Ordinary Level) around the age of sixteen. From there pupils may proceed to G.C.E. (Advanced Level) and Scholarship standard, gain entrance to university or technical colleges, and study for professional qualifications.

Selective central and secondary technical schools are reached by 6 per cent, at the most, of secondary children. To the layman the difference between the two is obscure. But the former provide a general education up to G.C.E. (Ordinary Level) or the Royal Society of Arts examinations, and run certain technical or commercial courses, such as engineering, building, housecraft, and commercial studies. The latter, which have developed from former junior technical schools in technical colleges, offer a basic general education leading to technical courses.

Secondary modern schools, the third type in this group, have been called the problem child of the 1944 Act. About 75 per cent of all pupils attend these schools, which developed from the former elementary schools. The best secondary modern schools offer a good general and social education, and at many the heads try to develop specialist courses. The inherent weakness is that the range of specialist subjects tends to be narrow, and that, as young people often leave at the end of the term in

* *Local Government Handbook*, Labour Party, 1954.

which they turn fifteen, the organization of the curricula for the last year becomes extremely difficult. In some schools heads succeed in building up G.C.E. and R.S.A. courses which attract and hold young people beyond the statutory leaving age. But the pull of economic forces is very strong.

Secondary modern schools come in for a great deal of unsympathetic criticism, yet they labour under great difficulties. Not only are pupils straining at the leash to leave school, but often they have entered initially with a sense of failure, having 'not made' the grammar or secondary technical schools. It should be remembered that these schools did not really begin until 1948, because only then, with their full complement of fourteen-year-olds, was it possible to plan and to carry through four-year courses. Educationists have had relatively little time, therefore, in which to think out the purpose of secondary modern schools clearly or to justify them.

L.E.A.s have attempted various developments at secondary level. Some group schools in their locality, to encourage specialization in different courses. Some develop bilateral schools, which have two of the three clearly defined sides – grammar, technical, or modern – or multilateral schools, which provide for all three types within one school, but in clearly defined streams. Yet others foster the 'lateral transfer'. By this means a child may be transferred to a different type of secondary school from that to which he was originally sent, if both 'exporting' and 'importing' heads are satisfied that he or she will benefit. Some L.E.A.s have an examination to justify these transfers, others effect change solely on interviews and the heads' recommendations.

Comprehensive schools

A new and important alternative to the tripartite system is comprehensive schools. They have given rise to deep and conflicting opinions in the educational world, and some authorities are sceptical as to their value. But they are being developed with zest and imagination in areas such as Anglesey, Coventry, London, and Manchester.

These large secondary schools vary in size from 900 to 2,000, are either co-educational or single-sexed, and will eventually re-cruit, mainly on a neighbourhood basis, children of differing ability. The curricula offer the widest range of choice in academic, technical, and practical subjects for children of di-vergent aptitudes and contrasting social background. Organiza-tion varies within each school. In many, pupils are grouped for academic subjects in highly selective classes: this means that children of similar ability and attainment work together, equal with equal. In all out-of-school activities – sports, clubs, social life generally – bright and backward work and play together.

For the first two years all pupils have a general education in which they study the same subjects at different paces. In their third or fourth year children begin to select and to reject certain subjects. And such is the specialist provision – and the calibre of specialist teaching staff – in subjects which range from Eng-lish, engineering, maths, and music to printing, physics, housecraft, and history, that for the first time, protagonists maintain, equality of opportunity becomes a reality.

Boarding schools

Boarding accommodation may be provided at the secondary stage for children for whom education as boarders is considered by their parents and the authority to be desirable. Some au-thorities have already established county boarding schools. But the cost per place is high, and on the whole, with notable ex-ceptions, L.E.A.s have regarded this permissive clause without enthusiasm.

Further education

Further education is the third stage specified in the Act. Until 1944 provision was permissive, now it is a major obliga-tion on L.E.A.s. Facilities must be available for:

(*a*) Full-time and part-time education for persons over com-pulsory school age, and (*b*) leisure-time occupation in such organized cultural training and recreative activities as are

suited to the requirements of any person over compulsory
school age, able and willing to benefit from the facilities.

Broadly, further education is either vocational or non-vocational. Vocational studies are either whole- or part-time, day or
evening; they relate to a particular trade or profession and lead
to specific qualifications. Non-vocational studies – and the line
is sometimes hard to draw – deal with hobbies and leisure-time
activities, such as judo, flower arrangement, boat building, bee-
keeping, carpentry, or choral singing.

The centres in which non-vocational skills are acquired vary
as widely as the studies, from adult men's and women's institutes, village halls, colleges of further education, and community centres, to adult education and technical colleges. The
Workers' Educational Association makes an important contribution to non-vocational work through lecture courses and week-
end schools.

County colleges and day release work

The Act specified that county colleges were to be established.
These were foreseen as centres where young people in employment would acquire 'such further education, including physical, practical, and vocational training as will enable them to develop their various aptitudes and capacities and prepare them
for the responsibilities of citizenship.' The introduction of
county colleges is still a pipe-dream. But the increase in part-
time day release courses – courses attended for one whole day
or two half-days each week by young people between the ages
of fifteen and eighteen, who have been voluntarily released by
their employers – indicates that there is substantial demand for
classes which ought to be met in centres such as the Act envisaged.

At present, part-time day release work is being carried on
mainly in day colleges, centres for further education, and technical colleges. Though neither universal nor compulsory, employers – and parents – are coming to recognize its worth. The
number of released students who study both vocational and
general educational subjects has increased from 42,000 in 1939

to over 350,000 in 1954–5. Many training and apprenticeship schemes – which cover some ninety industries – make this part-time study obligatory. Day release might now be described as a bridge leading to higher vocational study.

Vocational studies and youth work

The greatest volume of further education in the country is vocational – that is, mainly technical and commercial work – undertaken by means of part-time day, full-time day, or evening courses. The maintained (L.E.A.) establishments which students attend include Technical Colleges, Schools and Colleges of Art, Colleges of Commerce, and National Colleges of Technology (maintained by the Ministry). Courses lead to qualifications as varied as National and Higher National Certificates, City and Guilds Examinations, professional diplomas, membership of professional institutions, and University degrees. Some of the larger technical colleges have a wide range of science technology courses, including sandwich courses run in conjunction with industry, whereby students alternate six months' study with six months' industrial practice. A very recent innovation is the Diploma in Technology.

The recent Ministerial announcement (June 1956) for re-grading technical colleges (excluding Colleges of Art and Commerce) during the next five years as Colleges of Advanced Technology, Regional Colleges, Area Colleges, and Local Colleges is important. It is an attempt (albeit at present imperfectly thought out) to develop advanced technological courses, to maximize and rationalize the use of highly-qualified staff, and to relate the provision of courses both to the availability of students and to the needs of industry.

Youth work is a neglected aspect of further education. The need for extending facilities is pressing, for, by and large, L.E.A.s do little more than make piecemeal grants-in-aid to voluntary youth clubs, build occasional centres, and in some areas make school accommodation (and instructors) available for recreational purposes. Admittedly, there are exceptional L.E.A.s which, for example, run their own youth clubs, but over the country no positive policy towards the development of youth work is apparent. A national policy is needed which will deal with approved training courses for youth leaders, salary scales, the provision of premises (ideally some should be included in county colleges), and their distribution in relation to the voluntary clubs. With the secondary age bulge virtually upon us, the problem demands attention – and action.

FINANCIAL ASSISTANCE AND AWARDS

Every youngster of ability must, under the Act, be enabled to continue his or her studies after leaving school. Pupils must be enabled to take advantage, without hardship to themselves or to their parents, of any educational facilities available to them. To make this possible, financial assistance is given where necessary. L.E.A.s may grant scholarships, exhibitions, bursaries, and other allowances to pupils over compulsory school age.

Major awards are granted by L.E.A.s to students, normally over the age of eighteen, wishing to attend universities, technical colleges, and various courses of advanced study, subject to their being courses recognized by the Ministry and to the students having reached a certain academic level. L.E.A. grants are only made if the parental income is within an agreed scale. Recently the Minister recommended that assistance afforded by L.E.A.s should not be less than that of State scholarship awards.

The Ministry grants State and technical State scholarships for degree and advanced level courses; it also makes awards for post-graduate research and to 'mature students' – men and women over the age of twenty-five who have not been able to take University courses at the normal age.

Funds of charitable trusts are also available for educational purposes. A number of these are administered by L.E.A.s and should not be overlooked. Information on such aid is obtainable from local Education Officers.

HANDICAPPED CHILDREN

The provision for handicapped children, both at primary and secondary age, is established under the Act as an important care of L.E.A.s. Young people who suffer from any disability of mind or body must receive special educational treatment, either in school or elsewhere. The Ministry recognizes certain categories of handicapped children, specified under the School Health Service and Handicapped Pupils Regulations, 1953, as follows: pupils who are physically handicapped, deaf, partially deaf, blind, partially sighted, educationally subnormal (E.S.N.), epileptic, maladjusted, suffering from speech defect (not due to deafness), and delicate. L.E.A.s must provide education for children suffering from one or more of these defects, either in a maintained special day or boarding school or by placing them in independent *recognized* schools run by voluntary organizations.

Authorities may maintain school units in hospitals for children capable of benefiting from school, and may also organize home teaching. By the latter arrangement, teachers visit in their own homes children who 'by reason of any extraordinary circumstances' are unable to attend school. Special teaching may also be given within the framework of an ordinary primary school, such as special classes for the deaf or the partially sighted.

All L.E.A.s must ascertain what special education is needed for the children in their area. Accordingly they may have any child over two years old medically examined. Parents must always be informed by the L.E.A. when their children are so examined, and are entitled to be present at the examination. If it is decided that the child requires special educational treatment, the L.E.A. must notify the parents and ensure that special schooling is made available. If parents wish to make other educational arrangements, the L.E.A. must be satisfied that the alternative is in fact 'suitable'. Attempts are usually made to persuade parents to accept the L.E.A. or recognized provision; and if they are not prepared to do so, nor to offer a suitable alternative, the case must be referred to the Ministry.

If boarding provision is thought necessary, parents must make some financial contribution according to their means. Certain categories of handicapped children stay on at school until they are over sixteen. When they do leave, the L.E.A., the Youth Employment Officer, and the head co-operate to secure, wherever possible, a job, apprenticeship, or some form of further training.

A special clause of the Act deals with ineducable children. Any child of two years upwards who appears to be suffering from 'a disability of mind of such a nature as to make him incapable of receiving education at school . . .' must be medically examined. If he or she is then shown to be so incapable, the L.E.A. must be notified for purposes of the Mental Deficiency Act. A child is considered ineducable if he is both incapable of receiving education and if his disability makes it inexpedient for him to be educated in association with other children, either in his own or in their interest.

ANCILLARY SERVICES

The conception of education has widened and deepened since the first tentative legislation, which served mainly to keep children off the streets or from being nuisances, was passed. To-day, as a social service in the fullest sense, the Education Act provides not only for formal education but also for aspects of welfare which indirectly affect the education of young people.

The various services may be summarized as follows:

School Health Service

1. Medical inspection must be made available for every pupil at least three times during compulsory schoolage. It may also be provided for pupils at other maintained establishments (e.g. training colleges).

2. Dental Inspection similarly must be available for every pupil as soon as possible after admission to school. Other inspections are to be made as and when necessary.

3. Clothing may be examined in the interests of cleanliness, if thought necessary.

4. Particular attention must be paid to the disabilities of handicapped pupils.

L.E.A.s must accordingly establish a School Health Service and appoint a Principal School Medical Officer and a Principal School Dental Officer.

School Meals Service. Milk and midday meals must be supplied. Other meals and refreshments may be. Meals must be suitably varied and nutritionally balanced. Charges are made according to agreed scales. Milk, one-third of a pint, is supplied free daily.

Clothing grants may be given to any pupil on grounds of hardship if 'by reason of inadequacy of his clothing he is unable to take full advantage of the education provided.'

Transport. Free transport may be made available, providing the child lives more than three miles away from school. If it is thought necessary, reasonable travelling expenses may be paid.

Amenities for recreational and social and physical training must be provided for all young people. L.E.A.s may establish, maintain, or manage camps, holiday classes, playing fields, play centres and other places, including playgrounds, gymnasia, and swimming baths. L.E.A.s may also organize games, expeditions, or other activities, and may defray or contribute towards costs. This is an important imaginative clause, which makes many joyful things possible.

YOUTH EMPLOYMENT

The employment of young people is of direct concern to L.E.A.s. They have power to, and do, make by-laws restricting or prohibiting employment of children in any manner which is prejudicial to their health or 'likely to render them unfit to obtain the full benefit from the education provided.'

Vocational guidance is given through the Youth Employment Service. This service, authorized under the Employment and Training Act, 1948, may be administered by L.E.A.s direct or by the Ministry of Labour. (Local authorities have the choice.) Guidance and advice about the labour market are given to young people. Youth Employment Officers visit schools, to talk about careers, training, availability of jobs, and general economic prospects. Work is done in co-operation with the heads, parents, and industry, and particular care is given to guiding and aiding handicapped pupils.

ADMINISTRATION

Administration is a partnership between the central and local authorities – the Ministry and Local Education Authorities. The Minister is answerable to Parliament on national policy, and guided by his civil servants. Independently of this permanent secretariat, he is also advised by two standing committees of experts, the Central Advisory Councils for England and Wales. They give counsel both on problems referred to them (e.g. 'Early Leaving') and 'on such matters connected with educational theory and practice as they think fit'.

The Minister also has a large inspectorate, who visit, assess, and report upon education establishments all over the country. This body of highly qualified men and women, though technically of the Civil Service, are jealously proud of their traditional independence, which enables them to judge by their own standards and to report direct to the Minister. On general policy matters the Minister also consults local authorities and professional organizations.

There are 146 L.E.A.s in England and Wales. They it is – the county councils and county borough councils – who delegate the work of devising and supervising local educational policy to their Education Committee. This is a major committee in any council and is composed of elected and of co-opted members. Every L.E.A. must appoint a ' well-qualified' Chief Education Officer; and under the 1944 Act, in conjunction with this officer, had to produce comprehensive plans for (*a*) Primary and Secondary and (*b*) Further Education in their area. All local plans, which had to be submitted for approval to the Minister, are available locally on request.

Schemes of divisional administration have been introduced in most areas to humanize and to facilitate educational organization. The Welsh Department, with its own Permanent Secretary, is responsible for education in Wales and Monmouthshire. Here education divisions are grouped into regions.

Governing bodies

All schools must have governing bodies. Accordingly L.E.A.s appoint managers to primary – or groups of primary – schools, and governors to all secondary – or groups of secondary – schools, special schools, and technical colleges. If a maintained primary school serves the area of a minor local authority, such as a non-county borough, an urban district, or a parish, that minor local authority appoints one-third of the managers, and the L.E.A. the remainder. A minority (one-third) of managers or governors is appointed by L.E.A.s to voluntarily aided schools, but a majority (two-thirds) to controlled schools. Local authority nominees are usually local citizens.

Powers of managers and governors

The powers of managers and governors of county schools generally, though not extensive, are important. They serve as a close link between the specialists (the head, his or her staff, and the L.E.A.) and the man in the street. These powers, though broadly similar, are not identical. Governors and managers, in consultation with the head, must exercise the oversight of the conduct and curricula of the schools, and they have powers to pass resolutions regarding the welfare of their schools. In some areas they may spend certain (limited) sums on equipment, and may also authorize minor works and repairs to buildings. Many governors and managers keep a constant alert and interested watch on the upkeep and progress of their schools, and evidence a certain proud possessiveness, which is all to the good.

TYPES OF SCHOOLS

(*a*) *Maintained or county schools and maintained voluntary schools*

There are two categories of schools for which L.E.A.s have responsibility: maintained or county schools, and maintained voluntary schools. Nearly five million children attend county schools (primary and secondary) which were built by the School Boards or their successors, the L.E.A.s, and are maintained wholly by local authorities. Maintained voluntary schools were built by voluntary agencies, churches, or religious foundations, and are largely maintained by L.E.A.s. These schools may be of controlled, aided, or special agreement status, and are attended by over 1·6 million pupils. About one million are in Church of England voluntary schools, nearly 500,000 in Roman Catholic schools, and 140,000 in schools of other denominations.

In voluntary controlled schools the whole cost of maintenance falls on the L.E.A. Schools with aided status have heavier financial obligations. They pay 50 per cent of the external repair charge and alterations required by the L.E.A. to keep the premises up to standard. In both cases L.E.A.s are responsible for teachers' salaries, internal repairs, decorations, and all other expenditure. Special agreement schools are those towards which, under the 1936 Education Act, L.E.A.s must subscribe 50–75 per cent of the cost for new accommodation. Most such schools have yet to be built!

Religious instruction. Arrangements for religious instruction in county and voluntary schools differ considerably and are important. The whole procedure illustrates a compromise reached this century in the age-old battle between secular and religious control in State schools. The school day in both types of schools must begin with corporate worship, and religious instruction must be part of the curriculum. No pupil, however, may be compelled to attend a particular place of worship, nor may a particular form of worship be a condition for a child's entering any county or voluntary school. Pupils may be excused religious worship or religious instruction at the request of their parents and may be temporarily withdrawn from school to receive religious teaching elsewhere. In county schools, religious worship must not be denominational, and religious instruction is given according to an agreed syllabus drawn up by a panel of ecclesiastical and educational authorities. In controlled schools religious instruction of a denominational nature may be given twice weekly. In aided and special agreement schools most religious instruction is denominational.

(b) *Direct-grant and private schools recognized as efficient*

Outside the classification of maintained county and voluntary schools are direct-grant schools, private independent schools recognized as efficient (such as public schools), and unrecognized schools.

Direct-grant schools are so named because they receive grants direct from the Ministry; and as a *quid pro quo* they must offer 25 per cent of their places free to secondary pupils who have attended L.E.A. primary schools for at least two years. A further 25 per cent of reserved places may also be filled by L.E.A. nomination.

The total numbers catered for in the independent fee-paying schools are relatively small, perhaps 400,000 or 500,000. But, as H. D. Hughes wrote recently, '... the boys and girls in independent schools are a very important part of the country's sixth-formers ... a quarter of all the youngsters aged seventeen still at school are pupils at independent schools recognized as efficient. A quarter of all the university awards offered by the Ministry of Education 1953–4 were won by pupils from independent schools, in addition to closed scholarships where they predominate.' *

The cost of education in the private sector varies widely. Public boarding-school fees average £275 a year, though the upper limit is around £400, a level that preserves intact the

---

* *A Socialist Education Policy*, p. 21.

citadel of privilege. The private sector is a negation of educational equality.

Any L.E.A. may, with the consent of the Minister, pay fees (whole or in part) for pupils to attend independent schools. But this provision has been very little implemented over the country.

(c) Unrecognized private schools

Until now little control has been exercised over private schools which are not recognized as efficient. In 1957, however, all fee-paying schools must, under Part 3 of the Act, be registered and become liable to inspection by Her Majesty's Inspectors, who will 'assess the suitability of premises and accommodation, having regard to numbers, age, sex of pupils, the standards of instruction and the quality of the Head and teaching staff.' If standards are unsatisfactory official recognition of the school's efficiency will not be given. Under present circumstances, however, it is unlikely that high standards can be demanded, for the calibre of some of the worst State schools is so very low.

BUILDINGS

The Minister lays down standards to which buildings must conform. Accordingly regulations are issued which affect matters such as the cubic capacity per child, the circulation space in school premises, the design of buildings, the sanitary arrangements, playground areas, and the cost per place. But in spite of the basic standards required, the quality, age, design, and general personality of schools differ enormously over the country, both between and within local authority areas.

A high proportion of existing buildings are sub-standard by current regulations, but widespread remodelling has not yet been possible. Since the war all new schools have had to provide new (i.e. additional) accommodation, and it is unlikely that a real start to replace old and unsatisfactory buildings can be made before 1960. Some L.E.A.s and the Ministry have encouraged their own and private architects to experiment in design, materials, and colour. As a result excitingly successful new schools have been created. The child in a bright, light, modern 'glass' school is fortunate beyond dreams, but such luck does not come to everyone's son or daughter. It cannot be too strongly emphasized, however, that the most decrepit building can be a first-class school if the staff are keen and able.

TEACHING STAFF

Teaching staff are the joint responsibility of local and central authorities. But it is the Minister who must ensure that facilities for the training of teachers are sufficient. Accordingly he has powers to direct any L.E.A. to establish, maintain, or assist any training college. To-day all entrants to the teaching profession (in the public sector) at primary and secondary stages must be men and women qualified to teach, either by virtue of a University degree or by having completed a training course approved by the Ministry.

The appointment and payment of teaching staff (in the public sector), except in the case of direct-grant schools, are made by L.E.A.s. Conditions of employment and salary rates are settled by national agreement. The Burnham Committees (on which both L.E.A.s and the teaching profession are represented) – there is one on Primary and Secondary Schools and one on Technical Teachers – establish salary levels. These rates are subject to the Minister's approval, but once agreed must, since 1944, be paid by all L.E.A.s.

The degree of control exercised by L.E.A.s over the appointment and dismissal of staff varies with the status of a school. In a county school, however, an established (i.e. permanent) member of staff can be dismissed only for gross dereliction of duty, moral turpitude, moral offences, or for physically ill-treating a child. No woman may be disqualified from teaching in any county or voluntary school 'by reason only of marriage'.

Social Welfare and the Citizen

The curricula and activities of most schools are the responsibility of the head and the teaching staff, within a general framework laid down by the L.E.A. and the governors. Advice and guidance are given by Inspectors of the L.E.A. and by H.M. Inspectors. Teaching can be a stimulating if exhausting profession. Active professional organizations, specialist courses run by the Institutes of Education and by L.E.A.s, exchange teaching abroad, a wealth of publications, opportunities to implement new ideas and to experiment with new methods – these are factors which contribute to making it a challenging and provocative career.

The maximum size of classes is governed by Ministry regulations, although widespread staff shortages have made their general attainment impossible. The Ministry specified that the maximum number of pupils on the register of any class should be fifteen for the under threes, thirty for the three- to five-year-olds, forty in other primary classes, and thirty for secondary classes. But too often these maxima become the minima. In January 1955 over 44 per cent of all pupils in maintained schools were being taught in classes which exceeded these figures. The size of classes fixed for the physically handicapped is naturally much smaller, e.g. a maximum of ten for deaf and fifteen for blind children.

FINANCE

Education has long been financially starved in comparison with other items of national expenditure. In 1954, public authorities in England and Wales spent some £333 million on their education services. This represents approximately 3 per cent of the national income, and was equivalent to just over half the amount which citizens spent that year on cigarettes and tobacco. Capital expenditure, which amounted to £81 million, was less than one-sixth of the comparable figure for housing.

As with other aspects of education, finance involves a partnership between the central and local authorities. Of the £376 million spent in 1955, £233 million came from the Exchequer and £143 million from the local rates. About

40 per cent of all local authority spending is on education.

The formula which determines the Exchequer contribution towards the cost of L.E.A. primary and secondary schools (including nursery classes and special schools) is: £6 for every child plus 60 per cent of the net expenditure of the authority, less the local revenue obtained from a rate of 2s 6d in the pound. This formula aims to produce a fair distribution of grant between authorities whose resources and responsibilities (in the number of children to be educated) vary widely.

Several items in the education budget of an L.E.A. attract Ministry grant: 100 per cent of the expenditure on school milk and midday meals is met, and 75 per cent of that on the Youth Employment Service, while 75 per cent grants are paid on certain advanced courses of technological study and research. The cost of teacher training colleges is shared between all L.E.A.s in proportion to their school population. The Ministry pays 100 per cent grant on expenditure for 'the establishment, equipment, and maintenance of training colleges and halls of residence'.

Capital spending on, for example, new buildings, as distinct from current spending on salaries and overheads, is met almost wholly by borrowing. But before any authority may build a new school it must be included, with the Ministry's sanction, in a capital building programme for that authority. This in turn is related to the national pattern for building, which is largely controlled by the amount of capital expenditure approved for such projects by the Treasury.

It has been shown * that in terms of current purchasing power the expenditure per child at primary and secondary level is less than in 1938. Moreover, as a tax burden, the Education Service takes a smaller proportion of the national income than it did in 1938. Yet '... there is better value for money in education to-day, as compared with pre-war, than in any other commodity.' It is, however, worth remembering that the Minister estimated (February 1955), as 'a rough guess', that to implement the Education Act fully an additional £100 million a year was needed, apart from capital expenditure!

* *Education*, June 1953.

Social Welfare and the Citizen

CONCLUSION

Many hopes that arose directly from the terms of the 1944 Act remain unfulfilled. Schools 'sufficient in number, character and equipment' cannot become a widespread reality until many more teachers are available and the size of classes drastically reduced. Educational opportunity is likewise circumscribed by the inadequacy of the tripartite system (save where comprehensive schools are being developed) and the neglected quality of too many secondary modern schools. Buildings, equipment, and the general development of the secondary strata in particular, merit thought, encouragement, and expenditure. A national policy for youth work, and the development of county colleges as envisaged in the Act, call for attention. And at the other extreme is the need for more nursery and special schooling.

Educational provision is by no means fairly distributed over the country. Concerted effort must be made to secure less variation in the facilities offered by L.E.A.s. Accidents of geography ought not to be allowed to penalize a child's future.

Educational opportunity will remain unequal, however, so long as the dual system – that of fee-paying and non-fee-paying schools – exists within the Welfare State. Until all kinds of education are available to all children and the criteria for admission to any school are solely ability, aptitude, and general suitability, educational inequality will persist.

There is developing in England and Wales an integrated continuous – if too brief – system of education. And, although the Act is not fully implemented, there are written into its clauses powers which should oblige all L.E.A.s to provide suitable varied education for their citizens, young and old. The operation of those powers must be made effective, and not only economic resources are required to make this possible. Public opinion and parliamentary pressure should also play their part; John Citizen must recognize the unfulfilled promises implicit in the Act.

Demands on the Welfare State are many, and often mutually conflicting. But it is imperative in education that we continue to aim high. As H. C. Dent has written, 'Full implementation of the Act may make all the difference between a happy and glorious future for our country and an unhappy, inglorious one.' And to the cynic who asks why ceaselessly we strive let the glowing words of Ellen Wilkinson make answer:

'Our schools must have freedom to experiment, room to grow, variety for the sake of freshness, for the fun of it even. Laughter in the classroom, self-confidence, growing, eager interest, instead of bored uniformity. This is the way to produce from our fine stock the Britons who will have no need to fear the new scientific age, who will stride into it, heads high, determined to master science and to serve mankind.'

12

Aid and Advice

JOHN PAYNE

THE British people are rightly proud of their judicial system, but like most worthwhile things, its accessibility can be very expensive. The knowledge that 'the law courts, like the Ritz Hotel, are open to rich and poor alike' is cold comfort to the penurious litigant unable to afford lawyers' fees. In 1947, a committee under the chairmanship of Lord Rushcliffe reported that the provision of effective legal aid and advice for persons of limited means in Britain was inadequate. Although there were facilities for free legal aid in criminal cases, there was, apart from what was known as the Poor Persons' Procedure, no comparable service for bringing or defending civil proceedings. A limited amount of help was given at voluntary Poor Man's Lawyer centres by lawyers who gave free professional advice in their spare time; lack of funds prevented these centres from giving poor people active assistance in fighting their cases in the courts.

The Legal Aid and Advice Act was passed in 1949 to make legal aid and advice more readily available for persons of small or moderate means. There is a separate Act for Scotland. As will be seen hereafter, the legal aid facilities are not necessarily free, as applicants are subject to a means test. Although the Act received the Royal Assent on 30 July 1949, not all its provisions have yet been brought into force. At the time of writing, legal aid is available only for proceedings in the civil courts (other than the House of Lords and the Judicial Committee of the Privy Council). The purpose of this chapter will be to describe the facilities already available under the Act, and the remaining provisions for legal aid and advice not necessarily involving litigation which have yet to be brought into force. We shall also briefly refer to the provision of free legal aid in criminal cases.

Lastly, we will deal with the free legal advice and ancillary services provided by voluntary organizations.

I. THE LEGAL AID AND ADVICE ACT, 1949

(a) *Provision for legal aid in civil proceedings*

The Act provides for legal aid to be given to persons who wish to bring or defend proceedings before the House of Lords, the Judicial Committee of the Privy Council, the Supreme Court of Judicature, and any county court. The Supreme Court of Judicature consists of the Court of Appeal and the Queen's Bench, the Chancery, and the Probate, Divorce, and Admiralty Divisions of the High Court. Legal aid is also available in certain local civil courts which in some cases have rather wider jurisdiction than the county courts but do not rate so highly as the High Court. The legal aid scheme has not yet been extended to proceedings in quarter sessions, magistrates' and coroner's courts. It is intended that legal aid shall eventually be obtainable in the magistrates' courts for such matters as affiliation and maintenance orders, guardianship of infants, and the procedure for the recovery of possession of low-rated houses under the Small Tenements Recovery Act, 1838.

It is not within the scope of this chapter to set out the functions of the courts mentioned in the previous paragraph. The applicant for legal aid will merely wish to know whether the Act covers the remedy which he seeks from the courts. His legal adviser will help him to decide the appropriate court in which he should bring his action. The types of cases for which legal aid will usually be required include proceedings for damages for personal injuries, breach of contract, and divorce, judicial separation, and nullity. The experience of many legal practitioners tends to show that actions between landlords and tenants will probably attract numerous applications for legal aid. Disputes over the validity and construction of Wills come within the ambit of the legal aid scheme. It may at first sight seem surprising that legal aid can be obtained for bankruptcy proceedings. It should be remembered that the bankruptcy laws exist for the benefit not only of creditors but also for the protection of debtors. In many cases the most sensible course for a person who is failing in business is to file a bankruptcy petition, in order that his affairs may be sorted out under the direction of the Court, with a minimum of hardship to himself and his creditors. Too often he lacks the means to avail himself of this procedure. The Legal Aid Act remedies this anomaly.

It will be seen that the man knocked down by a bus is no longer prevented by the smallness of his bank balance from suing for damages for his injuries. The victim of a tricky clause in a hire-purchase agreement with harsh or dishonest dealers can seek the protection of the courts. The widow who has been unprovided for in the Will of a spiteful or eccentric husband can now obtain assistance to apply to the Chancery Division of the High Court for an order making provision for her out of his estate under the Inheritance (Family Provision) Act, 1938.

The Rent Restriction Acts, which give tenants considerable protection against eviction, are so complicated that expert professional help to invoke them is usually necessary. The ignorant and the needy may now obtain that help to secure their homes against unscrupulous landlords. 'Let justice be done though the heavens fall' can become a reality and not a juristic platitude.

There are, however, certain proceedings for which legal aid is not available. These include proceedings wholly or partly in respect of libel, slander, breach of promise of marriage, and enticement. Furthermore, if a disgruntled elector wishes to challenge a parliamentary or municipal election he must do so out of his own resources.

(b) Legal aid in matters not involving litigation

The Legal Aid and Advice Act provides for the service of a solicitor to be available to advise in taking steps to assert or dispute a claim, where the question of litigation does not arise or has not yet arisen, but if it did arise, the proceedings would be such that legal aid could be given in connexion therewith under the Act. Legal aid would not, however, be granted unless the applicant shows that he has reasonable grounds for the right which he seeks to assert. It will be appreciated that many disputes are resolved by negotiations between the solicitors for the parties without recourse to litigation. For instance, claims for personal injuries are often settled after interviews and correspondence between solicitors without a writ or summons being issued, but persons of limited means cannot afford to instruct solicitors to conduct negotiations on their behalf. Hence the necessity for the provision in the Act which, alas, has not yet been brought into operation. Its implementation should obviate a large number of actions and, incidentally, may relieve a certain amount of pressure on the Legal Aid Fund.

(c) *Legal aid under existing Acts*

For some years there has been provision for legal aid in criminal cases and appeals. The cost of free defence of poor prisoners is borne by local funds. A trial judge, a chairman of quarter sessions, or magistrates in a court of summary jurisdiction may grant appropriate free legal aid facilities to a prisoner who appears to be too poor to pay for the costs of his defence or appeal, or if it appears to be in the interests of justice that he should be given such facilities.

(d) *Provision of legal advice under the Act*

We have seen that financial assistance is available to those who wish to bring or defend actions in the civil courts or who defend criminal proceedings and, if necessary, appeal against convictions or sentences. Not all legal problems call for solution in the courts. For instance, an applicant for legal aid may merely wish to know the extent of his rights and obligations under a tenancy agreement. A widow may require some explanation of the procedure for obtaining letters of administration to her husband's small estate. An injured workman would welcome advice on the benefits he may be entitled to under the National Insurance (Industrial Injuries) Act or the possibility of making a claim for damages against his employers. A woman who has just remarried may want to know how she can change the surname of the children of her first marriage to that of her second husband. At present no facilities exist to enable persons of limited means to obtain such advice with the aid of State funds. Section 7 of the Legal Aid and Advice Act, when brought into force by regulations, will satisfy this urgent need of those unable to afford professional advice. A person seeking legal advice may be required under this section to show that he cannot afford to obtain it in the usual way and to pay a fee of half a crown or such other fee as may be prescribed for each interview.

Legal advice will be available in England and Wales for any person and outside Great Britain for any members of the forces.

(i) *Persons not members of the forces.* The advice, which is confined to questions of English law, will be given orally by a solicitor employed whole or part time at one of the legal advice centres which it is proposed shall be set up and organized by the Law Society. If it should transpire that an applicant for advice needs to bring or defend proceedings in the courts, the solicitor will assist him in completing a form of application for legal aid.

(ii) *Members of the forces.* In addition to advice on the law of any part of the United Kingdom, a member of the forces may, except where regulations otherwise provide, be advised on the law of any country or territory where he is serving. Regulations may also be made providing for legal advice on the law of any country or territory in which he has been resident whether in the course of his service or not. It will be appreciated that members of the forces stationed abroad are, like civilians, liable to need legal advice on their problems. For instance, if a soldier is involved in a motor accident in Cyprus or Malaya, his rights will be determined by local law. Regulations may be made to provide that advisers employed to give advice outside the United Kingdom to members of the forces shall act for those members in obtaining information needed to enable such advice to be given.

Although the advice given under section 7 of the Legal Aid and Advice Act is oral, the adviser may, if he deems it necessary, give a written note of his advice. This is a sensible provision as a layman could easily forget some important point in advice given orally on a complicated question of law.

Administration of Legal Aid Scheme. The Lord Chancellor may make regulations implementing the provisions of the Legal Aid and Advice Act. The Law Society, which is the professional body of solicitors, has been made responsible for the working of the legal aid scheme. On matters of policy it collaborates with the Bar Council, the body responsible for the barristers' branch of the legal profession. The scheme is administered by twelve Legal Aid Area Committees whose members are selected from both branches of the profession.

Area committees deal with the general administration of the scheme within their areas. They are responsible for the appointment and supervision of the work of local Legal Aid Committees. They prepare panels of solicitors and barristers participating in the scheme and arrange for the distribution, for the information of the public, of copies of or extracts from the lists of names and addresses of members of such panels. They investigate complaints against members of panels. These committees are charged with the responsibility of deciding on any steps to be taken to recover money due to the Legal Aid Fund.

It is with the local committees that the applicant for legal aid is directly concerned, as these are the bodies which consider his application. The members of these committees consist of representatives of both branches of the legal profession. From the information supplied on the application form and with their professional knowledge, they determine whether legal aid should be granted. Legal aid is not granted automatically. It may be refused if the local committee considers that an applicant does not have a reasonable case or if his financial circumstances are too affluent to warrant it. The committee determines the conditions on which legal aid will be granted. From an assessment of means made by the National Assistance

Board, it decides what financial contribution (if any) the applicant should make towards the cost of any proceedings. In addition to power to issue legal aid certificates, the committee may, in certain circumstances, revoke or discharge them.

APPLICATION FOR LEGAL AID IN CIVIL PROCEEDINGS

Application for legal aid in civil proceedings must be made on forms prescribed by the Law Society. Different forms must be used according to whether the applicant desires to bring or defend proceedings. There are separate forms for matrimonial causes (e.g. divorce, nullity, and applications to the Divorce Court for maintenance). The forms can be obtained from the office of the local Legal Aid Committee, the Law Society, from most voluntary legal advice centres or from solicitors, most of whom undertake legal aid cases. In practice many applicants consult solicitors of their own choice, who will assist them in completing the application form.

The forms clearly indicate the information which the local committee will require to enable it to consider whether legal aid certificates should be granted. It is not possible here to discuss all the forms but, as an illustration, we will consider the hypothetical case of John Brown who wishes to claim damages for injuries suffered in a motor accident.

He will be required to complete a form which is in four parts. In the first part he will give the following information:

1. His name, address and occupation.
2. The purposes for which he requires a civil aid certificate; i.e. to take proceedings in the High Court or County Court for damages for personal injuries.
3. The name and address of the person against whom he wishes to take proceedings.
4. The names and addresses of any witnesses. (He should attach their statements of evidence if available.)
5. A list of any documents to be used in evidence (e.g. correspondence, medical and police reports).

6. The name and address of the solicitor whom he wishes to act for him.
7. A statement acknowledging that the terms of a civil aid certificate may include his liability to contribute towards the costs of the proceedings.
8. A declaration that all the information supplied by him on the form is true to the best of his knowledge and belief.
9. An acknowledgement that he may be required to supply further information to the Legal Aid Committee or to the National Assistance Board.

In Part II of the form, John Brown will have to indicate whether he is a member of a trade union, ex-service organization, or similar body. If he belongs to such a body he must state whether he has applied to it for help and the result of such application. He must give particulars of any insurance policy which might cover the claim. He must also supply details of any previous application for a civil aid certificate.

In Part III he will set out a brief account of his accident and the injuries he sustained.

The information required in Part IV of the form is to enable the National Assistance Board to assess his means to determine what contribution he should make towards the cost of the proceedings. The details required include:

1. Particulars of dependants (e.g. wife and three children, ages 7, 9, and 12).
2. Whether his dependants live with him.
3. The yearly amount of rent paid by him or his wife.
4. (a) The capital value of the house in which he lives if owned by himself or his wife.
   (b) Particulars of outgoings such as rates and mortgage interest.
5. Particulars of his net annual income from all sources.
6. Details of any savings, capital, or house property (other than the house in which he lives).
7. Particulars of his wife's income and capital.
8. Any additional information about the financial circum-

stances of his wife or himself. For instance, one of them
may be assisting an aged or infirm relative.

The completed application form is sent by the applicant or
his solicitor to the secretary of the local Legal Aid Committee
who detaches Part IV of the form and remits it to the National
Assistance Board. The applicant will usually be requested by
the Board to attend an interview with one of its officials to
discuss his means. When this has been done the Board will
assess the applicant's means and notify the local committee.

If the local committee is satisfied that John has a reasonable
case and his financial circumstances entitle him to legal aid,
it will notify him of the terms on which it is prepared to grant
a civil aid certificate. He is given twenty-eight days within
which to accept the terms offered. He will be informed of the
amount of any contribution he may have to make towards the
costs of the proceedings. The contribution, which is usually
payable by instalments, varies in amount according to the
applicant's means.

The committee may, of course, refuse to grant a civil aid
certificate, but it must notify the applicant of the grounds for
its refusal, which may be one or more of the following:

(*a*) The applicant's means have been determined by the
National Assistance Board and exceed the upper limits of
disposable income and capital laid down by the Act.

(*b*) Legal aid is not available for the type of proceedings to
which the application relates (e.g. actions for libel or
slander).

(*c*) The applicant has not shown reasonable grounds for
taking, defending, or being a party to proceedings.

(*d*) The Committee considers that in the particular circumstances of the case it is unreasonable that the applicant
should receive legal aid.

An applicant whose application for legal aid has been refused
may appeal to the Legal Aid Area Committee within twenty-
eight days of such refusal. He may incidentally also appeal

against conditions which the local committee may have attached to a civil aid certificate which it has offered. Appeals will not lie against any determination of means made by the National Assistance Board or a decision of the local committee as to the amount of any contribution or the method by which it shall be paid.

In the case of an emergency, an emergency certificate may be granted, provided that the applicant can show:

(a) He is likely to fulfil the conditions under which legal aid may be granted under the Act and the regulations made thereunder.
(b) It is in the interests of justice that he should, as a matter of urgency, be granted a certificate.

An instance of the need for an emergency certificate would be in circumstances where an immediate application to the Court for an injunction to restrain the threatened commission of an irreparable act is imperative (e.g. someone is about to pull down or destroy property). As it may be three or four weeks before an application for a civil aid certificate is granted, it will be appreciated that but for the emergency certificate procedure, the issue of a definitive certificate may come too late.

ELIGIBILITY FOR LEGAL AID

The Legal Aid Act places an upper income limit for eligibility for legal aid which is £420 a year 'disposable income'. A person's 'disposable income' is assessed by a formula set out in regulations made under the Act. Broadly speaking an appli cant's disposable income means the gross income for the preceding twelve months of himself and his wife less various deductions for such items as income tax, rent, rates, and allowances for dependants. Thus although a man may earn £700 per year, his family circumstances and his financial commitments may be such that his disposable income which determines his eligibility for legal aid may be less than £420 per annum. There are circumstances in which a person may have a modest income such as a pension but possess considerable capital resources. It is for this reason that savings and other capital assets are taken into account when assessing eligibility for legal aid.

Although there is no upper limit for capital, applicants with more than £500 'disposable capital' will normally be refused legal aid. 'Disposable capital' means the capital resources of the applicant and his wife less deductions for such items as furniture, effects, tools of trade, an allowance of £75 for his wife or dependants and usually the house in which he resides. Anyone whose disposal income is less than £156 a year and disposable capital is less than £75 will receive legal aid without making any contribution towards the costs of proceedings. Every other person to whom legal aid is granted (called in the Act 'assisted persons') may be required to pay to the Legal Aid Fund all his disposable capital in excess of £75 and half the difference between his disposable income for a year and £156. Thus if an applicant has disposable capital of £200 and a disposable income of £250 a year, his maximum contribution will be £172. If the costs of the proceedings are unlikely to reach this figure, the amount of his actual contribution will be reduced. Furthermore, if his action is successful and costs are recovered from his opponent, he will obtain a refund from the Legal Aid Fund. According to the circumstances of the case, the local committee may require the actual contribution to be paid in instalments or the whole or part of it to be paid before the certificate is issued. The amount of the instalments, which are usually payable monthly and spread over a period of about twelve or eighteen months, varies according to the size of the contribution.

It will be noted that an applicant's disposable capital and income are aggregated with those of his or her spouse. This does not, however, apply in assessing the resources of (a) an applicant who requires legal aid for matrimonial proceedings; or (b) an applicant separated from his or her spouse. Furthermore, a spouse's resources are not taken into account if it would be inequitable or impracticable to do so.

If, after the issue of a civil aid certificate, the assisted person's financial circumstances change, his certificate may be amended or discharged. He is under a duty to notify any material change in his circumstances to the local committee who will then ask the National Assistance Board to reassess his means.

REPRESENTATION OF ASSISTED PERSONS

When the civil aid certificate has been issued, two copies will be sent to the solicitor nominated by the assisted person. Thereafter the normal professional relationship exists between the solicitor and the assisted person. There are, however, qualifications. The client does not pay any fees to the solicitor, who is paid for his services by the Law Society out of the Legal Aid Fund. If a solicitor has not been nominated, the local committee will assign a solicitor who is a member of the appropriate panel. The proceedings will be conducted in substantially the same manner as for a person who is not legally aided. A solicitor acting for an assisted person must, however, serve a notice on his opponent intimating that his client has been granted a civil aid certificate under the Legal Aid and Advice Act.

There is one qualification to the right of an assisted person to be represented by a solicitor of his own choice. If the contribution of an assisted person in matrimonial proceedings is £10 or less he will be represented by a salaried solicitor employed by the Law Society. A wife petitioner who has satisfied the local committee that her husband could pay costs if ordered to do so, may nominate her own solicitor, notwithstanding the fact that her contribution would not exceed £10.

In doubtful cases the local committee may attach a condition that proceedings must not be commenced under the legal aid scheme unless a barrister advises that the applicant has a reasonable chance of success. If he advises that the assisted person has no right of action, this fact must be reported to the local committee, who will usually thereupon discharge the certificate.

Let us return to John Brown, to whom we referred earlier. We will suppose that he was granted a civil aid certificate to issue proceedings in the Queen's Bench Division of the High Court for damages for the personal injuries which he suffered in his motor accident. He has paid to the Legal Aid Fund all his contribution, which we will assume amounted to £80. Some consolation for his suffering has been given to him at the trial of his action by the judge, who has awarded him damages amounting to £500, and ordered the offending motorist to pay 'party and party' costs. John Brown's solicitor then proceeds to 'tax' the costs. An official of the court known as a 'taxing master' assesses the amount of costs which is payable by the loser of the action. He does not necessarily pay the whole of the legal costs incurred on the plaintiff's behalf, but only roughly about two-thirds; these are known as 'party and party' costs. The proportion of the costs not recoverable from the loser is known as 'solicitor and client' costs. When these two sets of costs have been taxed, John's solicitor submits his bill to the Law Society. He must also remit to the Law Society the damages and costs which he has recovered from the defendant. The Law Society will retain for the benefit of the Legal Aid Fund the costs paid by the defendant, up to the amount by which his contributions fall short of the total costs, and will remit to John the damages and the balance of the costs, after deducting the amount of any unpaid contribution due by him. John's solicitor and counsel are paid by the Society. They do not, however, get all the fees to which they would be entitled if they acted for a client who was not legally aided, but only 85 per cent. It may be fairly said that the taxpayer and the assisted person pay 85 per cent of the costs of proceedings under the Legal Aid Scheme, whilst the remaining 15 per cent is in effect contributed by members of the legal profession in the form of a rebate of fees.

Discharge and revocation of certificates

A certificate is normally discharged when the proceedings to which it relates have been disposed of. The appropriate Area Committee may, however, discharge a certificate if an assisted person is more than twenty-one days in arrear with his contribution or any instalment, or if he has, against the advice of his solicitor and counsel, unreasonably insisted on carrying on the proceedings so as to incur unjustifiable expenses. A certificate may be discharged if the assisted person's circumstances improve to such an extent that his disposable income exceeds £420 a year.

The appropriate Area Committee may revoke the certificate of an assisted person who has, prior to the issue, wilfully made false representations in the information required to be supplied by him under the Legal Aid Regulations.

Discharge of a certificate brings the certificate to an end at the date of its discharge. The effect of revocation is that the assisted person is deemed never to have been an assisted person in the proceedings but his solicitor and counsel are paid their fees out of the Legal Aid Fund. The Law Society has the right to recover such fees from the assisted person.

LEGAL AID IN CRIMINAL CASES

The form of legal aid probably best known to the general public is the 'dock brief'. An unrepresented prisoner on trial at assizes or quarter sessions may, on payment of £2 4s 6d, choose any barrister present in court to appear for him. This custom has been regarded by the Bar as a form of voluntary social service. Dock briefs are welcomed by young briefless barristers eager to gain practical experience at the criminal bar. As the remuneration is so small, the undertaking of a dock brief by an established barrister with a flourishing practice may entail considerable financial sacrifice, as he may have to give up quite lucrative work while the case, which might last several days, is in progress. Dock briefs are less frequent these days in view of the other forms of legal aid now available.

Under the Poor Prisoners' Defence Act, 1930, a person charged with an offence triable by jury may apply, either at the preliminary hearing before the magistrates, or at the trial court, for a defence certificate. This certificate will give the applicant the right, without payment, to the professional services of a solicitor and counsel at his trial at quarter sessions or assizes. He is also entitled to a copy of the depositions of witnesses taken at the preliminary hearing when he was committed for trial. He is entitled to a defence certificate as of right, if the charge is murder. For charges other than murder, such a certificate will only be granted if the Court is satisfied that his means are insufficient to enable him to pay for legal aid. The Court has, however, a discretion to grant a certificate in other cases if it considers it desirable in the interests of justice.

The same Act empowers a magistrates' court to grant a legal aid certificate in respect of proceedings in that court. Normally only a solicitor will be assigned to conduct the case on behalf of the prisoner. In more serious cases counsel may also be assigned.

Free legal aid is also available in certain cases for appeals from the decisions of magistrates' courts (Summary Jurisdiction (Appeals) Act, 1933). The Criminal Appeal Act, 1907, confers on the Court discretion to grant legal aid for appeals to the Court of Criminal Appeal. It must grant legal aid for appeals in murder cases.

LEGAL AID AND ADVICE PROVIDED BY VOLUNTARY ORGANIZATIONS

Many bodies, such as trade unions, provide legal aid as part of the service for which members pay their subscriptions. In some unions negotiations for damages for injuries at work are conducted with employers or their insurers. If negotiations break down, a case is passed to the union's solicitors for legal action. Some ex-Servicemen's organizations supply their members with legal aid in fighting pensions appeals.

Some very useful and much needed work in the field of free

legal advice is still being carried on by numerous voluntary organizations. Some of the larger settlements such as the Mary Ward Settlement in Holborn, and the Cambridge House Settlement in Camberwell, employ full-time solicitors to give legal advice to those unable to pay the usual professional fees. These two centres are obliged to fix upper income limits which are graduated according to family circumstances. Those able to afford it are required to pay a very nominal fee to the centre for the assistance they receive. These centres sometimes arrange for their clients to be represented at magistrates' courts, or negotiate settlements of small claims.

Most free legal advice centres are obliged by lack of funds to confine their activities to oral advice given by lawyers who attend voluntarily in the evenings for this purpose. At the centre attached to the Katherine Low Settlement in Battersea, solicitors and barristers attend every Monday evening to give advice on a wide range of legal questions. No income limit is imposed nor any fee charged for advice, but a collecting box is placed in the waiting room for donations to the funds of the settlement, which relies very largely on voluntary subscriptions to carry on a wide range of social work catering for the needs of youth and the aged. In addition to oral advice, the lawyers draft letters and applications for legal aid under the Legal Aid and Advice Act, 1949. The principal topics on which advice is usually sought are matrimonial disputes, landlord and tenant cases, and accident claims. Some of the problems brought to free legal advice centres may seem trivial, but a chat with a poor man's lawyer can often dispel unnecessary but gnawing anxiety.

Many political organizations run legal advice centres. In most large towns in Britain Members of Parliament and local councillors conduct their own advice centres, to which their constituents can bring their problems on such questions as housing and pensions. It has been said that the modern M.P. is not only a legislator but also a welfare officer for his constituents.

Much useful advice work is being done by Citizens' Advice Bureaux, not only on legal questions but on the multifarious social problems which beset the citizen in an age harassed by housing shortages, government regulations, and complicated official forms. The increase in the divorce rate since 1939 has revealed the existence of an alarmingly high proportion of unhappy marriages in this country. It is becoming more widely recognized that many married couples need expert unbiased advice on the art of living happily together. The Marriage Guidance Council is doing much to save many marriages from ending in the Divorce Court. The Council also gives useful advice to those young couples about to get married who are sensible enough to realize that successful marriage is not necessarily the inevitable happy ending of a popular romance.

The Legal Aid and Advice Act, when fully in force, should ensure that poverty will not prevent a man from ascertaining his legal rights; but legal advice on tap for half a crown and litigation launched by a civil aid certificate will not satisfy the miscellaneous needs of John Citizen, which are so admirably catered for by voluntary organizations. Many of the problems for which help or advice is required are outside the scope of lawyers altogether. John Citizen will continue to look to his local Citizens' Advice Bureau, his M.P., or town councillor for advice on pensions, National Insurance benefits, or housing problems. If his marriage is in danger of breaking down, he will turn to the Marriage Guidance Council for help. And may he always do so, for the material benefits of the Welfare State, however generous, can never entirely supersede the friendly personal efforts of those whose sole aim is to do their neighbour a good turn.

13

Law and the Family

FRANCIS PETRE

IN the words of the popular song, 'Love and marriage go together', and so also in a less romantic (and less controversial) way, do Law and Marriage. For while marriage is a subject of keen interest to social workers and the clergy, it is also inevitably the concern of lawyers, since the whole domestic and family structure of Western society is based upon it. Indeed the claim to family relationship between two people is necessarily based upon lawful marriage, and so this chapter will deal predominantly with the relationship of a husband to his wife, both in its happier moments, and in more difficult times when the marriage is breaking up and continued cohabitation is no longer reasonably practicable. It will also touch upon the legal status of children and the duties of parents towards them. Finally, a brief account will be given as to where advice, whether legal, moral, or practical, can be obtained both by the rich and by people too poor to pay for the help they may receive.

We are dealing in this chapter with the matrimonial and domestic law of England, and it is interesting to trace back into history the antecedents of our present system of matrimonial law. This law has changed through the ages so as to become more and more a secular law, and it has now thrown off its religious beginnings. Thus a wedding in a Registry Office is just as effective in the eyes of the law as the most elaborate ceremony at St Margaret's, Westminster. However, the early matrimonial law of our nation was within the jurisdiction of the Ecclesiastical Courts, and these administered the Canon Law of the Catholic Church. After the break with Rome at the Reformation, the Ecclesiastical Courts retained their jurisdiction, and it was not until 1857 that they were deprived of these duties. Finally, in 1873, Parliament created the High Court as we know it to-day, and assigned divorce cases, together with probate and Admiralty matters, to one Division of this Court.

Just as the courts with jurisdiction in such cases were altered, so also has the law been changed, and this particularly during the last hundred years. It is generally correct to say that the law of a nation is no more than the set of rules composed by the people, or imposed by the rulers upon them, for the conduct of life, and as the outlook changes so also will the Law do likewise. Thus with the secularization of the courts has come the introduction of divorce and the loosening of the marriage bond. However, it is not the duty of this chapter to comment upon the trend of modern thought, but rather to state the law as it now stands. This law is concerned with the family, is enforced in the secular courts of the country, and is based upon the Statutes of Parliament and interpreted by the civil courts of England.

The courts with jurisdiction in family cases

Before the actual laws which can be enforced in these courts are dealt with in detail, it may be of assistance to see what these courts are and how they can be approached, from a practical point of view. As has been pointed out in the last paragraph, the High Court now has matrimonial jurisdiction in certain cases. It is empowered to hear cases of divorce, nullity, judicial separation, restitution of conjugal rights, jactitation of marriage, declarations as to the validity of marriage or the legitimacy of children, and certain other questions concerned with children's welfare.

In addition to the High Court, there are certain courts of inferior jurisdiction which can deal with family cases. Of these the magistrates' courts are the most important, for they can make non-cohabitation and maintenance orders which permit or enable spouses to live apart without loss of legal rights, and they can also deal with the custody of the children of the marriage. Magistrates' courts are local courts, and sit in most large towns. Cases are tried by two or more lay magistrates, or in some cases, notably in London, by one trained stipendiary magistrate.

In addition to magistrates' courts, another type of local court having jurisdiction in certain family cases is the county court. This can deal with declarations of a child's legitimacy, custody of children and, together with the High Court, can decide disputes which arise between a husband and wife as to property and possession of goods. Finally, both a county court and the High Court can enforce a valid separation agreement reached between two spouses.

The decisions of all these courts can be appealed against if proper grounds exist for disturbing the Court's finding, but we have not sufficient space to examine the rights and procedure on such appeals.

What constitutes a valid marriage?

Before the courts will treat a marriage as valid and properly effective certain essential elements must be present in the formation of the marriage. If any one of them is absent the purported marriage is in fact no marriage at all, and the parties to it are wholly unaffected by it. Hence they need not take any legal action to have it declared null and void, because it is so irrespective of any such declaration, but in many cases it is proper and wise to obtain a decree of nullity from the High Court to clarify the position beyond doubt.

Marriage has been defined as 'The voluntary union, for life, of one man and one woman to the exclusion of all others'. There are several essential factors in this union. Firstly the parties must have reached the age of sixteen; and if either of them is under twenty-one, the consent of the parents or guardian, or in some cases of a magistrate, must be obtained. Further, both parties must be unmarried, so that, if either has previously been validly married and the other spouse to that earlier marriage is still living, a decree of divorce must have been granted and made absolute. Further, it is essential to a valid marriage that the two spouses are not so closely related as to fall within certain prohibited degrees of relationship. These date from

1563 and are set out in the Book of Common Prayer, except in so far as they have been relaxed so as to permit a man to marry his deceased wife's sister or niece or a woman to marry her deceased husband's brother or nephew.

In order to perform a valid ceremony of marriage certain rules must be followed, and the ceremony must take place in a properly licensed place, such as a Church or a Registry Office. The rules as to the validity of a marriage ceremony, which are too detailed to be set out here, must be complied with. Finally, both parties to a marriage must consent to it freely. Thus they must both understand the nature and effect of the ceremony, so that if one party wrongly thinks for example that the ceremony is a conversion to Hinduism, the ceremony is not a valid marriage, for it would clearly be wrong to consider a man who had sought to espouse a new religion to be bound in marriage to a wife instead. Similarly if one spouse marries with a mistaken belief as to the identity of the other spouse, and not merely as to a quality, the marriage is invalid, as also if the consent is only apparent and has been got by threats or duress. Similarly where consent cannot be given because the mind of a party is clouded by insanity or intoxication, there is no real consent and the marriage is invalid. A person who is insane at certain periods may, of course, marry with full and proper consent during a lucid interval, though, as will be seen later, the marriage may be 'voidable'.

The above, then, are essentials to a valid marriage, and unless they are all present the marriage is void.

Marriages which may be 'avoided' after the ceremony

We now turn to 'voidable' marriages, that is marriages which are valid but which have an inherent fault, which enables the party not responsible for the defect to go to the Court and, as it were, to say 'Although this is a valid marriage I do not want to treat it thus because of such and such a defect in it.' In such cases that party petitions the Court for a decree of nullity, and if the petition is successful the marriage is declared null *ab initio*, that is from its inception, and is treated as if it had always been void. Thus a party who is by reason of such a defect permitted to claim a nullity may do so – but if this is not done the marriage remains a valid one.

There are five grounds upon which a petition for a decree of nullity may be based where the marriage was valid but an inherent defect exists. The first three of these can conveniently be treated together, because they are in many respects much alike. They each refer to the state of things at the date of marriage, and each of them gives the unaffected spouse the right to petition during the year immediately following the marriage – but no later. They are that one spouse was at the date of marriage suffering from recurrent epileptic fits or bouts of insanity, or was pregnant by a man other than her husband, or was suffering from venereal disease. In each of these three cases the spouse not so affected may seek nullity provided that he or she did not know of the state at the date of marriage, and that when it was later discovered intercourse was not consented to thereafter.

In addition a marriage may be treated as voidable in two other cases, namely, where it is not consummated by intercourse, owing either to impotence or to wilful refusal to consummate. Impotence presupposes incapacity, whether physical or mental, to consummate, whereas in cases of wilful refusal consummation is possible but not permitted by one party in face of the reasonably tactful and proper requests of the other party. In both cases a medical report can be ordered by the Court, but where the party against whom this is ordered refuses to allow it, the Court can nevertheless grant a decree. In cases of wilful refusal the refusal must have been continuous since the marriage, whereas a petitioner on the ground of impotence must prove such a state both at the date of marriage and of the presentation of the petition. The number of cases on these grounds could be greatly reduced if all spouses would take adequate advice on this subject before the marriage is finally celebrated.

We have now dealt with void marriages and with those that are valid but, having a defect at the date of the ceremony or continuously thereafter, can be subsequently 'avoided'. However, the vast majority of marriages are perfectly valid and give rise to certain important duties between husband and wife.

The rights and duties of spouses towards each other

The relationship of husband and wife carries with it certain rights and obligations which affect both parties, though in many different ways. For example, it is a husband's duty to maintain his wife for so long as she lives with him, or, where she lives apart from him, for so long as she does so with good cause or his consent. However, if the wife commits adultery she loses her right to maintenance. As the reverse side of this rule, it is the husband who is entitled to select where the parties shall live, though experience tells one that, in practice, this right of decision is very differently interpreted by the wife!

Each party to a marriage has a mutual right of cohabitation with the other – but, of course, no court of law would ever enforce such a right, for to do so would clearly be impossible and fruitless. However, as will be seen later, a party who is deprived by the other spouse of this right may be granted orders by the courts which ensure maintenance. The ancient figure of the head of the family who had the right to chastise his wife ('but not in a violent or cruel manner') has now passed away and is unrecognized by the law, and husbands are faced by wives who are protected both by their feminine wiles and by the courts.

The separation of a husband and wife by agreement

Although the courts will always attempt to keep a marriage intact, they nevertheless recognize that some marriages do break up so as to make continued cohabitation virtually impossible. Thus the law recognizes separation both where the spouses live apart by agreement and where they ask the court for an order permitting separation or dissolving the marriage ties. We will first deal with cases of mutual separation by agreement, because this form of separation avoids the unpleasant necessity of court proceedings. It is, of course, important

that such an agreement should be properly drawn up, so that
it provides for all the essential matters such as maintenance,
and, if there are children, their custody and keep. It may
amount to a separation agreement, that is, a mutual consent to
live apart, or it may be no more than a maintenance agreement,
which recognizes the separation but does not consent to it.
In the former case any existing state of desertion is terminated
and it may thus prevent a later divorce or judicial separation on
this ground.

Where an agreement has been made it can be enforced in the
same way as any other contract, namely in the High Court or
in a county court, but the somewhat simpler procedure available of enforcing a magistrates' court separation order cannot,
of course, be used, and this represents a disadvantage. It is
wise to obtain legal advice on the drawing up of an agreement,
because although it may appear a simple matter, unexpected
difficulties frequently arise if this is not done.

Separation as effected by the magistrates' court

This is a form of order which provides for separation and
which is frequently used by parties whose marriage has broken
down. It has many advantages, especially in that it is cheap,
quick, and easily enforceable, and it enables parties to live
apart, and to arrange for the children of the marriage. The
procedure in such cases is briefly that the spouse wishing for
an order visits the local magistrates' court and issues a summons there, with leave of the magistrates, on one of the grounds
on which such summonses can be framed. These are listed
below. A date is fixed for the hearing, and the summons is
served by the Court on the other spouse. At the hearing the
matter is tried by the magistrates in a private court, and if the
complaint is proved an order is made, binding the guilty
spouse. The order may be appealed against and may be later
varied or discharged. This subject is a very large and detailed
one and necessarily we will deal with it briefly, first considering
the grounds upon which a summons can be granted, then
discussing the nature of an order which can be made, and

finally touching shortly on the variation and discharge of such
an order.

The grounds upon which a magistrates' court can make an order

In order to obtain the grant of a summons in the magistrates' court, the party seeking to do so, known as the complainant, must allege that the other spouse, or respondent, has
been guilty of one of the following offences during the six
months immediately preceding the application for the summons. Where the offence is one that has continued over a
period of time, such as persistent cruelty, it must have continued into the six-month period. It will be noted that a wife
has more grounds open to her than a husband, for she has ten
grounds upon which she can seek an order, whereas a husband
has only three. A wife's ten grounds are:

1. That her husband has been convicted of an aggravated
   assault on her.
2. That he has been convicted of any assault on her for
   which he has been sentenced to pay a fine of over £5 or to
   a term of imprisonment.
3. That he has deserted her;
4. That he has treated her . . .
5. . . . or her child, with persistent cruelty.
6. That he has wilfully neglected to maintain her.
7. That he is an habitual drunkard as defined by the
   Habitual Drunkards Act, 1869, or is a drug addict.
8. That he has insisted on sexual intercourse knowing that
   he was suffering from venereal disease.
9. That he has committed adultery.
10. That he has compelled her to submit to prostitution.

A husband, on the other hand, may only be granted a summons on grounds Number 5, 7, and 9 above, namely persistent
cruelty to children, habitual drunkenness or drug addiction,
and adultery.

The above list is a formidable one and in the space available it would clearly be impossible to deal with each of the ten offences. However, four of the grounds dominate the lists at magistrates' courts, and it is these four which we will consider briefly. They are desertion, persistent cruelty to the wife, wilful neglect to maintain, and adultery.

Desertion. This ground is open to the wife only, in the magistrates' court, though it may form the basis of a High Court petition for divorce or judicial separation, presented by either the husband or the wife, provided certain conditions apply. In the magistrates' court the desertion need not run for any special period, but it must, of course, continue until the date of hearing.

Desertion has been defined as 'the intentional bringing to an end of cohabitation without cause and without the consent of the other spouse'. Thus it usually occurs because one spouse leaves the matrimonial home without good reason and against the wishes of the other. Nevertheless it is equally desertion if one spouse acts in such a way as to drive the other out of the home, whether by conduct or expulsive words. This latter form is known technically as 'constructive desertion'. Thus in essence desertion is an act which causes the spouses to part, and in rare cases this may happen even though they remain under the same roof, if they have parted in the sense that they lead wholly separate lives.

Where a husband is alleged to be in desertion, he may in defence reply that he had reasonable cause for terminating cohabitation. In order to succeed on this defence he must prove that his wife's conduct has made continued cohabitation a practical impossibility – by, for example, causing him to form the reasonable belief that she has committed adultery, or by refusing to live in the home offered by her husband, or in some cases by her persistent extravagance, or in many other ways.

Once a state of desertion exists it may be terminated in the following ways. Firstly the parties may resume cohabitation, though if this be only for a very short period and with the intention of attempting a reconciliation it will not necessarily end desertion. Secondly, where the party who is in desertion makes a genuine offer to the other spouse to return; then, if this is refused, desertion by the party making the offer is at once terminated, and the other party, by refusing the proffered cohabitation, is doing an act which causes the parties to remain separate and is thus placed in desertion. However, before an offer to return has any of the above effects it must be *bona fide*, that is it must be made with the honest intention of reconciliation and not for ulterior motives such as the avoidance of an anticipated Court Order. Finally, it is important to note that where a magistrates' court makes an order which includes a non-cohabitation clause, this prevents desertion running from the date of the order forward, unless it is varied in this respect or discharged.

Persistent cruelty. The second class of summons which is frequently met with in magistrates' courts is for persistent cruelty to the wife. This ground of complaint is open to a wife only, though either spouse can proceed on a summons alleging persistent cruelty to the children. The offence has two elements, namely 'persistence' and 'cruelty'. In order to satisfy the first of these, the acts of cruelty must show some degree of repetition or continuance, so that a single cruel act cannot constitute this offence – but two such acts may satisfy the definition of persistence.

What then is cruelty? It may best be described as conduct which causes 'danger to life, limb, or health, bodily or mental, or a reasonable apprehension of it'. Usually, of course, it consists of blows, but many other types of conduct may amount to cruelty, such as threats, false accusations, revolting behaviour whether sexual or otherwise, and extreme forms of sulking or nagging. While the cruelty may cause mental injury only, the words 'mental cruelty' have no magical significance in English Law, and they are often used to describe that state of affairs which exists when two parties exasperate each other by their behaviour and thus cause constant irritation and annoyance.

Wilful neglect to maintain. It has been pointed out that a husband has a duty to support his wife and children, and if he fails to do so properly he may be guilty of this offence. A husband cannot claim support from his wife, however, nor can a wife who has ceased to act as a wife towards her husband claim the benefit of her right as wife to maintenance. So, for example, a deserting wife cannot claim that she is entitled to maintenance. For this offence to be proved the Court must be satisfied that the husband is wilful in not providing reasonable maintenance. If he is out of work for good reason he may be unable to maintain her and his failure is not wilful, but where he could earn sufficient money to support and fails to make use of his opportunities he is guilty of this offence.

Adultery. Either a husband or a wife can obtain a magistrates' court order by proving that the other has committed adultery. This may be defined as voluntary sexual intercourse between two persons of opposite sexes, one or both of whom is married. The frequent difficulty in adultery cases is proof of the offence, because direct evidence is obviously very rare. Thus in practice evidence is given of circumstances which imply adultery, and the Court draws its conclusions therefrom. A few examples of circumstances which if proved may satisfy a court, are familiarity, close association, a night in the same hotel room, or the birth of a child to the wife of whom the husband could not have been the father. Admissions of adultery are also very frequently used in evidence. In the magistrates' court a party accused of adultery may defend by saying that the other party connived at it or conduced to it by certain conduct, or has acted collusively, in which case the Court will not make an order. These defences are considered later.

In the case of all the matrimonial offences referred to above, and more frequently in the case of adultery, the innocent spouse may forgive the offence by having sexual intercourse with the guilty one and otherwise acting as if the offence were completely forgiven. When this has happened the original offence, provided it was fully known about by the forgiving spouse, ceases to be a ground upon which a complaint can be made so long as the guilty party refrains from further matrimonial misconduct. It is said to be 'condoned' by the act of forgiveness, but where a later act of misconduct is committed it is 'revived' so that it once again becomes a ground upon which the complaint can be made to the Court.

Orders which can be made in the magistrates' court

Where the magistrates find that the complainant spouse has proved that the other spouse is guilty of one of the offences set out above, they will make an order containing certain specific terms. Firstly, they may order that the complainant be not bound to cohabit with the respondent. This is usual in cruelty or habitual drunkard or drug-addict cases, but is seldom used in other cases. It has been noticed earlier that this clause prevents desertion running, and it may thus impede later divorce proceedings. Secondly, the magistrates may make certain orders as to money. Thus they can order the husband to pay up to £5 per week to his wife, if and only if she has proved him guilty of an offence, and they can order him to pay up to thirty shillings per week in respect of each child, where she is granted the custody of the children by the Court. These orders often insist that the sums paid under them are paid through the office of the Court. Thirdly, the magistrates may make orders as to the children of the marriage in exactly the same way as they can under the Guardianship of Infants Acts (see later). Finally, the Court may make an order that one party pays the costs of the hearing, which usually amount to solicitors' charges, and the cost of taking out a summons, which is normally two shillings.

Variation and discharge of magistrates' orders

Once the magistrates have made their order it is at once operative if the parties are living apart, and unless discharged it remains so until one or other of the parties dies. However, if they are still living together it would lead to a terrible situation if the order were treated as being effective, and so it does not operate until they separate. If they remain together for three months after the order is made it is automatically discharged, and similarly even where it has become operative because the parties have lived apart, it is discharged if they resume cohabitation. An order may also be discharged where it was made in favour of a wife who has later committed adultery, unless she has done so because the husband has caused her to commit adultery by not paying the money he was ordered to pay under the order.

Orders may also be discharged, in certain cases, by application to the Court, where 'fresh evidence' can be given either of incidents which happened after the order or of which evidence was not reasonably available at the hearing for one reason or another. So also may an order be varied in its terms where fresh evidence is available, and if it is sought solely to alter the money payments ordered, fresh evidence is not necessary in theory, though in practice it is not advisable to approach magistrates for a variation of their order where the circumstances are exactly the same as those which prompted their earlier decision.

Appeals and enforcement

Very briefly a magistrates' decision can be appealed against if it is wrong either in law or in fact, but in the latter case it must be shown that there was not sufficient evidence to establish even a *prima facie* case. The appeal is to the Divisional Court of the Probate, Divorce, and Admiralty Division sitting in the Strand in London, from there to the Court of Appeal, and finally to the highest tribunal in the land, namely the House of Lords. Needless to say anyone considering appeal must have trained legal advice, and legal aid is available in such cases where the appellant is poor.

A husband who does not pay under an order made against him may be summoned for arrears, and he may have distress levied against his goods or be sent to prison in extreme cases. It is, of course, always wise for the order made against the husband to be one which he can pay – because a low order regularly paid is much more valuable than a large order which is not complied with.

DIVORCE

No order of the magistrates' court can undo the bonds of marriage in the eyes of the State, and in order to obtain such an order the jurisdiction of the High Court must be invoked. There are now six grounds upon which a marriage which is valid and not voidable may be, as it were, dissolved, and the parties made free to remarry once more. This branch of the Law is an accretion since the days of the Ecclesiastical Courts, for in those days the traditional point of view of the Christian Church was adhered to, which is that when a man and a woman marry they are united until parted by death. However, this view is now considered outdated except by a few, of whom the author is one, and divorce has become a common feature of our society. Indeed it is prevalent in all classes of society, and the attitude of the Established Church is sufficiently obscure to leave its members in doubt as to the morality of the position. The recent Divorce Commission recognized the dangers, and stated that if there were to be an increase in divorce it might be better to forbid it altogether in view of the deleterious effect upon family life. Nevertheless, it remains, and upon any one of six grounds properly married couples may have their marriages dissolved. Before a divorce can be obtained, however, the parties must have been married for three years, or alternatively the party petitioning for divorce must be able to satisfy the Court that the case is one of exceptional hardship or that the other party has acted in an exceptionally depraved manner. The Court will not permit a divorce within three years of marriage if it considers that it would be contrary to the welfare of the children or might prevent a reconciliation.

Grounds for obtaining a divorce

As has been stated there are six grounds upon which a divorce petition may be successful, and three of these are very

like three grounds for complaint before the magistrates. These
are dealt with first:

Cruelty. This is very similar to persistent cruelty, which was
described earlier as an offence which, if proved, would entitle
a magistrates' court to make an order. The only real difference is that in divorce proceedings the cruelty does not need
to be persistent, and one act, if really grave, could amount to
cruelty.

Desertion for three years. Once again desertion in the High
Court is very much like desertion in the magistrates' court,
but in the former it must be for a period of three years immediately preceding the presentation of the petition.

Adultery. This ground is the same in magistrates' courts as
it is in the High Court, except in one small matter. It was
noticed that the magistrates were barred from making an order
if the adultery was conduced to by the other party's conduct,
whereas in the High Court the judge has a discretion as to
whether to grant a decree in such cases.

Rape, sodomy, or bestiality. A wife who can prove that her
husband has been guilty of any one of these offences is entitled
to a decree of divorce.

Unsoundness of mind. Either spouse may be granted a divorce
if the other spouse is insane, and beyond cure, and has been
under care and treatment for the five years immediately preceding the presentation of the petition. In order to constitute
care and treatment the party alleged to be insane must either
have been undergoing compulsory treatment by reason of the
Lunacy and Mental Treatment Acts, 1890–1930, or, in cases
where it immediately follows compulsory treatment and not
otherwise, voluntary treatment under the Mental Treatment
Act, 1930.

Presumption of death. Where there is evidence upon which

a court can reasonably presume the death of the other party, it may do so, and then dissolve the marriage. In cases where the spouse whose death it is sought to presume has been absent and has not been heard of or seen by any of the persons who would normally have heard of him or her for seven years, the Court will automatically presume death.

Bars to the grant of a decree

Even where the petitioner in a divorce suit is able to prove that one of the grounds for the granting of a decree exists, the Court may not grant an order if a 'bar' to such a grant exists. Such a bar may be either 'absolute', that is one which is binding on the Court, or 'discretionary' so that the Court may act upon it if it thinks proper, but is not bound to do so.

Dealing first with absolute bars, which preclude a decree being granted – the first of these is an obvious one, namely that the Court has not jurisdiction to hear the case. As far as divorce cases are concerned, the Court will only have jurisdiction where the petitioner is domiciled in England or, in the case of a wife petitioner, where she has resided in England for three years.

Domicile is by no means easy to define, but very briefly it can be described as the country which a party would describe as his home. It will be the country in which that party was born until, by choice, a home is made in another land, whereupon domicile changes. A home is more than a mere residence and must be based upon a measure of and desire for permanence. A wife automatically has the same domicile as her husband, and if his changes so also does her own.

Apart from lack of jurisdiction there are three other absolute bars which are best considered together. These are connivance, condonation, and collusion. Connivance is the act of the petitioner in an adultery case, which preceded the adultery alleged, and which has caused it, whether by incitement or acquiescence in it. Condonation is an act, subsequent to adultery or cruelty, which amounts to forgiveness of the offence. Naturally, in order to forgive an offence it must be known of, and the act implying such forgiveness must be a substantial one, namely complete restoration of the relationship of husband and wife – though intercourse is not an essential element.

Finally, collusion is the arrangement between the parties to provide evidence on which a divorce can be granted. Thus the fabricating of evidence or acting in such a way as to provide evidence, is collusive – but merely to provide a statement as to events which have already occurred is not collusive, nor is discussion or other preparation for the future of the children or matrimonial property.

The bars upon which a court may exercise its discretion are, briefly, that the petitioner has delayed for an unreasonable time, or is guilty of adultery, cruelty, or desertion. Where a petitioner has committed adultery a discretion statement must be filed which sets out all such adultery. Generally speaking the Court will exercise its discretion in these cases. Finally, in cases of desertion, adultery, or unsoundness of mind, where such offence or condition has been caused in some measure by the conduct of the petitioner, then the Court may decide not to grant a decree on that ground.

Order of the court in divorce suits

Where the Court grants a divorce it pronounces a decree nisi, which means that unless certain unusual events occur, the divorce can be made absolute in six weeks and so finally dissolve the marriage and permit the parties to remarry. The Court may also make orders as to maintenance for the wife and no limit is placed on their amount, though if they are not reasonable, bearing in mind the means of the parties, they can be appealed against. Further orders as to the custody, access to, and maintenance of children may be made, and the Court can, as in the magistrates' courts, make orders as to costs. Finally, where the petitioner in an adultery case is a husband he may claim damages against the party with whom the adultery is committed, and the measure of the damages will be assessed in accordance with the estimated value of the wife to the husband at the date of the adultery and the means of the parties. Thus a loose-living wife whose marriage was already doomed at the time of the adultery will merit lower damages than a previously faithful spouse, enticed away by the co-respondent. It should be noted briefly that 'interim' orders can be made which operate between the time when the petition is filed and the date upon which it is finally made absolute.

OTHER HIGH COURT REMEDIES

In addition to divorce proceedings, other orders may be made in the High Court with reference to marriage. Thus a petition may be filed for Judicial Separation, and this may be successful on the same grounds as a divorce petition. The effect of such a decree is to provide for a separation between the parties, and it does not terminate the marriage, so that if they resume cohabitation the order may be discharged. There are certain advantages over a divorce which are worthy of notice. For example, there is no need for the parties to have been married three years, and it is sufficient to give the Court jurisdiction if they both reside in England. It is often used by a petitioner who is precluded on religious grounds from obtaining a divorce.

Another High Court remedy is restitution of conjugal rights. This is comparatively rare, and amounts to an application to the Court by one of two separated spouses for an order that the other resume cohabitation. This order cannot, of course, be enforced in that form, but if cohabitation is not resumed certain consequences follow, namely that the successful petitioner can obtain a judicial separation, or can get permanent alimony, or payments, or a settlement of property.

The last remedy in the High Court in matrimonial cases to which reference need be made is a decree in a jactitation suit, ordering a person, who has been alleging that he or she is married to the petitioner, to cease from making all such allegations in the future.

Needless to say this is an extremely rare remedy and the records of such cases are very few.

Law and the Family

Children

It is unhappily all too frequent for the relationship of husband and wife to be stressed to such a degree that the essential importance and unity of the family as a whole is forgotten. Where a man and woman marry and bring children into the world it is clear that they owe those children a very high duty to care for them, particularly in the early years when they are unable properly to look after themselves. Thus the parents must provide a home for their family and keep it in a proper and fit state, and they must not neglect them. Further it is the parents' duty to educate the children and to ensure that the statutory attendances at school are adhered to. All this is common sense and is normally done in a reasonable and happy home, as a matter of course. Where the parents are separated other considerations arise, and in such cases the custody of the child and the responsibility for it are, *prima facie*, vested by common law in the father as head of the family. This is an ancient idea and one which, no doubt, springs from the conception of the *pater familias* in Roman Law, which has so much influenced all later codes of law in Western Europe.

Although the father is thus considered to have custody in the absence of any court order, this preference for the father ceases to operate when proceedings in the magistrates' court or the High Court are taken in respect of the custody of any child. Once such a matter is before a court there is, by statute, one matter which is pre-eminently important, namely the well-being of the child concerned, and no other question can be considered in priority to that.

The question of the custody of a child may be raised in the courts either in conjunction with other proceedings concerning the marriage or separately. In the magistrates' court, therefore, on any matrimonial summons an order as to the custody of and maintenance for the children of the marriage may be made, and also either party may issue a summons under the Guardianship of Infants Acts dealing with these questions only. In both cases the orders which the Court can make are the same. Thus the magistrates may order that the custody be vested in either party and can order that, where the wife is granted custody, maintenance be paid to her up to 30s per week. The party who is deprived of the custody is normally granted access to the child either at reasonable times or at times specified by the Court. Where the access is to be 'reasonable' the advice of the Probation Officer is frequently of great assistance in reaching a working arrangement between the parties.

When the custody is dealt with in the High Court it falls within the province of the Probate, Divorce, and Admiralty Division if it is heard in conjunction with other matrimonial proceedings – but if the question is merely one of custody it comes before the Chancery Division. The interests of the child are paramount and the order which can be made is much the same as in the magistrates' court except that the size of the maintenance order is not restricted. Once such an order has been made the child may not be removed from England without the permission of the Court.

Matters concerning the children of a marriage are frequently decided by agreement between the parties, and it is often possible for them to make an arrangement which, in spite of the bitterness of matrimonial dispute, will clearly benefit the child.

Where advice can be obtained

Marriage is essentially a personal relationship and parties to it are often loth to take advice until matters have reached a hopeless stage. However, when troubles start there may often be a good chance of a reconciliation, and in such cases either the local clergyman or priest, or perhaps a doctor, may help to keep the marriage alive. There are also many Marriage Guidance Centres which will give experienced advice and will almost certainly have met very similar facts before, since broken marriages usually follow very well-worn tracks. Another very vital personality in the world of matrimonial advice is the Probation Officer, who is attached to the magistrates' courts and whose life is devoted to helping people in such difficulties. Interviews with such officers are confidential and, where reconciliation is sought by them, evidence of what is said at any interview between the Probation Officer and the party cannot be given in later proceedings unless this is agreed to by both parties. Thus in effect there is no danger of any admissions made in an effort to reach a reconciliation being later produced as evidence, against the will of either party. Often, however, legal advice is required, and in such cases a solicitor should be consulted. In selecting one it may be well to take advice from an officer of the court, a Citizens' Advice Bureau, or a person in public life. In addition to solicitors with private practices, there are legal advice centres which deal with cases at very low rates – but these are open to persons with small incomes only, such as, for example, old age pensioners, or wives who are not being maintained or have been deserted.

It has been noted that legal aid is available for all proceedings in the High Court, and this is obtained by application to the Local Committee, who consider both the means of the applicant and the nature of the case and decide whether to grant assistance. It is advisable to fill up the application form for legal aid with qualified assistance, so as to ensure that all the facts which are legally relevant are placed before the Committee for their consideration.

Where proceedings are taken in the magistrates' court no legal aid is available, but in a few cases the particular court in which the case is heard may have a fund to provide legal help to the very poor. This fund is used with the consent of the magistrate, and this is frequently given upon the advice of the Probation Officer. Husbands and wives appearing in these courts would be well advised to bear in mind the importance of the proceedings, and to obtain representation where possible if the case presents any difficulty, for the money order alone may, in the course of years, amount to several thousand pounds. It is an odd feature of our free legal aid schemes in this country that such large sums of money may be ordered to be paid in cases where often no financial assistance is given to the litigant, while in county courts, where the normal limit to the amount that can be claimed is £400, legal aid is available. Perhaps it is the fact of payment by weekly instalments which conceals the real nature of the order. Whatever the truth be, it is as well for the parties to take whatever steps they can to ensure a favourable result, because once made an order of this nature may persist till death.

SUMMARY

Looking back over this chapter it is displeasing to note how much of it is devoted to the breakdown of the marriage relationship and how little to its happier side. This is, of course, a false picture of marriage, but just as a book on medicine can make one wonder how one has survived the many diseases which are lurking just round the corner, so reading a lawyer's discourse on marriage may make it seem a perilous adventure. This is because the vast majority of normal cases are not referred to. Marriage is, of course, much more than a legal concept, since it is also a personal relationship and the natural foundation of a family. Hence, this chapter is called 'Law and the Family', and is not concerned only with a husband and wife, for the family is a group of people with closely knit interests, each dependent on the others, and any step which tends to disintegrate a marriage affects all the members vitally, and in particular the children. Thus, before any steps are taken, sincere thought should be given to them and advice taken so that nothing irrevocable is done which will be regretted later, and no innocent child is made to pay the price unnecessarily for the discords of its parents.

Any person who feels nervous of seeking advice should remember that although his own case seems very rare and important to him, it is one of many others, and those whose job it is to give advice will almost certainly have experience of other cases very much like it. This does not mean, however, that it is prudent to rush off to an adviser as soon as any difficulty appears, for every marriage has its less happy periods, and the sensible realization of this 'for better or for worse' is perhaps the greatest human safeguard of all to a happy married life.

14

Landlord and Tenant

PETER ARCHER

THE relationship of landlord and tenant exists when one person, who enjoys the exclusive right to possession of a piece of land or the whole or part of a building, grants that right for an ascertainable period in return for rent. The granting may be an oral one, or its terms may be set down in a written document. It may consist in the somewhat rambling conversation which takes place when a prospective tenant calls upon a landlord or agent. The parties are free within very wide limits to decide by agreement what the conditions of the tenancy are to be. Where there is no written agreement, any later dispute will be decided by such evidence as the recollections of the parties as to what was said, any letters exchanged, writing on rent books, lists of rules supplied to tenants, or notices exhibited on the premises.

Once in existence, a tenancy may be determined (legal phraseology for 'ended') in any of three ways. And until it is determined the tenant is entitled to possession of the premises, the landlord is entitled to his rent, and each party is bound by the agreed conditions of the tenancy. If it was granted for a definite period (e.g. ninety-nine years) it determines at the end of that period, and no notice is required. If it is a periodical tenancy, that is, a tenancy which is to continue indefinitely until either the landlord or the tenant gives notice to quit, it determines after a proper notice has been served and has expired. And if the tenancy is terminable by the landlord upon breach by the tenant of any condition of the tenancy, then upon such a breach the landlord may treat the tenancy as terminated.

A periodical tenancy may run from week to week, or year to year, or for any other period upon which the parties agree either expressly or by implication from their conduct. The importance of this is that a notice to quit, either by the landlord or the tenant, will be effective only if sufficient notice is given. Thus to terminate a tenancy from year to year or longer, at least half a year's notice must be given. Tenancies for periods of less than a year require notice of not less than the period of the tenancy. Thus a weekly tenancy requires at least a week's notice. The date from which the period is calculated is that on which the notice is served, i.e. when it actually reaches the other party. However, these rules apply only where the parties have not expressly agreed otherwise.

The notice may be either oral or in writing, but it must conform with certain rules. It must specify the day on which the tenancy is to end, and this must be the last day of a period of the tenancy (oddly enough) or the following day, in which case the notice is deemed to expire at the first moment after midnight. For example, the period of a quarterly tenancy beginning on 29 September will end on 24 December, and a notice purporting to determine the tenancy on 26 December will be invalid. Similarly, if a weekly tenancy runs from Monday to Sunday, the notice must expire on a Sunday or a Monday. However, it is immaterial that the actual date is not specified if it may be calculated from the terms of the notice, and where the correct day is in doubt it is advisable to use some general formula, e.g. 'at the end of the period of your tenancy which shall expire next after one week from the service of this notice'. Two alternative dates may be given, and the usual practice is to specify the particular date which is thought to be correct and add the general formula as an alternative. In the absence of agreement between the parties as to the date on which the period begins or ends, it is presumed, failing evidence to the contrary, that the day on which rent is normally paid is the first day of a period where rent is payable in advance (i.e. at the beginning of each period), and the last day of a period where it is payable in arrear (i.e. at the end of each period).

A landlord's notice to quit for a weekly tenancy may take some such form as the following:

To Henry Brown: I, John Smith, hereby give you notice to quit and deliver up possession of the basement flat at number 12 High Street, Barchester, in the County of Barset, which you hold of me, on the 12th day of August 1955, or at the end of the period of your tenancy which shall expire next after one week from the service of this notice.

(Signed) John Smith
Dated 3 August 1955

Although an oral notice is effective, if given in the proper form, it is usually advisable to serve notice in writing, retaining a copy. In order to prove that the other party has received the notice, he should be asked to sign a copy as a receipt, or it should be handed to him in the presence of witnesses. If neither of these methods is practicable, the notice should be sent by post and registered 'A.R.', which means that a form of receipt, signed by the recipient, is returned to the sender. Even after the termination of a tenancy, by notice to quit or otherwise, a new tenancy may be deemed to have been agreed upon if both parties continue to act as though there were a tenancy. Thus, if a landlord serves a notice to quit and after its expiry continues to accept rent, a new notice to quit may be necessary before he can lawfully regain possession. This is not so, however, where the acceptance of rent may be explained on some ground other than that the parties have agreed upon a new tenancy. So that if the tenant is protected by the Rent Acts the landlord may safely accept rent, since this may be explained on the ground that he has no option but to leave the tenant in possession until the county court has made an order for his eviction.

Liability for repairs

Having fixed the length and nature of the tenancy and the rent, the parties may proceed to agree upon any other terms. The most usual of these cover liability for repairs, and they may make such arrangements as they wish. In the absence of express agreement the general rule is that neither party may compel the other to repair, although in their common interest, they would be well advised to arrive at a reasonable compromise. To this rule there are a number of exceptions. Even where there is no express agreement the landlord is liable in certain cases.

(*a*) A landlord who retains under his own control some part ancillary to the premises, such as a common staircase in a block of flats, must not allow it to fall into such a condition that it becomes dangerous to the tenants. If he does so, he may be liable to pay damages to any tenants who are injured there.

(*b*) If in the case of a furnished letting the premises are not reasonably fit for occupation at the time when the tenancy is to begin, the tenant may refuse to take the tenancy. But, since he is not entitled to damages and there is no obligation when once the tenancy has begun, the exception offers small comfort to tenants during the present scarcity of accommodation.

(*c*) A landlord who lets a house for human habitation at a rent not exceeding £40 per year in London and £26 elsewhere must make and keep it reasonably fit for occupation. If he fails to do so, the tenant is entitled to damages. The rule is subject to certain limited exceptions. There is a similar obligation upon a farmer who lets a 'tied cottage' to an agricultural employee.

(*d*) A tenant may invite the local Public Health Authority (in practice the Public Health Inspector) to employ the powers discussed in Chapter 5. These are independent of any agreement between the landlord and the tenant, since the proceedings, if any, are brought not by the tenant but by the Health Authority. However, tenants are not always well advised to pursue this remedy. If there is a condition to that effect in the tenancy agreement, the landlord may recover from the tenant the cost of carrying out the work.

The tenant does not escape a share of implied liability.

(*a*) A tenant must not cause damage to buildings, and he must give them up at the end of the tenancy in the condition in which they were at the beginning, reasonable wear and tear excepted.

(*b*) An agricultural tenant must cultivate the land in a good and husband-like manner.

THE SCOPE OF THE RENT ACTS

The amount of rent to be charged is a matter for agreement between the parties, except that, if the tenancy is one to which the Rent Acts or the Rent Control (Furnished Dwellings) Act, 1946, apply, the rent may not be higher than that fixed by the Acts. Until the passing of the new Rents Bill, referred to below, the Rent Acts apply subject to certain exceptions, to all living accommodation the rateable value of which on 6 April 1939 (in London) or 1 April 1939 (elsewhere in England) did not exceed £100 and £75 respectively. If the premises did not exist in 1939 or had not then been assessed, the rateable value in question is the one at which they were first assessed. Subsequent re-assessments do not affect the question. The following are the exceptions:

(*a*) Where any part of the essential living accommodation is shared with the landlord the Acts do not apply. This strange rule originated with the Increase of Rent and Mortgage Interest (War Restrictions) Act, 1915, which set up the modern system of rent control (originally as a wartime measure). The Act was expressed to apply to 'a house or part of a house let as a separate dwelling', and the courts held that where accommodation was shared there was no letting 'as a separate dwelling'. Until 1949 the rule applied whether the sharing was with the landlord or with fellow-tenants, but in that year it was enacted that sharing with another tenant should not exclude the Acts. Living accommodation for this purpose includes a kitchen or a sitting-room, but does not include a bathroom, a lavatory, or a wash-house.

(*b*) Tenancies the terms of which include board, attendance, or the use of furniture are not controlled under the Rent Acts, although they are subject to a separate system of control, to be considered later. In order to prevent landlords excluding the Acts by installing a few odd pieces of furniture in the premises, it is provided that, in order to be exempted for this reason, the amount of rent which is fairly attributable to these items must form a substantial portion of the whole rent. There are no fixed

rules as to what constitutes a substantial portion, and those in
doubt should take legal advice, but a very rough-and-ready rule
is that, where the value of the furniture plus five times the
annual cost of any board or services is roughly equivalent to the
annual rent, the letting will probably be held to be furnished.

(*c*) Tenants of premises which are overcrowded or insanitary
as defined by statute are not protected against eviction, although while they remain in occupation the rent payable is
controlled in accordance with the normal rules.

(*d*) Tenancies which are rent-free or let at a rent of less than
two-thirds the rateable value of the premises are not within the
Rent Acts. Other premises to which the Rent Acts do not
apply are houses let with a substantial quantity of land on other
premises; farmhouses occupied by the farmer; public-houses;
parsonage houses; houses or flats let by local and county councils, new town development corporations, and certain housing
associations or trusts; and premises let to a limited company or
certain kinds of society. A further important exception is that
the Rent Acts do not apply to premises built after 30 August
1954. Those which are altered to such an extent that they cannot be said to be the same premises are treated for this purpose
in the same way as new premises.

The rent

Where the Rent Acts apply their effect is twofold: the landlord may not charge a rent in excess of a certain figure, known
as the 'recoverable rent', and he cannot evict the tenant, even
after the tenancy is determined, unless he can persuade the
county court that certain conditions apply. The recoverable
rent of the premises consists of two parts, known respectively
as the 'standard rent' and the 'permitted increases'. For the
majority of restricted premises the standard rent is the rent at
which the premises were let on 3 September 1939 or, if they
were not let on that date, the rent at which they were last let
previously. If at that date they had never been let, the standard
rent is that at which they were first let thereafter. But premises
which were let before 1923 may be 'subject to Old Control',
that is, they may have been rent-controlled before 1939. Their

standard rent is that at which they were let on 3 August 1914, or at which they were last let previously or first let thereafter. The tests for deciding whether premises are subject to Old Control are too complicated to be set out here, but it may be assumed that this is not the case if the rateable value on 1 April 1931 exceeded £45 in London and £35 elsewhere, or if they are registered as decontrolled on the registers which were kept by local councils between 1933 and 1939 and are still available for inspection. If they are not subject to Old Control and are within the Rent Acts, then the standard rent is normally established according to the general rule stated above.

There are certain exceptions to this rule:

(*a*) Where the premises let are part of larger premises of which a standard rent has been established, or where at the relevant date the premises were included in a single letting of larger living accommodation, whether or not the rateable value of this was within the Acts, the standard rent must be determined by 'apportionment'. This means that, upon the application of either the landlord or the tenant, the county court will decide what proportion of the standard rent applicable to the larger building (or, where this is not within the Acts, of the earliest rent paid for it) should be assigned to the premises in question.

(*b*) Where the rent of the earliest rent-controlled letting was less than the rateable value of the premises (but not less than two-thirds thereof, so as to exclude the Acts altogether) the standard rent is the rateable value at the time of letting.

(*c*) Certain premises which since 1952 have been owned by a local council or certain other public authorities, and subsequently sold to a private landlord, or which, since 1949, have been improved or reconstructed with financial assistance from the local Housing Authority (usually the local council), are subject to a standard rent fixed by the housing authority. This may be ascertained from the local council.

(*d*) Where it is not practicable to obtain the evidence necessary to apply the normal rule, the county court may fix a standard rent in accordance with that of similar premises in the neighbourhood.

(*e*) Finally, where the standard rent has been established by a letting beginning after 1 September 1939, and was not established under the provisions referred to in (*c*) above, either the landlord or the tenant may apply to the rent tribunal to fix a revised standard rent which in all the circumstances is reasonable. The standard rent may be revised in this way only once, and no further application may be entertained.

When the standard rent has been established (frequently after considerable research into the history of the premises) it remains to consider the permitted increases. These are justifiable on any of the following grounds:

(*a*) If the landlord has expended money in making improvements or structural alterations to the premises, an increase in rent is permitted. Where the premises are subject to Old Control, the rent may be increased by 6 per cent of any such expenditure incurred between 4 August 1914 and 2 July 1920, and 8 per cent of any expenditure incurred after that date. Where Old Control does not apply, the permitted increase is 8 per cent of any expenditure incurred since 2 September 1939. Landlords are thus encouraged to improve their premises, but this provision is confined to improvements and structural alterations and does not include repairs. Further, unless the tenant either agreed to the work or became tenant with notice that it had already been done, the county court may declare that the whole or any part of the work was in all the circumstances unnecessary, and the expenditure upon it does not qualify for the increase.

(*b*) Where the agreed rent is inclusive of rates (that is, where the landlord pays the rates) the rates payable at any given time in excess of the amount payable on 3 August 1914 (in the case of Old Control) and 1 September 1939 (in other cases) is a permitted increase. This is another way of saying that the landlord is entitled to the same rent, clear of rates, as he was in 1914 or 1939. If after an increase under this heading the rates are reduced, the rent must be reduced accordingly. For this purpose rates include water rates.

(*c*) In the case of Old Control only, a landlord is entitled to add to the rent 15 per cent of the 'net rent', that is, the standard rent less any sum paid out by the landlord in respect of rates. Furthermore, if he is wholly responsible for repairs, the landlord may add a further 25 per cent to the rent. Where the tenant is partly responsible for repairs, the rent may be increased by such proportion (being less than 25 per cent) as the parties agree, and, failing agreement, as decided by the county court. However, the increase is not recoverable if the county court decides that the premises are not reasonably fit for habitation or otherwise not in a reasonable state of repair. Alternatively, the tenant may ask the local Public Health Department to grant a certificate that the premises are not in a reasonable state of repair and, if the certificate is granted and served on the landlord, the increase will not be payable until the landlord convinces the Health Authority that he has remedied the state of disrepair. The landlord may, however, seek to prove in the county court that the Health Authority was wrong in granting the certificate, which will then be discharged. This is in the nature of an appeal, and the Court will not lightly overrule the health authority.

(*d*) Again only in the case of Old Control, a tenant who sublets any part of the premises may increase the rent recoverable from the sub-tenant by 10 per cent of the net rent of that part. His own landlord may increase his (the tenant's) rent by 5 per cent of the same sum; that is to say, the landlord is entitled to half the increase.

(*e*) If certain services are provided by the landlord, but not of sufficient value to exclude the Rent Acts, he may apply to the rent tribunal to authorize such increases as it considers fair. The tribunal will usually authorize an increase of the amount by which the cost of the services at the time of application exceeds their cost in 1939 or at any later date when the services were first provided. It appears that only one increase may be authorized under this heading, and that there can be no further application in respect of further increases.

(*f*) In 1954 provision was made to recompense landlords for money spent on repairs. A figure is assigned to all premises, known as the statutory repairs deduction (commonly abbreviated to the S.R.D.). This is determined by the gross annual value of the premises and may be ascertained from the local council. If, during a period of twelve months falling within the previous fourteen months, the landlord has effected repairs to a value of at least three times the S.R.D., the annual rent may be increased by twice the S.R.D. The repairs increase is not recoverable until the landlord has served upon the tenant a notice in the prescribed form showing how the increase is calculated, and a declaration that the necessary sum has been spent upon repairs and specifying the repairs. These forms are obtainable from most stationers, and since they set out all the important provisions these will not be dealt with here. The 1957 Rent Bill contains proposals for the repeal of these provisions. In any event they do not apply to Scotland, which has a separate Act.

(g) The recoverable rent is in respect of particular premises let on particular conditions. If any of the conditions are altered by agreement between the parties, so that the tenancy is less advantageous to either the landlord or the tenant, the recoverable rent must be adjusted accordingly. This is so if, for example, rates are paid by the tenant instead of the landlord, or if the landlord begins, by agreement, to supply hot water. The value of any 'transfer of burden' is decided by the county court.

Increases are also possible in certain circumstances where railway employees occupy accommodation belonging to the Transport Executive, and where tenants of certain business premises, in making improvements, increase the burden of rates payable by the landlord.

A landlord is not entitled to any permitted increase under headings (a), (b), or (c) unless he first serves a formal notice of increase in the prescribed form. This may be obtained from most stationers. It must be served upon the tenant at least four weeks before the date on which the increase is to begin or, where the increase is in respect of rates, at the same time as would be necessary in the case of a notice to quit. A notice of increase also operates as a notice to quit, so that after it has expired the landlord is entitled to possession if he has grounds for claiming possession under the Rent Acts, and no further notice to quit is necessary.

The Rent Acts limit the rent which a landlord may charge.

They do not enable him to recover more than the rent agreed between the parties. If the agreed rent is less than the standard rent, the landlord is not entitled to demand a higher rent unless he first determines the tenancy by serving a notice to quit or otherwise, and the tenant then agrees to stay on at the higher rent. A tenant whose tenancy has been determined, and who but for the Rent Acts would have no right to remain in the premises, is known as a 'statutory tenant'.

However, there would be no point in limiting rents if landlords were entitled to demand large sums as a condition of granting a tenancy at all. Consequently, the Rent Acts provide that it is illegal for a landlord to demand a premium (that is, a sum of money) as a condition of granting or renewing a tenancy. This is so even when it is disguised, for example, as an excessive price for furniture and fittings. There is an exception where the premium was paid for the grant of a tenancy of fourteen years or more before 2 June 1949. A tenant is entitled to accept a payment from the landlord as a condition of vacating the premises, and if he is not already a statutory tenant he may require payment from a prospective new tenant of the same premises.

Rent overpaid in excess of the recoverable rent, or increases in respect of which a proper notice of increase was not served before the date of payment, may be recovered from the landlord at any time within two years of the payment. They may be recovered either by legal proceedings or by deduction from the current rent. Premiums paid in contravention of the Acts may similarly be recovered or deducted from rent, and in this case there is no two-year limitation period, so that they may be recovered, like ordinary debts, at any time within six years. Further, it is a criminal offence to charge an illegal premium.

Security of tenure

A tenant of premises to which the Acts apply is secured against eviction unless the landlord satisfies the county court both that he has grounds under the Acts for claiming possession and that it would be reasonable in all the circumstances to make the order which he claims. Further, the Acts exist to protect tenants. They do not confer rights to possession which the landlord would not otherwise have. Thus, where a landlord claims possession, it is necessary to decide first whether but for the Acts he would be entitled to possession, i.e. whether the tenancy has been determined in one of the ways discussed above or whether a notice of increase of rent (which also operates as a notice to quit) has at some time been served. If this is so, it must next be asked whether the Rent Acts apply. If they do not and no other Act confers security upon the tenant, then the landlord is entitled to an order for possession. If they do apply, then it becomes relevant to decide whether the landlord can show a ground for claiming possession under the Acts.

Possession may be claimed on any of the following grounds:

(*a*) That any rent is unpaid or any obligation of the tenancy broken. The Court will not usually consider it reasonable to make an order for possession unless rent is persistently unpaid after being demanded, or the breach of obligation is deliberate or occasions great inconvenience.

(*b*) That the tenant or any person living with him is guilty of nuisance or annoyance to neighbours (not to the landlord, unless he happens to be a neighbour). There is no ready guide to the conduct which falls within this category, but a tenant whose conduct seriously inconveniences his neighbours will, if his landlord can be persuaded to bring proceedings, lose his security.

(*c*) That the tenant uses the premises in a manner which is illegal (e.g. for immoral purposes of a criminal nature) or causes or permits the premises to deteriorate (as opposed to merely becoming dirty).

(*d*) That the tenant has given the landlord notice to quit and the landlord has incurred liabilities on the expectation of having vacant possession, as, for example, if he has contracted to sell the premises with vacant possession. The tenant is not permitted to change his mind to the prejudice of the landlord.

(*e*) That the tenant has assigned or sub-let the whole of the premises without the consent of the landlord. The Acts are intended to protect tenants who require the premises for living accommodation, not to assist those whose interest is simply a business one.

(*f*) That any part of the premises is an off-licence and the tenant carries on the business in such a way as to place the licence in jeopardy.

(*g*) That the tenant holds a 'service tenancy' (i.e. that he is an employee of the landlord, who lets the premises to him in consequence of the employment) and the employment has terminated. (If, however, the employee occupies the premises not as a tenant but as a mere licensee, then the Acts do not apply at all. Normally this will be so if the employee pays no rent, but that is not conclusive, and it is better in cases of doubt to take legal advice.) Alternatively, if the County Agricultural Committee or the Minister of Agriculture grants a certificate that the premises are required for a person whose employment is necessary for an agricultural holding. In either case the landlord is entitled to possession only if he proves in addition either that he reasonably requires the premises for an employee in the full-time employment of himself or one of his tenants, or that he is to supply living accommodation as a condition of future full-time employment.

(*h*) That the landlord reasonably requires the premises for occupation by himself, his son or daughter over eighteen years of age, or one of his parents. Even so, the landlord will not be granted an order for possession if he bought the premises after 6 December 1937 (in the case of Old Control) or (otherwise) 1 December 1939, and the tenancy existed at the time of the purchase. He will not therefore be permitted to purchase and obtain possession at the expense of a sitting tenant. Nor will an order be granted where the judge is satisfied that greater hardship would be caused by granting the order than by refusing it. If the landlord obtains an order for possession under this heading or under heading (*g*) by misrepresenting the facts, he may find himself liable to pay damages to the tenant.

(*i*) That the tenant charges a sub-tenant rent in excess of the recoverable rent for the sub-tenancy. Those familiar with the parable of the Unmerciful Servant will require no explanation of this rule.

(j) That suitable alternative accommodation is available to the tenant, whether offered by the landlord himself or by someone else. The alternative accommodation need not be of the same standard as the premises of which possession is required. Whether it is reasonable depends upon all the circumstances. A part of the existing premises may, in certain circumstances, constitute suitable alternative accommodation. But the alternative accommodation will not be considered suitable unless it is itself protected by the Rent Acts. This is one ground among others for claiming possession. Contrary to general belief, it is not a necessary condition where any of the other grounds exist.

Where an order for possession is granted against a tenant, it does not operate against his lawful sub-tenant unless the sub-tenant was made a party to the proceedings and a ground was shown for claiming possession against him. He becomes tenant of the head landlord on the terms on which he held from the tenant. If he was protected by the Rent Acts against the tenant, he is equally protected against the landlord. This is so, however, only if his sub-tenancy was 'lawful', i.e. if the tenant was not forbidden by the terms of his tenancy to sub-let, or if he has not sub-let the whole of the premises without the landlord's consent. But a sub-tenancy which was originally unlawful may become lawful if the landlord, with knowledge of its existence, continues without protest to accept rent from the tenant.

A contractual tenant (that is, a tenant who has not become a statutory tenant) has an interest which (subject to any conditions of his tenancy) he may sell, part with in any other way, or leave by Will. If he dies leaving no Will, it passes to his next-of-kin unless the landlord takes steps to determine it before letters of administration are granted relating to the estate. A statutory tenant has no interest which he can sell or otherwise assign. However, on his death the statutory tenancy may pass to his widow if she is residing with him at his death or, if the tenant leaves no widow, or was herself a woman, to any member of the family who resided with the tenant for at least the six months prior to the death. Thus the death of a statutory tenant does not necessarily add to his family's problems that of being homeless. If there is only one member of the family who qualifies, no problem arises. If there are a number of claimants and they fail to agree among themselves who is to succeed to the statutory tenancy, the dispute is determined by the county court. But where all the possible claimants agree which of them is to succeed, the landlord is not entitled to object. Where a contractual tenant dies leaving a member of his family who, had he been a statutory tenant, would have succeeded to the statutory tenancy, that member is entitled to remain in occupation as statutory tenant whoever succeeds to the contractual tenancy. The rights and obligations of the new contractual tenant are thus virtually suspended. There is one important qualification to the rule. A statutory tenancy may pass in this way only once. It therefore becomes necessary to decide who was the first statutory tenant. If after his death the tenancy has passed once, it cannot pass again on the death of his successor. However, the law relating to this subject is so complicated that those who find themselves in such a position would do well to seek legal advice.

The landlord of every rent-protected tenancy must supply the tenant with a rent book containing all necessary information, and to fail so to do is a criminal offence. Printed rent books are readily available at stationers', and if the landlord exercises normal care in filling in the information required he is not likely to find himself in breach of the law. Since a clear rent book frequently serves the tenant as a reference in obtaining other accommodation, the tenant is protected against inaccurate entries. It is a criminal offence for a landlord to show as arrears of rent any sum which is irrecoverable under the Rent Acts.

Furnished lettings

Thus the tenant of unfurnished accommodation is adequately protected, although he may need to pursue complicated and expensive research in order to clarify his rights. Many landlords prefer, however, to avoid the restrictions of the

Rent Acts by letting their premises furnished. Until 1946 a tenant of furnished accommodation was protected in only two respects. Where the premises would have been rent-controlled if let unfurnished, the landlord is not entitled to a profit in excess of the profit reasonably to be expected from a similar letting in the year ending 1 September 1939, or, where they would have been subject to Old Control, to a profit of more than 25 per cent in excess of the profit reasonably to be expected from a similar letting in the year ending 3 August 1914. Where a rent has been charged which yields a profit in excess of that permitted, the tenant may within two years recover the excess in the county court. And in the case of any premises which would have been controlled if unfurnished, a landlord who charges a rent yielding a profit which in all the circumstances is extortionate is guilty of an offence for which he may be fined in the magistrates' court, and the magistrates may order any excess paid within the preceding two years to be repaid.

But it is not easy for tenants to provide the evidence necessary to prove that these provisions have been contravened, and in any event they do not protect them against eviction by the landlord. In 1946, however, Parliament set up a system of rent tribunals, the powers of which were originally connected only with furnished tenancies, but which have since acquired the additional powers mentioned above. Any tenancy including furniture or services may be referred to the rent tribunal by either the landlord or the tenant, or indeed by the local council. This is so even though the premises are not substantially furnished (so that the tenancy may be within the Rent Acts) and although living accommodation is shared with the landlord. The tribunal will give each party an opportunity of making a statement, and normally it will inspect the premises. It will then decide the reasonable rent for the tenancy. It may reduce the rent or leave it unchanged, but it may increase it only if the landlord provides services the cost of which has increased since 3 September 1939, and then by not more than the amount of such increase. When the rent has been decided it is entered in a register kept by the local council, and the landlord may not afterwards charge a rent in excess of the registered rent. To do

Landlord and Tenant

so is a criminal offence, and the tenant may recover the excess. The registration does not operate retrospectively, so that the tenant cannot recover any rent which he has paid before the decision of the tribunal.

If the premises are subsequently re-let on different conditions (e.g. if they are refurnished differently) the tenant, or any subsequent tenant, or the landlord, may ask the tribunal to reconsider the rent. And upon reconsideration the tribunal may increase or reduce the registered rent or leave it unchanged. The registration is only in respect of the particular premises considered, so that if they or any part of them are let along with other premises the registration does not apply. There are provisions forbidding premiums, as in the case of unfurnished lettings.

Where a tenant or the council refers a tenancy to the tribunal, any notice to quit served by the landlord after the reference has been made does not operate to determine the tenancy until three months after the tribunal has given its decision, unless the tribunal directs that a shorter period be substituted for the three months. The tenant is thus given a limited security of tenure. Further, if any notice has been served or is served afterwards, the tenant may apply for an extension of his security, and the tribunal may continue to extend it for periods of up to three months at a time.

However, this right is subject to certain qualifications. If upon any application the landlord convinces the tribunal that in all the circumstances the tenant ought not to be given security (or further security) it may be refused; and if, upon the original reference, the tribunal directs that a shorter period be substituted for the three months, no further security may be granted at the expiry of the shorter period. Again, security may be given only against a notice to quit. If the tenancy is determined in some other way (as for breach of covenant or, in the case of a tenancy for a fixed period, by the expiry of the period) there is no security. Finally, if the landlord serves a valid notice to quit before the tenancy is referred to the tribunal and does not then accept rent or otherwise recognize a new tenancy, the notice will expire in the usual way and the tenant has no security. However, if a reference is made after the service of a notice but before it has expired, then, although the tenant has no security, the tribunal is entitled to fix a reasonable rent, which will be registered and bind the premises for the future.

The Rent Bill, 1957

There is now before Parliament a Bill which, if it becomes law in its present form, will exercise a considerable effect upon the law relating to landlord and tenant, and therefore upon the social and economic life of the country.

It is proposed to restrict in three ways the property to which the Rent Acts apply. First, the Bill seeks to decontrol all property the rateable value of which on 7 November 1956 was in excess of £40 (in London and Scotland) or £30 (elsewhere). For the majority of such property, there will be no legal restriction upon the rent chargeable or the landlord's right to terminate the tenancy and recover possession. But tenants of controlled property at the time when the Bill takes effect are not to be evicted without fifteen months' notice, nor may their rents be increased except upon similar notice. Secondly, no tenancies beginning after the Bill is passed will be subject to the Rent Acts. Finally furnished tenancies will be controlled only if their rateable value is such that they would have continued to be within the Rent Acts if unfurnished.

The rents of tenancies which remain controlled will be calculated in a different manner. The basic rent will be calculated by multiplying the gross annual value by two where the tenant is not responsible for repairs, by $\frac{4}{3}$ where the tenant is so responsible, or by a proportion between these figures where the responsibility is shared. Further, if the landlord is responsible for internal decorations, the proportion will be $\frac{7}{4}$. To this basic rent sums will be added in respect of any services or furniture supplied by the landlord, any rates paid by him, and 8 per cent per year of the cost of any necessary improvements which he executes. The first 7s 6d of the increase will be payable only after three months' notice, and the remainder after nine months' notice in the proper form, and it will not be recoverable while any work requires to be done under a certificate of disrepair.

Where a tenant is protected against eviction, either by the Rent Acts or under the provisions applying to furnished lettings, the landlord may not take any steps to interfere physically with his enjoyment of the premises. If he does so, the tenant may ask the Court (usually the county court) for damages and for an order known as an injunction, forbidding the landlord on pain of imprisonment to interfere further. In other cases, where the tenancy has been determined and there is no question of security, the landlord may lock the door of the premises against the tenant, or may enter while he is out and place his belongings outside, provided that he does not damage them unnecessarily. But he may not enter by force while the tenant is in possession. The police will not intervene except to prevent a breach of the peace, but it is usually safer to bring legal proceedings for possession.

All the provisions discussed in this chapter apply only to a tenancy. It is possible for an occupier of property to grant to another a right to reside there without creating a tenancy. A person who sleeps on the premises but does not have the exclusive use of a particular room or rooms may not be a tenant at all, but a lodger, and, in any event, if the parties intended that the occupier should retain complete possession and control of the premises subject only to the right of the other party to stay there, the relationship will be that, not of landlord and tenant, but of licensor and licensee, and a licensee will not be protected in any of the ways set out above. But the parties cannot exclude a tenancy merely by saying so, and if they have in fact created one it does not matter what they have called it.

It has been possible here to refer only to the provisions which apply most frequently, but there are others relating particularly to leases for more than twenty-one years and to business and agricultural premises. Either a landlord or a tenant who is in need of advice will normally find a sympathetic and helpful clerk at the rent tribunal, the town hall or council offices, or the county court. And the landlord or tenant who feels that everyone is against him and that the authorities are unhelpful is usually (though not always) the party who has been unreasonable in his demands.

15

Men at Work

JOHN PAYNE

INTRODUCTION

IN the mid-twentieth century, when the combined effect of social legislation, the strong bargaining power of organized labour
and full employment has earned the British worker a reasonable standard of living, we tend to take for granted the hard-
won safeguards for his industrial well-being which have been
created by legislative and trade union activity. The earliest
statutory incursions into industrial relations were not designed
to further the interests of the worker. As the ravages of the
Black Death in 1349 had created an acute labour shortage, Parliament passed the Ordinance of Labourers and, in 1351, the
Statute of Labourers, which empowered justices of the peace
to assess the wages of workers in husbandry and certain other
occupations at rates in force before the Black Death. In the sixteenth century, State intervention in the regulation of wages
and conditions of employment was extended. The great industrial changes of the eighteenth century increased the com-
plexity and tempo of the economic life of the country. As large
numbers of men, women, and children crowded into the 'dark
satanic mills' to work new mechanical processes and to produce
a greater variety of goods, wage regulation by justices fell into
disuse. The concentration of workers in mill, factory, and mine
produced many industrial problems: what was a worker to be
paid; what hours was he to work; to what extent should his
health and safety be protected by State action from those new
mechanical monsters which the Luddites hated and feared? In
this chapter we shall examine the measures which have been
taken to deal with these problems.

Among the topics we shall consider will be the safeguards of

225

the British worker's working conditions, his pay packet, his rights of association with his fellows to protect his economic interests, and the machinery for settling his disputes with his employer. We shall also refer to the provisions which have been made to restore to working life the unfortunate worker temporarily removed from it by accident or disease.

CONDITIONS AT WORK

The whole pattern of working life was completely changed by the textile mills, the foundries and factories whose smoking chimneys began to blacken our Midland and Northern landscapes at the opening of the nineteenth century. The factories which needed more and more 'hands' found a large reservoir of cheap labour in the 'pauper apprentices', thereby relieving parishes of the burden on their rates. Manpower was also provided by those thousands who, deprived of their 'acre and cow' by the growing enclosure movement, were driven from the countryside into the grim crowded towns. It was recognized that these new mill-workers should not be the completely unprotected hostages of the Industrial Revolution. Thus we find that the first milestone of our factory legislation, the Factories Act, 1802, was designed for 'the health and morals of apprentices and others'. It applied to cotton and woollen mills and factories which employed three or more apprentices and twenty or more other persons. The Act provided that the walls of such factories should be limewashed twice a year and that the buildings should be reasonably ventilated. The apprentices' hours of work were regulated; they were to be given clothing and religious instruction or rudimentary education. To ensure compliance with the obligations under the Act, visitors appointed by the local justices of the peace were empowered to inspect the mills and factories.

Industry expanded at such a pace in the next thirty years that more detailed factory legislation became necessary. Under the Factories Act, 1833, four paid Government inspectors were appointed to inspect factories employing children and young persons and to make regulations for implementing the provisions of the Act. The hours of work of children and young persons in certain industries were to be limited and children under the age of eleven were not to be employed unless a surgeon certified that they were fit to be so. Thanks to the enthusiasm of such reformers as Lord Shaftesbury, parliamentary intervention in the industrial field expanded. In the hey-day of *laissez-faire* the Welfare State was being created. The Factories Act, 1844, for the first time provided for the guarding of moving machinery; accidents causing injury to workers were to be notified to the factory inspectors; inspectors could take steps to obtain compensation for injured workers. Successive Acts extended the scope of factory legislation to a wide range of industries and introduced more stringent measures to protect the health and safety of workers.

The present-day protection of the factory worker's conditions is contained in the Factories Acts, 1937 and 1948. More detailed provisions to meet the varied requirements of specific industries are embodied in regulations made under these Acts from time to time by the Minister of Labour and National Service, who in 1946 took over this function from the Secretary of State. For instance, provision for the safety of workers on building sites is made in regulations for the building trade. In the compass of this short chapter it is, of course, only possible to refer to the general principles laid down in the Acts. The principal Act is the Factories Act, 1937, which modifies and amends previous legislation. A 'factory' is broadly defined by section 151 as 'any premises in which, or within the close or curtilage or precincts of which, persons are employed in manual labour in any process for or incidental to the following purposes, namely: (*a*) the making of any article or part of any article; (*b*) the altering, repairing, ornamenting, finishing, cleaning, or washing, or the breaking up or demolition of any article; or (*c*) the adapting for sale of any article; being premises etc. in which the work is carried on by way of trade or for purposes of gain and to or over which the employer of the personnel employed therein has the right of access or control.' It was realized that this definition was not comprehensive, so Parliament, in order to include some industrial undertakings which might otherwise be exempt, specified that certain premises employing manual labour should be deemed to be a 'factory'. They include, *inter alia*, shipyards and dry docks in which ships are constructed, repaired, or broken up; premises in which articles are sorted as a preliminary to the work carried on in any factory, or in which bottles or containers or packing articles are washed or filled, or in which yarn or cloth is made up or packed. The Act covers the premises of a transport, industrial, or commercial undertaking in which is undertaken the construction, reconstruction, or repair of locomotives, vehicles, or other plant used for transport purposes or as ancillary to such undertaking; it does not, however, apply to premises where only cleaning or running repairs are carried out. Among the types of premises covered by the Act are those used for the purpose of printing and bookbinding for gain, the storage of gas in a gasholder having a storage capacity of not less than 5,000 cubic feet, and for making and mending nets incidental to the fishing industry. It is necessary to determine whether premises in which a worker is engaged are a factory in order to ascertain whether any injury sustained at work is due to his employer's failure to comply with any provision of the Act. If the premises are not covered by the Act, the worker's remedies will be governed only by general Common Law principles relating to negligence.

Parliament has enacted that the attention of factory workers should be drawn to the existence of the Act designed for their protection. As it would be obviously impracticable and useless to erect notices containing the text of a complex Act with 160 sections and four schedules, section 114 of the 1937 Act compels the posting at the principal entrances of factories of an abstract of the Act, notices of the address of the factory inspector for the district and of the name and address of the examining surgeon for the factory, and every notice and document required by the Act to be posted in the factory. The inspector may order these notices to be posted in parts of the factory other than the entrances. The notices must be posted so that they can be conveniently read by employees.

We will now briefly refer to some of the principal provisions of the Acts. Parts i to iv set out provisions for the health, safety, and welfare of workers; Part v, the notification of accidents; Part vi, the employment of women and young persons; and the remaining eight parts deal with administration and enforcement and miscellaneous matters. It has been recognized that the nature of certain industrial processes makes it impossible for factory occupiers strictly to comply with some of the requirements of the Act. The Minister is empowered to grant exceptions from such requirements where he is satisfied that the circumstances warrant it. The reader should refer to the Acts, the regulations made thereunder, and the standard textbooks for details.

The Act lays down in general principle certain minimum standards to protect the health of workers. Factories must not be so overcrowded as to risk injury to health. A reasonable temperature in workrooms must be maintained, but not in such a manner as to be offensive or injurious to employees; in workshops where the employees are seated or where work does not involve serious physical effort, a temperature of at least 60° after the first hour whilst work is going on must be maintained to satisfy the requirements of the Act. In order that workers may be satisfied that the temperature is adequate, at least one thermometer must be readily available in each workroom. The Minister of Labour has power to make regulations for the adequate ventilation, and for standards of sufficient and suitable lighting, of factories. Sufficient sanitary conveniences with proper separate accommodation must be available for persons of each sex.

The Factories Act, 1948, has empowered the Minister to make regulations or orders for the medical supervision of factories where it appears that there may be risk of injury to the health of employees from any substance or material to be used or handled there.

The complexities of modern industrial processes and the operation of complicated and dangerous machinery have increased the risk of accidents at work. The Act imposes in general terms an obligation on factory owners to provide adequate safeguards. Not only does dangerous machinery have to be adequately fenced, but vessels containing certain fluids must as far as practicable be securely fenced or covered, or such precautions taken as to prevent workers from falling into them. As young persons are unlikely to have the same degree of skill or prudence as older workers, the Act insists that they should have proper training and supervision when working at dangerous machinery. The worker must have safe access to his work and his employer has an overall duty to make the place of work safe. The Act contains more specific provisions for factories where steam boilers, noxious fumes, and inflammable substances are used in the course of work. The local authority has power to approve and inspect fire-escape facilities in certain cases.

The Act prescribes certain conditions for the welfare of factory workers, who must be supplied with adequate drinking water, washing facilities, and accommodation for clothing not being used in working hours. Female workers must be provided with seating accommodation where their work makes this possible. At least one first-aid box should be provided for each 150 workers. There are numerous detailed provisions relating to the conditions and hours of employment of women and young persons.

Accidents occurring in factories have to be recorded by employers and notified to Government inspectors. These inspectors have power to inspect factories and to take legal proceedings for any breach of the Factories Acts or regulations.

There are statutory provisions regulating safety in mines and conditions in shops. Unfortunately, despite the long and intensive campaign of the Clerical and Administrative Workers' Union, successive Governments have not been persuaded to introduce similar legislation to ensure decent working conditions for the millions of office workers.

THE WAGE PACKET

Wages and salaries form part of workers' contracts of employment with their employers. In industries and undertakings employing large numbers of workers these are usually determined by collective bargaining between associations of employers and trade unions. Wage agreements which are reached by voluntary negotiations have no legal sanction, but depend on the good faith of both parties. Agreements for the wages and working conditions in many industries are made by Joint Industrial Councils consisting of employers' and workers' representatives. Some large industries have worked out their own systems of collective bargaining. For instance, the wages of workers in a large section of the engineering industry are determined by negotiations between the Engineering Employers' Federation and the Confederation of Engineering and Shipbuilding Unions. The rates of pay in the printing and building industries are regulated by complex voluntary wage-negotiating machinery. Wage-negotiating machinery in road haulage and agriculture has been set up by statute.

In certain industries where there is no wage-negotiating machinery the Minister of Labour has power to set up Wages Councils. Workers in industries for which Wages Council Orders have been made are entitled to be paid the wages laid down by such a council even if they have agreed to work for smaller amounts. Wage rates recommended by a Wages Council and confirmed in a Wages Council Order made by the Minister are incorporated into the contracts of service of workers in the industry affected. Employers who neglect to comply with such an order are liable to a penalty. Workers may ascertain from their trade union or the Ministry of Labour whether a Wages Council exists in their industry.

Wage-regulation machinery has been set up by statute in certain industries. For instance, under the Catering Wages Act, 1943, a Catering Wages Commission can inquire into the wages and working conditions of sections of workers in the catering industry and, if satisfied that no adequate wage-negotiating machinery exists, can recommend the establishment of a Catering Wages Board. Such boards, which consist of employers' and workers' representatives, can make recommendations as to remuneration. When such recommendations have been confirmed by a Ministerial order, they constitute the statutory minimum conditions of pay for the class of workers to which they relate and supersede any less favourable rates payable under existing contracts of service. Employers in paying the statutory minimum are not allowed to take into account tips which employees may receive in the course of their duties.

Collective bargaining is often criticized on the ground that it reduces the more highly-skilled worker to the level of his less conscientious or able workmates. In practice, however, the system ensures that everyone shall be paid a decent living wage, without prejudice to the right of an employer to reward his more competent employees on a scale above the recognized minimum rate.

Before the war most manual workers were not paid during holidays. The Holidays With Pay Act, 1938, for the first time ensured that workers in industries covered by Trade Boards received holiday pay. Trade Boards were superseded in 1945 by Wages Councils. In industries covered by Wages Councils the minimum length of holidays and payment during them have statutory force. Some industries such as building and civil engineering, have set up their own voluntary holidays-with-pay schemes.

Even in the days before the size of workers' pay packets was determined by collective bargaining or statutory wage regulation, Parliament took steps to safeguard their contents. In the early nineteenth century unscrupulous mine and mill owners would compel their workers to purchase goods from their own shops at an inflated price, which would be deducted from their wages. The Truck Act, 1831, made such deductions illegal. The Act does not apply to domestic servants, but to any 'person being a labourer, servant in husbandry, journeyman, artificer, handicraftsman, miner, or otherwise engaged in manual labour.' A workman is entitled to be paid in the current coin of the realm and can recover from his employer the amount of any illegal deduction. It is not, however, unlawful for an employer to supply his workmen with goods or services provided he does so for a reasonable amount. For instance, he may provide meals at an agreed sum, which must not be deducted. It is lawful for him to pay the worker £8 per week and in addition to supply him with meals which are reckoned at, say, 10s per week. This secures the worker's liberty of action to deal with his wages to his own satisfaction. Employers cannot arbitrarily deduct fines from wages. If it is customary to impose fines for breakages or indiscipline, the employer's right to do so must be incorporated in the worker's contract of service, or a notice of the existence of such a right prominently displayed in the place of work.

There are many qualifications of the prohibition of deductions from workers' wages, too numerous and varied to enumerate here. It should, however, be remembered that employers have a statutory obligation to deduct income tax and National Insurance contributions.

TRAINING AND REHABILITATION IN INDUSTRY

As man-power is a precious national asset, Governmental action has been taken to find employment for the disabled, who might otherwise fret away in enforced idleness. Under the Disabled Persons (Employment) Act, 1944, the Minister of Labour is required to keep a register of persons disabled by injury, deformity, or disease to such an extent as seriously to reduce their chances of earning a livelihood. The Ministry may also provide or contribute towards the cost of vocational courses for the industrial rehabilitation of industrial workers. To obtain registration as a disabled person, a person must be so substantially physically handicapped that he is unlikely for a period of at least six months to be able to obtain or to keep a job. Employers of twenty or more persons are obliged to offer jobs to a specified quota of the disabled. And the Government has formed a company called Remploy Ltd which has factories employing disabled workers.

The Ministry of Labour can also provide training schemes for workers who cannot find employment in their normal calling. To facilitate the mobility of labour, the Ministry also has power under the Employment and Training Act, 1948, to assist by grants or loans persons obliged to move in order to obtain employment.

The special problems of young workers under the age of eighteen are dealt with by the Youth Employment Service. Many Local Education Authorities employ youth employment officers to advise school-leavers on the choice of jobs.

INDUSTRIAL DISPUTES

It was a logical development of the establishment of machinery for collective bargaining in many industries and undertakings that provision should be made for reference of disputes to an arbitrator acceptable to both sides. Among the industries which have voluntary arbitration machinery are coal-mining, railways, building, textiles, iron and steel, boots and shoes, tailoring and furnishing. Arbitration is usually undertaken by a small committee consisting of representatives of the workers and employers. In the railway industry, for instance, disputes can by consent of both parties be referred to the Railway Staff National Tribunal, which consists of a chairman, appointed by agreement or by the Minister of Labour, and two other members, one selected by the British Transport Commission and the other by the railway trade unions. Arbitration is not confined to industry, as the pay, hours of work, and annual leave of non-industrial civil servants may be decided by reference to the Civil Service Arbitration Tribunal. Provision for the settlement of disputes by joint consultation in the publicly-owned industries has been written into the legislation nationalizing them.

Since 1896 the Government has taken an increasingly active part in industrial peacemaking. The Industrial Relations Department of the Ministry of Labour has been set up to assist and advise on the setting up of voluntary conciliation machinery and joint consultation in industry. Its conciliation officers are available for consultation and assistance in the event of the breakdown of voluntary arbitration. The Minister of Labour and National Service may intervene in industrial disputes by conciliation, arbitration, or the appointment of a court of inquiry or a committee of investigation.

(a) *Conciliation*

The Minister will not normally intervene unless he is satisfied that no voluntary conciliation machinery exists or that it has broken down. Under section 2 (1) (*b*) of the Conciliation Act, 1896, he has discretion to take such steps as may seem expedient to induce the parties in dispute to meet under the chairmanship of an independent person, in an effort to resolve their differences. After consideration of all the circumstances, including the adequacy of an existing means of conciliation, he may at the request of either party 'appoint a person or persons to act as a conciliator or as a board of conciliation'. The Industrial Courts Act, 1919, also empowers him to take any such steps as seem to him expedient to promote a settlement of a trade dispute reported to him by or on behalf of one or other of the parties. The Act defines a trade dispute as 'any dispute or difference between employers and workmen, or between workmen and workmen, connected with the employment or non-employment, or the terms of the employment, or with the conditions of labour, of any person.'

(b) *Arbitration*

The Conciliation Act, 1896, and Industrial Courts Act, 1919, provide for the reference, with the consent of both parties, of a dispute to arbitration. Although the arbitration award under either of these Acts is not legally binding on the parties concerned, in practice it is usually accepted. When accepted, its terms are incorporated in the contracts of employment of the workers covered by the award.

The Minister of Labour may refer cases for arbitration to either the Industrial Court, one or more persons appointed by him, or to a Board of Arbitration.

(i) *Industrial Court*. The Industrial Court was set up by the Industrial Courts Act, 1919, as a permanent and independent tribunal. As it is not a court of law its decisions are not binding as are the judgements of Her Majesty's judges. If, however, one of its awards has been accepted and acted upon by the parties concerned, it forms a term or condition of the contract of employment. The members of the Court, which may sit in two or more divisions, are appointed by the Minister of Labour. The Court consists of an independent chairman and two other members, one each from panels representing employers and workpeople. If the Court cannot agree on an award, the Act provides that the Chairman, acting with the full powers of an umpire, may decide the issue. Some Acts of Parliament, setting up machinery for regulating wages, provide that disputes which cannot be resolved otherwise should be referred to the Court (e.g. the Bacon Industry Act, 1938, and the Cinematograph Films Acts, 1938 and 1948). Other matters, such as the hours of duty of drivers of certain vehicles, differences about the conditions of persons employed under the National Health Service Acts, and the modification of pre-war trade practices, are specified by various statutes for reference to the Court in the event of dispute. In addition, some agreements between trade unions and employers provide for the reference of disputes to the Court and for the acceptance by both parties of its findings.

(ii) *Single arbitrators.* The Minister may refer disputes to a single arbitrator. He may be assisted by assessors, who do not, however, take part in framing the award.

(iii) *Boards of Arbitrators.* Disputes may, with the consent of both parties, be referred by the Minister to *ad hoc* arbitration boards. Their composition follows the usual tripartite pattern.

(c) Courts of Inquiry

Under Part II of the Industrial Courts Act, the Minister of Labour is empowered to inquire into a trade dispute whether reported to him or not. He may appoint a Court of Inquiry to report its findings to him. In practice he would do so only if attempts at conciliation had failed. The consent of the parties to the appointment of the Court is not required. Although the Court is not appointed to act as conciliator or to make an arbitration award, it may make recommendations for a settlement.

Neither party is, however, obliged to accept any such recommendations. The Act requires that any report of a Court of Inquiry shall be laid before both Houses of Parliament. Examples of such reports are inquiries into disputes arising out of the alleged refusal of D. C. Thomson & Co. Ltd to recognize trade unions and to employ their members, the pay claims of the railway unions in 1955, and the decision of certain printing trade unions to 'work to rule' in 1956.

Compulsory arbitration

All the methods of arbitration and conciliation previously referred to are purely voluntary. The State has, however, provided for compulsory arbitration. In order to prevent any stoppages of work due to industrial disputes, the Conditions of Employment and National Arbitration Order, 1940 (Order 1305), made strikes and lock-outs illegal and provided for compulsory arbitration. In 1951, the right to strike was restored, but new compulsory arbitration machinery was set up by the Industrial Disputes Order. Industrial disputes may be referred by the Minister to the Industrial Disputes Tribunal, whose members are drawn from a panel of independent members appointed by the Minister and from panels of employers' and workers' representatives, who are also appointed by the Minister after consultation with the British Employers' Confederation and the Trade Union Congress respectively.

A 'dispute' under the Industrial Disputes Order, 1951, means 'a dispute between an employer and workmen in the employment of that employer connected with the terms of employment or with the conditions of labour of any of those workmen.' Unlike its predecessor under Order 1305, the Tribunal has no jurisdiction to consider such matters as the employment or non-employment of workers, or the claim of a trade union to the right to represent workers in a particular industry. The existence of a trade dispute may be reported to the Minister on behalf of one of the parties by (*a*) an employers' organization representing employers involved in the dispute, or (*b*) an individual employer in dispute with his employees, or (*c*) a trade union representing a substantial proportion of the workers involved in the dispute. Reports must be in writing and contain such particulars as the Minister may require. The Minister must in the first instance satisfy himself that any existing voluntary arbitration or conciliation machinery has been resorted to and failed. If the dispute has already been settled by joint negotiating machinery or an award under the Conciliation Act or Industrial Courts Act, it cannot be dealt with under the Industrial Disputes Order. If he is satisfied that all available means of conciliation and arbitration have failed, the Minister must within fourteen days of the dispute being reported to him refer it to the Industrial Disputes Tribunal. Should the Minister consider that either party to the dispute is applying coercion by a strike or lock-out, he may delay the reference to the Tribunal or, if already referred, may request the Tribunal to stay its proceedings until the strike or lock-out ends. The terms of award of the Tribunal are incorporated in the contracts of employment of the workers affected by it, and can only be varied by subsequent agreement between the parties or a fresh award.

TRADE UNIONS

The right of workers to combine to improve their working conditions has been won by trade union pioneers in the face of considerable opposition. The Combination Acts of the early nineteenth century considerably inhibited the activities of trade unions, and it was not until 1875 that they acquired a legal status which gave them any real freedom to take effective action on behalf of their members. To-day, industry has expanded to such an extent, and its wage structure is so complex, that it is inevitable that the wages and working conditions of the majority of workers should be determined by collective bargaining between employers' associations and trade unions. As the wages bill forms a substantial item in the cost of production, the activities of trade unions play a significant part in the life of the nation.

The Trade Union Act, 1913, defines a trade union as 'any

combination, whether temporary or permanent', whose principal objects are 'the regulation of the relations between workmen and masters, or between workmen and workmen, or between masters and masters, or the imposing of restrictive conditions on the conduct of any trade or business, and also the provision of benefits to members'. Although, according to statutory definition, employers' associations are trade unions, we are here concerned only with workers' organizations. Trade unions differ greatly in their structure. Those known as industrial unions organize into membership workers of all categories in a particular industry (e.g. the National Union of Mineworkers and the National Union of Railwaymen). Many of the older unions confine their membership to workers in a particular craft. Two of the largest unions, the Transport and General Workers' Union and the National Union of General and Municipal Workers, recruit workers in many occupations engaged in a wide range of industries. There are also federations of unions in certain industries which exist to discuss matters of common interest or even to promote joint wage negotiations for all the workers in those industries. The largest of these is the Confederation of Engineering and Shipbuilding Unions, which conducts negotiation on behalf of thirty-nine affiliated unions having members in the engineering and shipbuilding industries. Similar federations exist in the building and printing trades.

In law there are two types of trade unions: those which are registered with the Registrar of Friendly Societies under the Trade Union Acts and those which are unregistered. As all unions of any importance are registered, we will confine our remarks to such bodies. The advantage of registration is that the union can sue in its registered name and can own property which is vested in trustees. In order to be registered a union has to satisfy the Registrar of Friendly Societies that its principal objects are the statutory objects referred to at the beginning of the preceding paragraph.

Membership of a trade union is in effect a contract between all its members, whose rights and liabilities towards each other are defined by its rules. The rules must set out the objects of the union, the purposes for which its funds may be used, and the conditions on which members may claim benefits. Any action of the union which is not authorized by the rules may be challenged in the courts by any aggrieved member. The rules must clearly state the procedure to be adopted for their own alteration, amendment, or rescission.

A member may not be fined or expelled from the union unless this is permitted by the rules. A wrongly expelled member may obtain in the courts a declaration that his expulsion was illegal, an injunction to restrain the union from excluding him from membership, and an award of damages caused by his expulsion. The importance of these legal remedies lies in the fact that in industries where the 'closed shop' principle applies, the withdrawal of a union card means the loss of employment.

A trade union may apply its funds to any purpose it wishes, provided that such purpose is not contrary to its rules. It may not, however, use its general funds for political purposes. Like other influential pressure groups, trade unions further their social and economic interests through political action. This usually takes the form of financial support for candidates at parliamentary and municipal elections and contributions to the funds of political parties. This can only be done, however, out of the union's political fund, whose establishment must be authorized by a resolution passed on a ballot of a majority of the members voting. Rules providing for the setting up and administration of a political fund must be approved by the Registrar of Friendly Societies. Trade contributions and 'political levies' must be kept distinct. A member who does not wish to pay a political levy may 'contract out' of doing so and merely pay his trade contribution.

A registered trade union may sue and be sued in its own name on its contracts. Although it can sue for damages for tort (an actionable wrong other than breach of contract or trust) it cannot be sued (Trade Union Act, 1906). But for this statutory protection, trade unions and their officials who call their members out on strike might be sued for damages for inducing breaches of contracts of employment.

Trade unions provide a wide range of benefits for their members. In addition to negotiating wages and conditions of employment, some of the wealthier unions have sickness and unemployment benefit sections which supplement the State insurance scheme. Many of them have educational schemes which enable their members to attend classes, week-end and summer schools organized by the Workers' Educational Association and the National Council of Labour Colleges. The T.U.C. has set up training courses at Clapham in trade union and production topics for the benefit of active rank-and-file trade unionists. Most unions assist their members in legal proceedings concerned with their employment.

CONCLUSION

In this short chapter it has only been possible to refer briefly to the matters which affect the citizen in his working life. Although there is great scope for improvement, it will be seen that much has already been done to protect the health, safety, working conditions, and wage standards of the British worker. Both sides of industry have by their own efforts and with Government assistance evolved methods of settling their disputes with a minimum of inconvenience to the general public. But social legislation and arbitration machinery, important as they are, are insufficient without goodwill and tolerance. The intervention of the Welfare State in industrial life is no substitute for common sense and mutual understanding.

16

Property and Town Planning

J. E. SIDDALL

THIS chapter will be devoted to some of the relations between local authorities and the individual as the occupier or owner of property, apart from the general law relating to public health and local Acts and Regulations, and it should be borne in mind that local legislation may in some areas be quite extensive, not always merely supplementing, but in some cases even amending the general law. It would also be not inappropriate to point out that in addition to what has been shown in a previous chapter, that all public health matters are not necessarily found under the Public Health Acts, similarly, the Public Health Acts cover many matters which are not ordinarily regarded as health, whereas they do affect the public, for example highways, wires across streets, cellars under streets. Only if the word 'health' is understood as 'weal' does the position become apparent.

CONDITION AND REPAIR OF PROPERTY

Affecting the citizen from many aspects are the Housing Acts, which for some part of their course, in so far as they may affect repairs to dwelling-houses, run concurrently with the Public Health Acts, but they go much further and their scope is wider. Section 2 of the Housing Act, 1936, prescribes the liability of the lessor of the small house to his tenant, a liability which, if the breach of his obligation has been made known to him, may affect him in damages. Following upon this personal liability of the landlord to the tenant is the borough or district council's duty to inspect the houses in the borough or district with a view to ascertaining whether any of them is unfit for human habitation. From that inspection flow the duties of the council which may result in a house, or even an area of houses, being repaired or even demolished.

A report is normally prepared by the Medical Officer of Health or the Health Inspector and is considered by the council. If the council is satisfied upon such a report that any house is in any respect unfit for human habitation it shall serve on the person having control of the house a notice to execute various works specified in that notice. If, however, the local authority considers on the report from its official that the house is not capable of being repaired at a reasonable expense, it must then go on to make a demolition order. As to what constitutes reasonable expense there must be considered the cost of the repairs and the value which it is estimated that the house will have when the works are completed, and in this connexion the value of the house when completed must be read in the light of the fact that it will continue to be let and at a controlled rent. From any decision of the local authority on this point the owner has a right of appeal to the county court, where the judge may vary the local authority's decision and may even substitute a decision that the house cannot be rendered fit at reasonable expense. If no appeal is forthcoming, then the landlord will either do the work or the local authority will serve a further notice to enter, doing the work itself and recovering from him the cost, about which there are further rights of appeal.

On the other hand, it may well be that the local authority has come to the conclusion that it would be unreasonable to demand a repair, and in these circumstances, after giving an opportunity for the owner to be heard, may proceed to make a demolition order, that is to say an order that within a certain specified time the property shall be vacated and demolished. One of the effects of the Rent Restriction Acts to-day, as opposed to twenty years ago, is that owners are more likely now to request demolition orders in lieu of repair notices, for much property has become, or is in process of becoming, unremunerative, particularly with the increasing cost of building repairs. It might be, however, that the property which had become unsatisfactory as a dwelling, comprises one of a block, or

represents merely certain rooms in a house which is otherwise
satisfactory, and in this case the local authority in lieu of making a demolition order may make a closing order. Again, an
owner attending before the local authority may have his
undertaking not to relet the premises as a house accepted, and
subject to conforming with the Town Plan these may be of use
to him for storage or other purposes. It may be, however, that
it is not an individual isolated house which is unfit, but that
there is a whole area of them, and in this case the local authority
may by order define these houses as a clearance area. In considering a clearance area, not only the individual defects of the
houses are taken into account, but also the narrowness or bad
arrangements of the streets. When such an order has been
made it is the subject of a public inquiry by the Minister of
Housing and Local Government, at which any person interested can be heard. Not merely has the Minister full power to
amend the order in the area affected, or indeed to refuse to
confirm it altogether, but he may also authorize the paying of
compensation, not only for certain owner-occupiers under the
Slum Clearance (Compensation) Act, 1956, but also under
section 42 of the Housing Act, 1936, where the property has
been well maintained. The Council must also undertake to
house the various occupiers of the property concerned and
must subsequently secure that the vacated houses are demolished. Instead of securing demolition by the owners, the local
authority may proceed (in addition to making the clearance
order) to make a compulsory purchase order of the land
comprised in the clearance area, and when they do this they
may at the same time purchase any land surrounded by the
clearance area, or adjoining it, so as to make the area affected
of a convenient shape for redevelopment. In view of restrictions now imposed by planning and the growth of one town
into another in so many areas to form the huge urban masses
known as 'conurbations', there is often little room for new
building unless every economy is taken with existing clearance
areas so that they may be utilized for the future. When they
are to be developed, the local authority purchases at site value
(except where the 1956 Act authorizes a higher payment) and

this prevents not merely an owner's being left with perhaps the liability for demolition and an unsaleable site, but also the growth of derelict areas in the town.

At another point the local authority's jurisdiction touches the landlord and the tenant. Where a house is overcrowded, the local authority's duty is to secure an abatement of over-crowding, and again not merely may it give evidence of the existence of overcrowding conditions as a reason for the landlord to secure vacant possession despite the Rent Restrictions Acts (as to which see Chapter 14) but may also take steps itself to secure the abatement. Certain housing offences referred to in Chapter 14 may also be prosecuted by the council, for example the absence of the necessary statutory information in the rent book.

The question of the older house, the accelerated rate of decay owing to compulsory lack of maintenance during the war years, and certain properties becoming increasingly uneconomic to the owner, have all tended to reach a point where properties may well fall into disuse faster than they can be replaced by the industry, even without regard to the economic factor. Beginning with the Housing Act, 1949, and increased in 1954, provision has been made by which owners of property may obtain grants towards the provision of further amenities which will bring the houses up to a satisfactory standard, so that they will last for not less than fifteen years. The grant may be as much as 50 per cent of approved expenditure in appropriate cases, and the local authority's grant is to a large extent recouped by the Government. There are certain restrictions: the maximum rent is fixed by the local authority, the grant is repayable by the landlord if the property is sold and not used for letting purposes within a certain time, and, of course, the works in question must really be of improvement and not merely to put the property into repair. Again, there is provision whereby the local authority may lend money for putting the property into repair and may itself purchase properties and put them into repair. The tenants may thus find that their landlord is replaced by the local authority.

DEVELOPMENT AND PLANNING

It may well be, however, that the purchase of land or a house is desired, and here great care should be exercised.

First of all, once the desirable site or property is seen, before any written undertaking is exchanged, deposit paid, or contract entered into, it cannot be too strongly urged that the would-be purchaser should consult his solicitor. In many cases the position is quite clear, and the formalities of inquiries before contract and searches, in which the solicitor will indulge, may seem superfluous, but the odd case in which they are necessary will justify the care taken in all. It must be realized that all land, built upon as well as unbuilt, is to-day subject to planning control, and it may be subject to compulsory purchase, that is to say designated for the carrying out of some statutory public purpose.

A Development Plan has been prepared by every Planning Authority, and has now in most cases been approved by the Minister of Housing and Local Government, as a result of a survey. This plan indicates the manner in which the land covered by it is to be used and the stages, the first one of five years, in which it is to be carried out. The plan has been prepared pursuant to the Town and Country Planning Act, 1947 (as amended), and is subject to review every five years. This Act, which had several forerunners, brought about a dramatic change. Under it the Planning Authority is not the borough or district council, but the county borough or county council, a much bigger authority, and, in the case of the county council, one with headquarters often a considerable distance away from the various points in the county affected by a proposal. On the other hand, in many counties there exist what are known as delegation schemes by which the local borough council and perhaps other district councils carry out as agents for the county council certain of the provisions of the Act and the plan made thereunder, and usually the plan, if it has been made and approved, is available for inspection in the offices of the local district council. Therefore, as a preliminary, it is often well worth while to inspect the plan and see for what purpose the land in question has been zoned. It must be realized at the outset that the mere fact that it is an existing house or shop or factory does not necessarily mean that it has been approved for that purpose in the development plan. Its use may be one which does not conform with the plan; for example, one or two isolated houses in an industrial area might very well not conform, and the whole area in the plan may be zoned for industry. It is then necessary to ascertain whether it is proposed to remove this non-conforming use within the first five years from approval of the plan, or if not, at what date.

Again, it might be that the property in question has been designated for compulsory acquisition, for example for the purposes of a road-widening scheme, and in these circumstances a little reluctance might be felt if a permanency were desired. Of course, compensation would be payable, but while the original provisions of the 1947 Act (which restricted compensation to the value of the existing use of the land) have for the most part been repealed, in so far as public acquisition is concerned, the compensation payable is still not the same as might perhaps be the open market price, but represents the existing use plus an amount attributable to approved development value. In this case, therefore, if it is decided to proceed with the purchase, inquiry should also be made whether there is an accepted 1947-established development value attached to the property which is the 'unexpended balance of development value'. If the property is old, further inquiry in this connexion might well be made at the local council offices as to the prospects of clearance or demolition, although these again would be matters revealed by the searches made by the solicitor, for here again the question of compensation might, as mentioned before, be restricted to site value.

It might be, however, that the purchase contemplated would be either of a plot of ground or of a house which it is desired to turn into a shop, in other words that there was to be some development of the property. Now, if there is to be development of the property, whether by building or by changing the use, as for example if it were desired to use one room as a workshop or to build on a front and convert into a shop, then in this and every other similar case planning permission must be sought. Development is defined in section 12 of the Town and Country Planning Act, 1947, and it means the carrying out of building, engineering, mining, or other operations in on, over, or under land, or the making of any material change in the use of any buildings or other land. That definition is very wide, and to avoid doubt, a material change of use of a building is also defined to include the use as two or more separate dwelling-houses of any building previously used as a single dwelling-house; and the deposit of refuse or waste material on land also involves a material change of use notwithstanding the fact that the land is comprised in a site already used for that purpose. On the other hand, this omnibus definition is slightly reduced in that if the external appearance of the building is not affected (unless a scheduled building), works which affect only the interior may be carried out for maintenance, improvement, or other alteration, for example installing a bathroom. Secondly, various works by highway and statutory authorities, the use of any buildings or other land within the curtilage of a dwelling-house for any purpose incidental to the enjoyment of the dwelling-house, and the use of any land for the purposes of agriculture or forestry are not 'development', and finally, the Minister may make an order dealing with any specific class of buildings or other land. Thus, generally speaking, it will be realized that development is very strictly controlled, and the last class, now set out in the Use Classes Order of 1950, would have to be accurately defined and would include only the building of certain small ancillary buildings, e.g. a small greenhouse, and reference to the district council offices should again be made.

It may sometimes be difficult to ascertain whether the purpose for which the premises are in use is the 'existing use', but this is very important; for notwithstanding anything in the first part of section 12 as to the obligation to obtain permission for development, the permission is not required where it is proposed to use the land for the normal use for which it was being employed, provided that was in conformity with previous planning control, although it may have been used temporarily for some other purpose on the actual appointed day, that is to say 1 July 1948. Secondly, permission is not required where on the appointed day the property was used normally for one purpose, but had also been used, whether at regular intervals or not, for any other purpose and it was proposed again to use it for that purpose. For example, many towns have visiting fairs, such as a statute fair, which will use land or streets for the purposes of the fair on these infrequent occasions. Thirdly, land on the appointed day might have been unoccupied, and again permission is not required to use it for the purpose for which it was last used. It should be observed that a resumption of use cannot arise if it were not in accordance with previous planning control, if any, and in any event if the land was unoccupied on 7 January 1937, and has not been occupied since that day, permission to develop must be sought.

Having concluded that the proposals definitely involve development, the necessary steps to secure the consent of the Local Planning Authority must be taken unless the case is one of those minor ones which falls within the definition of permitted development under Section 3 of the Town and Country Planning General Development Order and Development Charge Applications Regulations, 1950. Presuming that it does not come within the latter category, the would-be developer, who need not have a legal interest in the land he desires to develop – in fact he can even make his application without the knowledge of the owner of the land – makes his application for permission in accordance with Article 5 of the General Development Order, 1950. He can obtain the application form either from the Local Planning Authority or from the district council, with whom the application is to be lodged, and it is the latter whose approval also under building by-laws must be obtained. The application form is printed, and must normally be lodged in triplicate together with such necessary plans and drawings as the Local Planning Authority require, and other information for which the form will make provision. In addition to the district council's approval for the purposes of the building by-laws, industrial buildings of over 5,000 square feet will require a certificate of the Board of Trade. The application having been lodged, unless agreement is reached in writing for deferment, or the applicant receives a decision within two months (generally speaking) he will be deemed to have been refused consent, and in case of refusal he has, of course, two further steps open to him. The applicant may either appeal to the Minister against the refusal (or deemed refusal) of planning permission, or in certain cases, and here again it is advisable to take legal advice, he may be in a position to serve a purchase notice on the Local Planning Authority provided he does so within six months. The effect of this is that if the Minister confirms the purchase notice the local authority (not necessarily the Local Planning Authority) must purchase the property as if it had made a compulsory purchase order.

It should be noticed, too, when considering the grounds of an appeal, that not merely may the outright refusal be appealed against, but also conditions may be attached to the consent which the applicant may consider onerous and against which he desires to appeal. The appeal itself, of which due notice will be given, is usually heard by an Inspector from the Ministry of Housing and Local Government. He will hear both parties, and their counsel or solicitors; and other persons affected by the decision, for example neighbours, may also be heard. In due course thereafter the Minister announces his decision, which is final. In a restricted number of cases it may be that the application will be decided by the Minister in the first instance, but the vast majority of applications are decided by the Local Planning Authority and the decisions accepted by the applicants concerned.

It would not be inappropriate to consider the position of the Local Planning Authority, or, where this jurisdiction is delegated to the borough or district council, the position of that council in considering an application. Its discretion is by no means unlimited even apart from the fact that the possibility of an appeal is always present. Section 9 of the General Development Order of 1950 instructs the authority on this. Before granting permission for development in any of the cases which follow, whether unconditionally or subject to conditions, a Local Planning Authority shall (the obligation will be observed) consult with the following authorities or persons. If development is likely to affect land in a neighbouring Local Planning Authority, with that authority; if development is likely to create or attract traffic affecting a trunk road or level crossing, with the Minister of Transport; with the local Highway Authority where that is likely to be affected; with the National Coal Board where it is in the area of a proposed coal working; where it is within two miles of Windsor Castle, Windsor Great Park, or Windsor Home Park, or within half a mile of any other royal palace or park and which might affect the amenities, with the Minister of Works; where it is in a metropolitan borough and would conflict with existing development or affect streets, with the council of the borough; and with the Nature Conservancy where it is in an area of special interest. There may be additional cases, too, where notification is given, and there are special provisions for development affecting trunk roads and special roads. The Local Planning Authority must also have regard to the provisions of its development plan, although this is not conclusive, and it must give consideration to any special directions received from the Minister, for example, special areas in proximity to airports, or defence directions. It must also give consideration to whether the building affected is a special building, being one of special architectural or historic interest, the Minister having compiled lists of such buildings. Alterations thereto, including demolitions, are prohibited without consent and render a person contravening liable to a penalty not exceeding £100 and possible reinstatement. Certain trees and woodlands are also preserved. Having arrived at its decision, the Local Planning Authority must notify the applicant in writing of the decision at which it has arrived and within one month he may lodge the appeal to which reference has already been made.

The foregoing has applied to cases where there is not the deemed planning permission. There is, however, a not inconsiderable number of cases where the 1950 Development Order,

to which reference has also already been made, makes provision
for the consent not being required, and in those cases the Local
Planning Authority or the Minister does not need to give permission. The full list is set out in the schedule to the Order. It
is not proposed to give the complete list here, and the schedule
should in all cases be consulted. The first, and the one most
likely to be employed, is the enlargement, improvement, or
other alteration of a dwelling-house so long as the cubic content of the original dwelling-house is not exceeded by more
than 1,750 cubic feet or one-tenth, whichever is the greater
(to a maximum of 4,000 cubic feet). The erection of a garage,
stable, loose box, or coach-house, within the curtilage is treated
as enlargement. The height of the new building has not to
exceed the height of the original building, nor has it to project
beyond the forwardmost part of the front. Also within the
curtilage there may be erected, constructed, or placed any
building or enclosure required for a purpose incidental to the
enjoyment of the dwelling-house as such, including the keeping
of poultry, bees, pet animals, birds, or other livestock for the
domestic needs or personal enjoyment of the occupants of the
dwelling-house. The conditions are the same as those which
apply in the case of the first category (and this class must not
include any of that first category), and the height must not
exceed 12 feet.

Class II, defined as Sundry Minor Operations, includes the
construction of gates and fences or other means of enclosure,
also the painting of the exterior of any building or work otherwise than for the purposes of advertisement, announcement, or
direction. Advertisements will be referred to separately.
Class III consists of changes of use and certain changes of use
are permitted, as already stated, where one type of shop, for
example a grocer's, may be changed for use as a butcher's,
without the necessity for permission; but there are others in
respect of which there are restrictions. On the other hand, it
may be changed from a fried fish shop, a tripe shop, a pet
animals shop, or a cats' meat shop, to any other type of shop.
A general industrial building may be changed to a light
industrial building, and similarly there may be a change

within Class I from use as a restaurant. Class IV deals with temporary buildings and uses, Class V uses by members of recreational organizations, Class VI agricultural buildings, works, and uses, Class VII forestry, Class VIII development for industrial purposes. Many of the other classes deal with development by statutory authorities and undertakers, including mineral workers and aerodromes.

Generally speaking, therefore, in the absence of the consent of the Local Planning Authority, or of the deemed consent just referred to, failure to obtain consent is a bar to the development, and this provision may be enforced by the Local Planning Authority by means of what is known as an Enforcement Notice. Whether or not the work is 'development' may already have been determined by the Local Planning Authority pursuant to section 17 of the Town and Country Planning Act, 1947, and, of course, any necessary appeal must have been finally determined. Where development has taken place since 1 July 1948 without permission or without compliance with some condition annexed to the permission, provided it is served within four years of such development being carried out or with non-compliance, the Local Planning Authority may serve an enforcement notice on the owner and on the occupier of the land affected. Both 'owner' and 'occupier' are defined by the Act. The enforcement notice must specify the development which has been carried out or the condition which has not been complied with, and it is a document which must be most carefully drafted and must strictly comply with the legal and factual position. There will be a date specified in the notice itself (not less than twenty-eight days from service) and also a further period within which the person served may restore the land or comply with the condition. Before that date the person served may appeal against the enforcement notice to a magistrates' court and until that appeal has been determined the enforcement notice is of no effect. The enforcement notice may be challenged on the grounds that that which is proposed is not development, or that there is permission, or that permission is unnecessary, and if successful the magistrates will quash the enforcement notice. If, however, it is not quashed, or not appealed against, the Local Planning Authority may enter on the land and carry out any necessary works or demolition to comply with the notice, and recover the cost, or in certain circumstances, for example wrongful use, may take proceedings involving a fine and perhaps a continuing penalty.

Advertisements are subject to a separate code embodied in the Town and Country Planning (Control of Advertisements) Regulations, 1948, as amended. An advertisement displayed in contravention of the regulations renders the person guilty liable to a fine not exceeding £50 or 40s per day. There are also certain areas of special control which may be defined by the Local Planning Authority and approved by the Minister. Again, there are various advertisements in respect of which, as in the case of the ordinary development of land, there is a deemed consent. These are in various classes, as, for example, Class I which includes direction and bus stop signs, Class II professional and business plates, Class III advertisements of a temporary nature, Class IV business premises advertisements relating wholly to the business carried on or to the goods sold, and Class V flag advertisements over the building occupied by the person displaying it. Existing advertisements, that is to say those displayed on 1 August 1948, are now subject to challenge by notice served by a Local Planning Authority and requiring application for an express consent to be made. In certain circumstances compensation may be payable.

The subject of compensation under the Town and Country Planning Act, 1947, as amended by the Town and Country Planning Act, 1953, and the Town and Country Planning Act, 1954, is a most difficult one. The original position with regard to claims for loss of development rights is in process of being determined, and whilst there are still two codes of compensation for the acquisition of land, whether it be by public authority or privately, generally speaking development rights now remain in the land. Where development has been permitted and permission then withdrawn, and where again the development was not temporary, and existed prior to the coming into effect of the 1947 Act and was then prohibited, and in a very strictly limited number of cases where planning permission is refused,

there may be a claim for compensation against the Planning Authority. A prospective purchaser, too, may also ascertain under section 33 of the 1954 Act from the local borough or district council whether that council proposes to acquire the land, the subject of the application, within the next five years or whether it has been notified by a public authority which possesses compulsory purchase powers that such authority proposes to acquire it within the next five years. This means that at any rate for the time being the potential purchaser will be aware of the intentions of the local authority. A negative answer followed by a compulsory purchase order by that local authority within the period may enhance the purchase price.

BY-LAWS AND STREET WORKS

It has already been mentioned that where the work of building is involved, in addition to complying with town planning law, the appropriate plans, and not just (say) an outline application or an application for change of use affecting town planning only, must be submitted to the local authority, i.e. the borough or district council. A decision on whether the plans conform with the building by-laws will be sent within one month. Building by-laws deal with such matters as the materials from which the premises are to be built, drainage, load-bearing requirements, weather resistance, fire resistance, roofs, chimneys, space about buildings, ventilation, height of habitable rooms, sanitary conveniences, wells, and rainwater tanks. In other words, they form a code of workmanship and materials, subject to enforcement throughout the course of construction of the building to try to ensure that the houses to be built do not suffer from inherent defects from the beginning.

It may be, however, that the site selected is on an obviously unmade road. The status of the road is again a matter about which the solicitor acting for the purchaser would make enquiries from the local authority, and a road which is unadopted may be a very expensive matter for the purchaser. In all areas there is in existence the power of the local authority to call upon the frontagers to meet the cost of making up the private streets to its satisfaction before it adopts, i.e. assumes responsibility for them. The Public Health Act, 1875, is in force except where the Private Street Works Act, 1892, has been adopted. Section 6 of the latter states that where any street or part of a street is not sewered, levelled, paved, metalled, flagged, channelled, made good, and lighted to the satisfaction of the urban authority, the urban authority may from time to time resolve with respect to such street or part of a street to do any one or more of the following works – to sewer, level, pave, metal, flag, channel, or make good, or to provide proper means for lighting such street or part of a street; and the expenses incurred by the urban authority in executing private street works shall be apportioned on the premises fronting, adjoining, or abutting on such street or part of a street. The quotation from the Act has been deliberate to show the extent of the liability which may be incurred in this connexion, and it is well worth while to appreciate that such matters as lighting and sewering as well as metalling can be the subject of private street expenses. The local authority may recover the cost from the frontagers, and such cost can also be a charge upon the premises concerned. There is procedure for objections and for appeals again to a magistrates' court.

Incidentally, when giving consent to development of un-made roads, the local authority can in most cases require the developer to deposit with the local authority, or secure, sufficient money to meet potential road charges.

That care is necessary in the purchase of land may well arise also from the fact that in addition to the ordinary general district rate some land is subject still to tithe, to drainage rates, to liability for a bridge, or perhaps to maintain part of a church, a sea wall, or, under the Thames Conservancy Acts and the like, to riparian works.

It is also desirable to draw attention to the powers of local authorities with regard to land, particularly where it adjoins a highway. A local authority may lay down building lines and improvement lines with regard to the relative building position and the future width of the street. It may declare a lane which has existed for some time to be a new street pursuant to the Public Health Act, 1925. The local authority can give directions so as to prevent the obstruction of the view at crossings, and prohibit the planting of high hedges or the building of high walls which would have this effect. It may call upon owners and occupiers to trim trees and cut hedges. It is not lawful without the consent of the local authority to fix or place overhead rails, beams, pipes, cables, wires, or other similar apparatus over, along, or across any street (unless the person concerned is a statutory undertaker), and the local authority may make by-laws for the prevention of danger or obstruction to persons using any street or public place from posts, wires, tubes, aerials, or other apparatus in connexion with or for the purpose of wireless telegraphy or telephony installations.

When new premises are being constructed there is also involved the supply of water to such premises. If water is not readily available in the road opposite the house, it may be that a main will have to be brought some distance. Whether the water supplier is the borough or district council, a statutory authority, or a company, it can call upon a developer, i.e. a builder, to guarantee a return of $12\frac{1}{2}$ per cent for eight years on the capital outlay in which the water undertaker is involved. The Water Act, 1945, should be consulted if the demand of this guarantee is made by the water undertaker. On the other hand, the applicant can call upon the water undertaker in certain circumstances to provide him with water, subject to these rights of the water undertaker as to guaranteed reimbursement.

PAYING FOR PROPERTY

The financing of the new premises – or existing premises – should also be considered. Local authorities who have decided to operate the Small Dwellings Acquisition Acts, 1899 onwards, may make advances of not exceeding 90 per cent of the value to an applicant who is going to occupy the house himself. A small dwelling is restricted to one having a value of £5,000; and, where, for example, the premises comprise both a house and a shop, the house part may be treated separately for the purpose of an advance. A local authority which has not adopted the Small Dwellings Acquisition Acts can however operate under the Housing Acts, and in this instance may make advances to housing associations, in respect of houses which are not necessarily going to be dwelt in by the applicant personally, and also to two persons jointly, for example where a husband and a wife decide to make the purchase jointly. Again, the purchaser may desire to obtain a loan from a building society, and in this connexion it will be remembered that many local authorities will guarantee the loan up to 95 per cent of the value, and enquiry in both the local authority offices and of the building society should be made if it is desired to take advantage of these joint facilities. It is also worth while, in connexion with building societies, to note the provision of section 9 of the Building Societies Act, 1939. Where a society makes to a member an advance for the purpose of defraying the purchase price of freehold or leasehold property, the society shall be deemed to warrant to the member that the purchase price is reasonable, unless, before any contract requiring the member to repay the advance is entered into, the society gives to the member a notice in writing in such form as may be prescribed, stating that the making of the advance implies no such warranty. Finally, provision as to repayment should be borne in mind. With a fixed mortgage negotiated privately, unless notice is given, only the interest is payable each year. Local authority mortgages are usually repayable on the annuity system, that is to say equal monthly amounts of principal and interest combined, and the Small Dwellings Acquisition Acts make special additional provision for the repayment of lump sums by the borrower. Building society repayments are normally of a somewhat similar type, although based upon the number of shares held. It should not be forgotten, too, that default in interest payments can, under the Small Dwellings Acquisition Acts, lead to proceedings for possession being taken, and that whether the lender be society, local authority, or private person, a mortgagee has very valuable remedies of sale, of foreclosure, and of private debt recovery for any unrealized balance. A mortgage also implies the keeping up of an insurance policy, maintaining of the property in a good state of repair and condition, and the discharging of current liabilities, for example ground rent, rates, and taxes.

17

National Service

EVAN STONE

THERE can be scarcely any homes in Great Britain which have not been affected by conscription, in that some member of the family has had to serve his country for a period of years.

Conscription, or National Service, is regulated by the National Service Acts, 1948–55. Never before in British history has conscription been considered necessary in time of peace, and indeed conscription in wartime was unknown in Britain until the First World War. However, owing to the political situation and Great Britain's commitments overseas, successive governments have considered that it was necessary to retain national service in peace time, although it has not unnaturally been unpopular, not only with those most directly affected, but also with employers, and with universities and other educational establishments. This change from the traditional methods of recruiting men for the armed forces in time of peace is such a radical one that it is important to examine its workings.

The 1948 National Service Act states that every male British subject ordinarily resident in Great Britain, who has reached the age of eighteen and has not yet reached the age of twenty-six (except for registered doctors and dentists, for whom the upper age limit is thirty) is liable to be called up in the forces of the Crown for two terms of service. Both of these upper age limits are subject to extension by any period of postponement of call-up on the grounds of hardship. The two terms of service are made up as follows: (a) a term of whole-time service in the regular forces; and (b) a term of part-time service in an auxiliary force, such as the Territorial Army.

Certain persons are not liable to be called up, and these include:

1. persons employed in the government service of a Domi-

nion or British Protectorate, and who are resident in Great Britain solely by virtue of their employment;

2. persons in holy orders or regular ministers of any religious denomination;

3. persons subject to the Lunacy and Mental Treatment Acts, 1890 to 1930, or the Mental Deficiency Act, 1913;

4. persons registered under the National Assistance Act, 1948, as blind persons.

The 1948 National Service Act defines the meaning of the phrase 'ordinarily resident in Great Britain' by stating that a person who is resident in Great Britain shall be deemed to be ordinarily resident unless he is able to bring himself within some clearly defined exceptions. These exceptions are that if a person is merely resident for the purpose of attending a course of education, or the circumstances of his residence are such as to show that he is residing there for a temporary period only, or is a person who is either a citizen or national of any part of Her Majesty's Dominions outside Great Britain under any Act in force there, or born or domiciled in such a Dominion, Protectorate, or mandated territory, and has been resident in Great Britain for less than two years, then he is not deemed to be 'ordinarily resident' within the meaning of the Act.

The position which the courts attach to temporary residents, and the position of citizens of Eire ordinarily resident in Great Britain in relation to their liability for National Service, was considered in the case of Bicknell *v.* Brosnan. In that case a man born in 1931 in what was then the Irish Free State but is now the Republic of Ireland, lived there until 1949, when he came to England and worked as a builder's labourer. Apart from one month's holiday in Ireland, he had resided in England since May 1949, though he intended ultimately to return to Ireland and make his permanent home there. In September 1952 he was served with a written notice by the Ministry of Labour and National Service, requiring him to submit himself for a medical examination in October. He replied to the notice by sending a letter saying that the papers were no concern of his, that he was an Irish citizen, which meant that there was no claim on him and no medical examination.

The Lord Chief Justice, giving the judgement of the court, said that clearly 'a temporary resident' for this purpose means a person who is paying a visit, whether for social or business purposes, and merely making a short stay. This is emphasized by the fact that a person resident for the purpose of attending a course of education, which might easily last three or four years, is specially exempted by the Act. Lord Goddard went on to point out that the man was here for an indefinite period, and the fact that he intended to return to Ireland at some future date, did not make him a temporary resident within the meaning of the Act. Nor could he say that he was not 'a British subject'. The Court decided that the effect of the British Nationality Act, 1948, is that 'a national or citizen of the Republic of Ireland who is ordinarily resident in Great Britain, of the appropriate age and not in one of the excepted classes, is subject to the National Service Act. ....'

In a more recent case, in 1955, called Ullah *v.* Black, the Divisional Court dismissed an appeal from a Pakistani, and held that a citizen of Pakistan, whose residence in Great Britain was not of a temporary nature, was liable for military service under the National Service Act, 1948.

The House of Lords recently decided in a Scottish Appeal, the question whether the offices of a 'congregation servant' and a 'pioneer publisher' of Jehovah's Witnesses brought the holder of these appointments within the exception: 'a regular minister of any religious denomination'. In this case, Walsh *v.* Lord Advocate, the House of Lords decided that the functions performed by a person holding the appointments referred to did not bring him within the exception, which was confined to persons having a spiritual status apart from other members of their denomination, whereas, in the organization of Jehovah's Witnesses, all members on baptism are recognized as ministers commissioned to preach the Gospel of the Kingdom.

The 1948 Act lays down the procedure to be followed for call-up, and requires all male persons who have reached the age that the Minister lays down from time to time, not being less than seventeen years and eight months, to register, and anyone who fails to comply with this requirement commits an offence. After registration a person normally receives a notice requiring him to submit for a medical examination. Anyone who fails to submit himself for a medical examination is liable if convicted to be sent to prison for not longer than two years, or to a fine of not more than £100, or both, and if dealt with summarily by magistrates, to imprisonment for not longer than twelve months, or a fine of not more than £50, or both.

After having been medically examined, a person liable for call-up will receive an enlistment notice, which will state that he is to be called up in one of the regular forces as may be specified in the notice, and it will further require him to present himself at such a place and at such a time and to such authority as will be stated. Once having been served with an enlistment notice the person is normally deemed to have been duly enlisted for service in the force specified, as from the day on which he has to report for duty. Normally an enlistment notice does not require a person to report earlier than fourteen days after the date of the service of the notice.

The 1955 National Service Act makes provision for extending the present upper age limit for liability for National Service, in the case of persons who are absent from Great Britain in the last year of their liability. The men who are affected by the Act are those who reach the present upper age limit on or after January 1955, and who are absent for not less than twenty-eight days in the last year of their liability for call-up, and who either were liable to be called up immediately before reaching the age limit, or would have been so liable but for the fact that they are then not ordinarily resident in Great Britain (in the latter case, after having been ordinarily resident in Great Britain at some time after reaching the age of seventeen years and eight months). As has already been noted, the present upper age limit is twenty-six in the normal case, and thirty for registered doctors and dentists, both being subject to extension by any period of postponement on grounds of hardship.

The method of applying for postponement of call-up on the ground of exceptional hardship is to apply for a postponement certificate, and the Minister then normally refers the application for decision by a Military Service (Hardship) Committee.

An applicant for a certificate, and the Minister, if he considers it necessary, may, if aggrieved by the decision of the Committee, appeal to an umpire or deputy umpire appointed under the 1948 Act, and his decision will be final.

We must now consider the position of those who are conscientious objectors. If anyone who is liable for call-up claims that he conscientiously objects (*a*) to being registered in the military service register, or (*b*) to performing military service, or (*c*) to performing combatant duties, he may apply to be registered as a conscientious objector in a special register kept by the Minister. Where anyone applies to be registered, he will, provided that his application has been made in the proper way and in the proper time, have his name provisionally registered. This having been done, the applicant for registration has to apply, in the prescribed manner and within the prescribed period, to a local Conscientious Objectors' Tribunal, setting out to which of the three matters referred to he conscientiously objects. If he fails to do this, the Minister will remove his name from the register. Either an applicant who is aggrieved by any order of a local tribunal, or the Minister, may appeal to an appellate tribunal, and its decision is final. The local tribunal or the appellate tribunal may make various types of order if satisfied that the ground on which the application was made is established. They may direct that the applicant shall be registered without conditions in the register, or that he be conditionally registered until the end of twelve months and sixty days, the condition being that he must undertake work specified by the tribunal of a civil character and under civilian control, until the end of that period, and submit himself to such medical examination at such time and place as the Minister may direct for the purpose of ascertaining his fitness for that work, and at the end of that period he shall be registered without conditions. The third type of order that the tribunals may make is that the applicant be registered as a person liable, or prospectively liable, to be called up for service, but to be employed only on non-combatant duties. Thus it can be seen that Parliament has made provision for those persons who are liable to call-up, but nevertheless have conscientious objections which fall into one of the categories enumerated above.

In any case where, during the course of his service, a person is selected as a candidate for a commission, either during his term of full-time or part-time service, it is not to be a condition of his acceptance that he shall perform additional whole-time service, after the completion of his term of whole-time service.

Local Education Authorities have a duty under the Education Act, 1944, to secure the provision of adequate facilities for further education for their area, but this duty does not extend to anyone during his period of National Service, and while actually undergoing his service he is exempt from compulsory attendance for further education. The Service authorities, however, have a duty, so far as may be practicable, to provide further education as envisaged in the 1944 Education Act.

The National Service Act also provides for the safeguarding of employment of those who have been called up, and for their reinstatement in civil employment after their term of whole-time service. The Act obliges employers to take a person back into their employment where the man who has been called up makes an application to his former employer, in the employment in which the applicant was last employed before the beginning of his call-up, on terms and conditions not less favourable to him than those which would have been applicable to him in that job had he not been called up for National Service. If, however, it is not reasonable and practicable that the applicant should be taken into employment in that occupation and on those terms and conditions, then the employer is obliged to employ him on the most favourable terms and conditions which are reasonable and practicable in his case. Furthermore, the employer is obliged to take an applicant into employment at the first opportunity at which it is reasonable and practicable to do so. Where an employer has taken back a former employee, he is obliged under the Act to employ him for the following twenty-six weeks or so much thereof as is reasonable and practicable, subject to certain provisos. If a person who has been called up under the provisions of the 1948 Act claims that his rights of reinstatement provided in the Act are being denied him, he may apply to a Reinstatement Committee and the Committee will determine the question. Where the Committee is satisfied that the former employer has failed to discharge his obligations, it has power to make an order requiring employment to be made available, and in addition or as an alternative, as it thinks fit, an order requiring compensation to be paid for any loss suffered or likely to be suffered by him, but not exceeding the amount of the remuneration which in the opinion of the Committee he would have been entitled to receive. Furthermore, if the employer of a person liable to be called up terminates his employment without his consent before the date on which he is required to present himself, and does so solely or mainly because he is going to be called up, then the employer is guilty of an offence and liable to a fine of £50, and the Court has power to order the employer to pay, by way of compensation, a sum not exceeding five weeks' remuneration to the person who has lost his job.

This is one more instance of the way in which those who are called upon to serve the community are protected as befits its members.

18

The Law and the Motorist

EVAN STONE

THE inventor of the internal combustion engine can scarcely have appreciated a minute part of the true significance of his invention. In relation to motoring alone, it has been of great social and economic importance. It has also had an enormous effect legally, both from a civil and a criminal point of view; indeed it is hardly too much to say that, but for the coming of the motor car, our courts, both civil and criminal, would have had considerably less to do.

It is important, therefore, to examine briefly the way in which the law affects the motorist and road users generally. Every person who applies for a driving licence has to sign a form, which, among other things, states whether or not he has read the Highway Code. This, as everyone should know, is published by Her Majesty's Stationery Office, at the price of sixpence, and represents perhaps the best value obtainable to-day for the price: who will deny that the saving of life on the road is a matter which ought to concern us vitally, regardless of the cost? The Highway Code, then, contains something for all road users, and indeed reading it and carrying out its injunctions is a matter which should come high on our list of priorities. The Road Traffic Act, 1930, states in section 45, that 'a failure on the part of any person to observe any provision of the Highway Code shall not of itself render that person liable to criminal proceedings of any kind, but any such failure may in any proceedings (whether civil or criminal, and including proceedings for an offence under this Act) be relied upon by any party to the proceedings as tending to establish or to negative any liability which is in question in those proceedings'. Thus although the Highway Code has not the force of law it is nevertheless issued with the authority of Parliament.

The main Acts of Parliament at the present time which

directly affect motorists are the Road Traffic Acts, 1930–56, and the latest of these, the Road Traffic Act, 1956, makes several major changes in the law.

There are also a number of Statutory Instruments or Regulations, made by the Minister of Transport and Civil Aviation, which are most important to all motorists. The Road Traffic Acts and the Statutory Instruments lay down certain standards of conduct and impose duties upon motorists in the interests of the community at large, and are not concerned with compensation for particular individuals who have been injured or have suffered damage as a result of someone's negligent driving, except that third party insurance has now been made compulsory. However, the Road Traffic Act, 1930, requires any driver involved in an accident in which any damage or injury is caused to any person, vehicle, or animal, to stop at once, and if asked by the police or anyone having reasonable grounds for asking, to give his name and address, the vehicle owner's name if different, and the registration mark of the vehicle. If there is no one there to take particulars, then these particulars and a report of the accident must be given to the police as soon as practicable, and in any event within twenty-four hours. Failure to do this renders a driver liable to a fine of £20 for a first offence and £50 or three months' imprisonment for a second offence. Furthermore, if a person is injured and the driver does not produce his certificate of insurance at the time to the police, or to any person with reasonable grounds for requiring its production, it must be produced to the police, either when reporting the accident to them within twenty-four hours, or within five days of the accident, at any police station the driver may select. However, provided that the parties to an accident exchange the necessary particulars, and the certificate is produced at the time, it is not necessary to report the accident to the police.

Generally speaking, though, the Road Traffic Acts and Regulations are concerned with the criminal, rather than civil, aspects of motoring. Every motorist is required to have a proper insurance, which covers liabilities in respect of third party risks when the vehicle is driven by himself and any other person who may use it. He must also make sure that his driving licence is a current one, is for the class of vehicle which he intends driving, and has been signed in ink. The Motor Vehicles (Construction and Use) Regulations, 1951, provide that the condition of the vehicle and any trailer it may be pulling, and all parts and accessories, must be such that it is not likely to be a danger to the driver and other persons, and in particular refer to the condition of brakes and steering, tyres, windscreen and wipers, mirror, horn, speedometer, silencer, to noise and fumes, and to the load to be carried. The lights and reflectors and anti-dazzle requirement of vehicles' headlights are dealt with in detail in the Road Transport Lighting Acts, 1927-53, and the Road Vehicles Lighting Regulations, 1954, and though these matters have not been dealt with at length, enough has been said to show that Parliament and the Ministry of Transport and Civil Aviation have not been slow to provide the motorist with standards, and that failure to comply with them can result in criminal proceedings.

So far, we have not considered the position of the motorist while he is actually driving, and we shall now deal briefly with this. Apart from murder, the most serious offence with which a motorist may be charged is that of manslaughter, sometimes known as motor manslaughter. There have been cases where a person has been charged with murder, the weapon used being a motor car, a reminder that the motorist controls a lethal weapon, but such cases fall outside the ambit of our discussion here. Manslaughter by motor vehicles is the unlawful killing of a person whose death has been caused by a vehicle which has been driven either with criminal negligence or with such a degree of recklessness that the driver has shown a complete disregard for the safety of others. The punishment for manslaughter is entirely in the discretion of the judge who tries the case, save that the maximum penalty is imprisonment for life.

By section 8 of the 1956 Road Traffic Act, a new offence of causing death by the reckless or dangerous driving of a motor vehicle is created. This offence carries a maximum penalty of five years' imprisonment. The section provides for an alternative verdict of dangerous driving, where the jury are not satisfied that the driving of the motorist was the cause of death, but are satisfied that he was driving recklessly, or at a speed or in a manner dangerous to the public. The offence of dangerous driving now carries increased maximum penalties, and upon conviction before magistrates a first offender may be fined £100, with or without imprisonment for up to four months, and for a second offence he may be imprisoned for up to six months. Anyone convicted of this offence before a judge and jury may be imprisoned for up to two years. The particulars of such a conviction must be endorsed on his licence, and for a subsequent offence he must, unless there are special circumstances, be disqualified from holding or obtaining a licence for a period of not less than nine months, unless it is more than three years since he was last convicted of this offence.

It is quite a separate offence from that of 'being drunk in charge', that is, being in charge of a motor vehicle on a road or other public place (but not necessarily driving it) while under the influence of drink or a drug to such an extent as to be incapable of having proper control of the vehicle. The 1956 Act provides a new defence, in that, if a driver can prove that there was no likelihood of his driving the vehicle while unfit, and that he had not driven it after becoming unfit, he is deemed not to have been in charge of it. For this offence, the punishment on conviction before magistrates is a fine not exceeding £50 or up to four months' imprisonment, and for a second or subsequent conviction, a fine not exceeding £100 or up to four months' imprisonment, or both. Before a judge and jury, an offender may be sent to prison for up to six months, or fined, or both.

The Road Traffic Act, 1930, also deals with the offence known as careless driving, which is 'driving without due care and attention or without reasonable consideration for other road users', and requires all drivers to observe speed limits, traffic signs and signals, and the directions of a police officer controlling traffic, to stop when signalled to do so by a police officer in uniform, and to have side and tail lamps alight at night.

There are a number of regulations which require motorists, among other things, to be in such a position that they can exercise proper control of their vehicle, and retain a full view of the road and traffic ahead; and to give precedence to a pedestrian who is on an 'uncontrolled zebra crossing', i.e. a 'crossing marked with black and white stripes, studs and lighted beacons at which there is no police officer directing traffic'; while the Street Crossing Patrol Act, 1953, requires drivers to stop when requested to do so by a school crossing patrol. Motorists are also forbidden to sound their horns at night (11.30 p.m. to 7 a.m.) in a 'built-up area', which is defined as a road with a system of street lighting not more than 200 yards apart.

Quite apart from the offences that a motorist can commit while he is in the motor car, there are a number of legal requirements, such as obtaining a driving licence, which must be renewed annually, and passing a test as to his competence to drive, which must be satisfied before the motorist actually starts to drive his car. A provisional licence to drive for three months, accompanied by an instructor, entitles a learner to drive until he has passed his driving test, though until he has passed the test he must display 'L' plates on both the front and rear of the car as a warning to others. No person under the age of seventeen years may drive a car. As previously stated, every motorist who drives must make sure that the car which he is driving is insured against third party risks, and is duly licensed, and there is now a standard tax of £12 10s per annum, no matter what the horse power of the car may be.

A very frequent traffic offence on our crowded roads is that of causing an obstruction to passing traffic, an offence which is likely to increase rather than decrease, owing to the great increase in the number of cars on the road, and the fact that the parking problem is already a serious one in most of our towns and cities. It is also an offence, of a more serious nature, to drive someone else's car without his permission, though not such a serious offence, of course, as that of stealing someone's car.

What has been said with regard to motor cars is in the main also applicable to motor cycles, although a person may lawfully drive a motor cycle at the age of sixteen years. Only one passenger may be carried on a pillion seat, and that passenger must sit astride the seat, unlike passengers in some continental countries. Further, the pillion seat must be a proper seat.

So far we have been considering, for the most part, the criminal aspects of the law, inasmuch as it affects, or is likely to affect, the motorist, but we must now consider briefly the position of the civil law and the motorist. We have already noted that Parliament requires every motorist to insure with an authorized insurance company against any liability that he may incur by causing bodily injury to, or the death of, any third person. An injured person, therefore, or the dependants of a person killed, intending to bring an action for negligence, need not generally concern themselves with considerations as to the means of the motorist, and whether he has sufficient money to pay, for it is the insurance company which has to pay. In order to recover damages, however, it is not enough for the plaintiff to show that he was injured by the motorist who is being sued. He must prove that he was injured by the negligence of the motorist, and the onus of proving the existence of negligence is placed upon the party alleging it, i.e. the injured person. It is not for the motorist to prove to the satisfaction of the Court that he was not negligent, and if the plaintiff fails to prove that the motorist was negligent then he will be unable to recover any damages at all. Prior to 1945 and the passing of the Law Reform (Contributory Negligence) Act, if the driver could prove that the injured party, either vehicle or pedestrian, was partly to blame, the driver escaped any liability to pay damages, even though he was the major cause of the accident. But the position now is that if negligence is proved on both sides, the Court has power to apportion the relative degree of blame, in terms of hard cash. Thus if the judge decides, having heard the evidence, that the plaintiff was 50 per cent to blame, he will award a sum as damages which reflects the plaintiff's share of the blame for the accident. For example, assuming that for a case of 100 per cent liability the judge would award £1,000 damages, then if in the same case he came to the conclusion that the plaintiff was 50 per cent to blame, he would only recover £500.

We should also take notice of another important reform in relation to compensation, namely the creation in 1946 of the Motor Insurers' Bureau, which was set up by the leading insurance companies in order to provide compensation for those who, having been injured by a motorist and having proved negligence on his part, discover that the motorist has failed to insure himself against third party risks. The Motor Insurers' Bureau exists to compensate such injured persons, in the way in which they would have been compensated had the motorist been properly insured.

Finally, in this necessarily brief and incomplete outline of the Law and the Motorist, we must consider some of the new provisions of the 1956 Act, other than those with which we have already dealt. The Act now applies to pedal cyclists the statutory provisions relating to reckless, dangerous and careless driving, and driving under the influence of drugs. It gives constables the power to stop cyclists and require them to give their names and addresses. The Act also refers to pedestrians, who commit an offence if they disregard certain directions of a policeman controlling traffic. Local licensing authorities are enabled to refuse a provisional licence to anyone who has held such a licence within the preceding twelve months, and has also, within the twelve months preceding the coming into operation of that licence, held a previous provisional licence, unless he has applied for a driving test to be taken within six months after his application for a licence, and has either taken the test within the currency of his last provisional licence, or can show reasonable cause for not having done so.

The Act makes several other important extensions to the existing law, which cannot be considered in any detail, though in the main they are designed to make the roads safer for all road users; and in some cases it increases the penalties for

Social Welfare and the Citizen

certain driving offences, and makes more stringent provision as to driving disqualifications (including disqualification until the offender has passed a driving test). All of these should make motorists more careful, and ensure that if they fail to maintain the highest standards, they will not resume their inconsiderate activities without having felt the full effect of the law.

Appendix of Addresses

This list is not by any means exhaustive of the addresses where those in need will find help, but the appropriate organization on the list will supply any further addresses which may be necessary.

British Legion: 49 Pall Mall, London SW 1

Family Planning Association: 64 Sloane Street, London SW 1

Law Society: Chancery Lane, London, WC 2

Marriage Guidance Council: 78 Duke Street, Grosvenor Square, London W 1

Motor Insurers' Bureau: 60 Watling Street, London EC 4

National Association for Mental Health: 39 Queen Anne Street, London W 1

National Council of Social Service (Incorp.): 26 Bedford Square, London WC 1

National Institute for the Deaf: 105 Gower Street, London WC 1

National Old People's Welfare Council: c/o National Council of Social Service, 26 Bedford Square, London WC 1

National Society for the Prevention of Cruelty to Children: 15 Leicester Square, London WC 2

Royal National Institute for the Blind: 224 Great Portland Street, London W 1

St. Dunstan's: 191 Marylebone Road, London NW 1

Salvation Army: 1 Vandon Street, London SW 1

Workers' Educational Association: 27 Portman Square, London W 1

Women's Voluntary Services: 41 Tothill Street, London SW 1

Index

Index

279

Index

Some other Pelican books
are described on the
next few pages

THE QUEEN'S COURTS

PETER ARCHER

A365

The British genius for government, which has combined democracy and personal freedom with orderly administration, owes much to English ideas of law. These in turn are the products of the legal profession. And that system has been determined less by abstract speculation than by the practical working of the law courts.

An account of the institutions which produced the criminal trial for the protection of the citizen against unlawful interference alike by wrongdoers and the police, and the civil action for the effecting of justice between citizens, is not a static picture. English law embodies generations of experience, but it is constantly adapting itself to new situations, and the twentieth century has witnessed the birth of numerous tribunals which have taken their place alongside the ancient courts.

Of all these, their work, and their place in English life, this book sets out to tell. It concludes with a comparison between the legal institutions of this country and those which function in different settings for different ways of life.

PATIENTS AND DOCTORS

KENNETH WALKER

A387

Mr Kenneth Walker regards the relationship between
the patient and his doctor as being essential to successful treatment, and he has written this book specially for
the Pelican series in the hope of enlightening readers on
this important subject. There is, he declares, a great
deal of misunderstanding on the part of patients concerning the functions and the methods of the medical
profession, and this book can be regarded as being a
popular guide to doctors and their ways. But if mis-
understandings occur they are not necessarily always
on the side of the patient, for medical men often fail to
appreciate the difficulties and the confusions of their
patients in their dealings with the medical profession,
and particularly with medical institutions such as
hospitals and health services. The author of this book
is deeply concerned with the marked deterioration in
the patient-doctor relationship which has occurred
since the passing of the Health Act. He is equally disturbed by the decline in the prestige of the very person
upon whom the successful working of that Act entirely
depends – the family doctor. Kenneth Walker has a
gift for making difficult matters clear and he writes
lightly and amusingly both of patients and of his own
colleagues